FAMILY
THERAPY

*Principles of Strategic
Practice*

FAMILY THERAPY

Principles of Strategic Practice

Edited by **ALLON BROSS, M.S.W.**

Foreword by **PEGGY PAPP**

THE GUILFORD PRESS

New York   London

First published in the United States in 1983 by
The Guilford Press
A Division of Guilford Publications, Inc.
200 Park Avenue South
New York, N.Y. 10003

© 1982 Methuen Publications
(A division of The Carswell Company Limited)

LIBRARY OF CONGRESS CATALOGING IN PUBLICATION DATA
Main entry under title:

Family therapy.

   (The Guilford family therapy series)
   Includes bibliographies and index.
   1. Family psychotherapy—Addresses, essays, lectures.
I. Bross, Allon, 1951–   II. Series. [DNLM:
1. Family therapy. 2. Models, Psychological.
WM 430.5.F2 F1985]
RC488.5.F3343 1983   616.89′156   82-21060
ISBN 0-89862-045-7

Contributors

Michael Benjamin, M.A.
Family Sociologist, Department of Sociology, University of
Toronto, Toronto, Ontario.

Allon Bross, M.S.W.
Director, Ontario Family Guidance Centre Inc.,
Georgetown, Ontario. Lecturer, Renison College, University
of Waterloo, Toronto, Ontario

Susan Cohen, M.S.W.
Dellcrest Children's Centre, Toronto, Ontario

Peter Gove, M.S.W.
Ontario Family Guidance Centre Inc., Georgetown, Ontario

Pam Grosman, M.S.W.
Department of Social Work, Hospital For Sick Children,
Toronto, Ontario. Lecturer, Renison College, University of
Waterloo, and Ryerson Polytechnical Institute, Toronto,
Ontario

Patricia H. Lindsey, M.S.W.
Hospital For Sick Children, Toronto, Ontario

Peggy Papp, M.S.W.
Nathan Ackerman Institute of Family Therapy, New York,
New York

Michael Rothery, M.S.W.
Assistant Professor of Social Work, Faculty of Social Work,
Wilfrid Laurier University, Waterloo, Ontario

Nina Woulff, Ph.D.
Director, Dartmouth Branch, Atlantic Child Guidance
Centre, Halifax, Nova Scotia. Instructor, Family Medicine
Centre, Dalhousie University, Halifax, Nova Scotia.
Associate Fellow, Institute of Rational-Emotive Therapy,
Halifax, Nova Scotia

Adele Wolpert-Zur, M.S.W.
Department of Social Work, St. Joseph's Hospital,
Hamilton, Ontario

Foreword

Over the past few years the trend in family therapy has been towards a brief, problem-focussed, action-oriented therapy that is characterized as strategic. This has engendered a great deal of excitement and enthusiasm as well as confusion and questions. The excitement and enthusiasm have been produced by the rapid, sometimes magical results that can be achieved by these methods in certain situations. The confusion and questions have resulted from the misunderstanding and misapplication of these ideas to the detriment of the family and therapist alike. In the numerous articles and books describing this approach, most of the emphasis has been placed on the concepts and interventions, and little attention has been paid to the therapist who is attempting to put these concepts into practice—to his/her training, experience, skills, talent, all of which contribute to either a successful implementation of the ideas or to what is described in this book as "therapist's errors."

This book by Allon Bross is above all a teaching book. Few authors have taken as much pains as Bross to explicitly detail the complex process of putting concepts into practice. Included are all the details that most authors take for granted or forget and that beginners don't know. This makes it perhaps the most comprehensive book to date to be written on strategic therapy. Beginning with the basic assumptions derived from systems theory, the reader is meticulously instructed on how to assess a family, formulate a hypothesis, gather information, design tactics and strategies, recognize sources of therapeutic error, deal with resistance, and terminate.

Additionally, by including the theme of "therapist's errors" as an integral part of therapy, this book makes an important contribution to the understanding and application of the strategic approach. In certain chapters, Bross and Benjamin outline the various stages of therapy in which the therapeutic errors are most likely to occur, specify the reasons for them, describe the effects of the errors on the treatment process, and suggest how to avoid them. Therefore, the outline should prove invaluable to those who intend to learn this approach.

The book is full of case studies to illustrate these various stages. Among these, the case report on the "Systemic Treatment of Hysterical Paralysis" is of particular interest, as it describes the formidable task of taking into account the larger system in which the family is embedded. The context of treatment is a psychiatric in-patient ward which has its own homeostasis. Not only does the symptom serve a function in maintaining the homeostasis of the family system, but it also serves a function in maintaining the homeostasis of the psychiatric system. Through a series of skillful manoeuvres, the team of therapists manages to deter either system from interfering with the alleviation of the symptom. The case calls into question the medical perspective on hysterical paralysis which is oriented towards an individual diagnosis and treatment. It also raises intriguing questions regarding symptom selection and development, with the authors suggesting that this may be connected to the family's developmental stage or that it may have symbolic importance and be a metaphor for other family processes.

For either beginning therapists who wish to learn the basics of strategic therapy or for experienced therapists who wish to clarify their thinking and improve their skills, this book can serve as a basic text and can be referred to again and again.

PEGGY PAPP
Nathan Ackerman Institute
of Family Therapy
New York, N.Y.

Preface

In teaching and training mental health professionals, graduate, and under-graduate students in family therapy, I became keenly aware of the need for a basic text on the subject, one that could be used as a springboard to practice. This book was written in an effort to meet this need. It provides a pragmatic guide to the implementation of the principles of Strategic Family Therapy for the advanced family therapist and for those beginning a family therapy practice.

This text is divided into three parts. Part One is organized to present the fundamental concepts for the practice of family therapy. The chapter "Family Therapy: A Recursive Model of Strategic Practice" presents our model of family therapy practice. This chapter divides the therapeutic process (including both the family and therapeutic systems) into six phases. The model attempts to be balanced and comprehensive, and expli-cates the relationships between assessment, diagnosis, and intervention. Because no model of clinical practice, including our own, exists in the theoretical vacuum, the chapter "General Systems Theory, Family Systems Theories, and Family Therapy: Toward an Integrated Model of Family Process" rationalizes our practice model by grounding it in some body of theory that explains family functioning, family dysfunction, and the concept of change. This chapter reviews and evaluates four family systems theories and their pertinent related concepts. The author, Michael Benja-min, describes a recursive model of family process centred on five multi-dimensional constructs. Lastly, his model of family functioning is connected to our joint model of clinical practice.

Part Two of the text elaborates the content of Part One. The chapter "Family Therapy: A Typology of Therapist Error" is a new contribution to the ever-expanding family therapy "puzzle." This article draws attention to therapist error as it relates to therapeutic outcome. Five major sources of therapist error are outlined and discussed with relevant case examples. The chapter "The Formation of the Reconstituted Family System: Processes, Problems, and Treatment Goals" explores the processes and problems associated with the reconstituted family paradigm. This chapter highlights three transitional stages in the formation of the reconstituted family and goes on to review the clinical implications for the family practitioner. This chapter is illustrative of one family constellation which is given in-depth research and a clinical review. Elaboration of two techniques in family therapy are presented in the chapters "Contracts and Contracting" and "Paradox: A Common Element in Individual and Family Psychotherapy." These chapters were selected as representative of two polar techniques both of which can be used with success. The former is illustrative of a positive co-operative intervention whereby the therapist works in co-operation with the client in order to achieve treatment success. The latter refers to a negative co-operative intervention and explains the variety of rationales of working with clients whereby they can reject an intervention and move towards the therapeutic goals.

Part Three of the text comprises five selected case studies. Each case study illustrates the process of therapy from beginning to end and furthermore attempts to emphasize and highlight the different clinical perspectives. "The Systemic Treatment of Hysterical Paralysis: A Case Report" highlights the strategic treatment model with a difficult and rare symptom and goes on to discuss some of the problems of doing this kind of therapy in an in-patient psychiatric ward. "Strategic Intervention with an Individual: The Issue of Intimacy" illustrates the use of a strategic approach in therapy while working with the individual. "Ritual, Reframing, and Written Prescriptions: The Techniques of Strategic Family Therapy" underscores the use of a peer consultation group in the treatment process and the implementing of a number of therapeutic techniques discussed in the Strategic Family Therapy model. "Strategic Family Therapy . . . Feedback and Response" looks at both the therapist's and client's perspectives as they push and pull in a joint effort to reach the goal of the treatment. Lastly, "Intergenerational Continuity and Strategic Family Intervention" explores the intergenerational continuity of dysfunctional families.

Having "sown the seeds" of understanding in the articles in this text, a manual summarizes the key content areas in point form. My intention is for the practitioner to employ this manual as a reference for practice.

This text is filled with paradoxes. I will list them, for they are the assumptions upon which the text is based:

First, few of the ideas expressed about families and family treatment in this text are mine; they are all borrowed from those who have impressed me enough to affect the direction of my practice. The originators of the concepts are given credit as thoroughly as possible.

Second, this text is *not* designed to be exclusively scholarly (those scholars who read the text will surely note this); it is written as a pragmatic guide to strategic family treatment.

Third, it would be wrong, after reading this text, to assume that the work is "easy." It takes hard work, practice, and repetitive failure; however, the goal is attainable.

Fourth, there are many people from whom I have learned directly and many more from whom I have learned indirectly. I have also learned from those who have taught me what *not* to do. I thank you all.

Lastly, while no book can directly further skill development, this text provides the basic knowledge that is necessary to learning how to do family therapy.

The completion of this text has been made possible by those in my life who have supported, guided, and contributed to this endeavour.

Thank you, Fern, for your tireless revisions of the manuscript; Mike Benjamin, for your contribution to the evolution, organization, and completion of this text; and those contributors (listed page xii) whose work will speak for itself.

I would like to dedicate this book to the most important people in my life: my mother, my wife Pnina, and my children, David and Adee.

ALLON BROSS

Contents

The Family Therapist's Reference Manual, 218
Allon Bross

FAMILY
THERAPY

Principles of Strategic Practice

PART 1
THE BASICS

1

Family Therapy: A Recursive
Model of Strategic Practice

Allon Bross and Michael Benjamin

This article explicates a recursive model of family therapy practice. This takes the form of both a flow chart and a substantive discussion. By dividing the therapeutic process into six phases, the model is both balanced and comprehensive; demonstrates an explicit linkage between assessment, diagnosis, and intervention; involves a series of nested feedback loops; and directly attends to the issue of therapist error.

Introduction

Over the past two decades, family therapy has gradually but inexorably been accepted into the mainstream of modern psychiatry and clinical practice (47). While the course of this transformation has been anything but smooth, the results among professionals and students alike has been unequivocal. This includes the explosive proliferation of books and journals on the subject, the development of training programs, the availability of academic courses, the establishment of treatment centres, and the evolution of a large and growing population of "beginners" who seek instruction and training in the art of family therapy.

In this context, however, a problem arises. At present, an increasingly large number of models of clinical practice is available, including the psychodynamic models of Ackerman (1) and Bowen (13), the communication approach of Satir (67, 68) and Haley (40), the structural approach of Minuchin (56, 57), the strategic approach of Watzlawick (84, 85), Selvini-Palazzoli (71), and Erickson (38, 25, 26, 27), the behavioural approaches of Stuart (78), Leiberman (51), and Patterson (62), and so on (89, 9, 4, 34).

Collectively, these models have contributed immeasurably to our understanding of the logic and practice of family therapy. In our experience, however, all are vulnerable to criticism on one or more grounds with respect to the ease with which they may be taught to a "beginner." While several of the authors seek to offer a comprehensive approach to family therapy (e.g., Minuchin), most do not. Consequently, there is much variation amongst the models, with some emphasizing conceptual matters rather than techniques (Ackerman), others emphasizing technique at the expense of assessment (Watzlawick, Selvini-Palazzoli), or diagnosis (Satir). While some authors attend to both assessment and technique, the connection between the two is not always made clear (Erickson and Rossi).

Further, few of the models are explicitly recursive in the sense that later information may inform earlier conclusions regarding family assessment or task selection (Bowen, Haley). Finally, while all of the authors pay at least some attention to the issue of client resistance, none of them explicitly acknowledge the notion of therapist error, a consideration of general importance especially with respect to "beginners."

These considerations suggest the need for a model of family therapy practice which is both balanced and comprehensive, demonstrates an explicit linkage between assessment, diagnosis, and intervention, is recursive in design, and which explicitly attends to the issue of therapist error. In what follows below, we present and explicate such a model, both in diagrammatic and substantive form.

Like those listed above, the model to be discussed is empirically derived, based on clinical contact with a large number of families over a period of five years and a large number of students during the same interval. Its chief advantage is not so much in its content, for we borrow heavily from the authors named above, but rather in its organization and integration of ideas and techniques. Concomitantly, feedback from our students suggests that the model is relatively easy to teach and that it remedies many of the problems of consistency and continuity that characterize existing models.

A Recursive Model of Strategic Practice

In diagrammatic form, an overview of our recursive model of family therapy practice is seen in Figure 1.1. Before proceeding with its explication, several features of the model are worthy of note. First, the various numbered components of the "block model" (77), resolve into the six major phases into which the therapeutic process is divided. Second, the model is explicitly recursive in the sense that it consists of a series of nested feedback loops. By analogy, therapeutic intervention is thus conceived in ballistic terms in which repeated correction in "aim," based on the accurate interpretation of feedback from therapist-client interaction, increases the probability of "hitting" the "target." Finally, the accuracy of the therapist's interpretation of feedback is left neither to chance nor solely to experience; but, rather, the model has built into it a series of nested "error" loops, which are intended to force the practitioner to consistently monitor and evaluate his or her performance. These loops, in turn, provide an operational means by which the practitioner can distinguish between client behaviour that reflects either client resistance or therapist error.

Assumptive Base

All existing models of family therapy practice contain within them two sets of assumptions: one pertaining to their relative degree of commitment to system theory and one pertaining to their model of clinical practice (53). In most instances, such assumptions are either left implicit or passed over

Figure 1.1
A Recursive Model of Family Therapy Practice

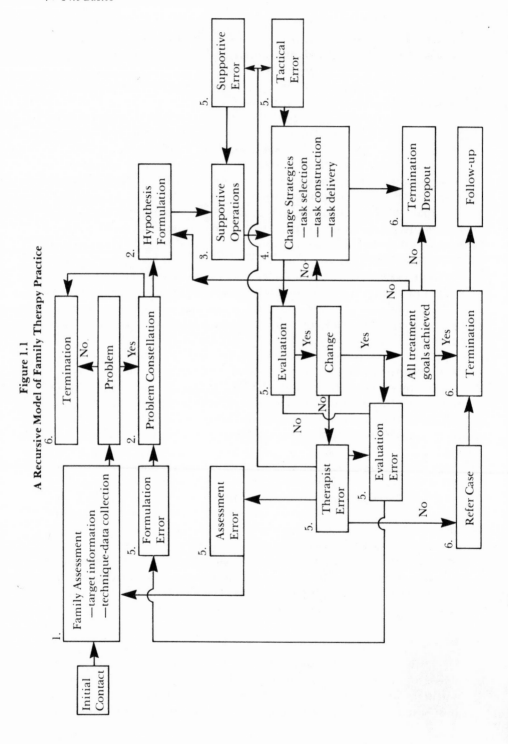

lightly. This is extremely unfortunate, for it is essential that all therapists, especially "beginners," be as clear as possible regarding the assumptive base of the practice model that they employ. It has been our experience that such a grounding facilitates learning the model in question and sensitizes the "beginners" to instances in which they may inadvertently act or think in ways that contravene these assumptions.

Accordingly, we begin explication of the recursive model of family therapy by discussing the twin sets of assumptions on which it is grounded.

Systems Theory Assumptions

Contrary to its name, general systems theory (GST) is not a theory in the proper sense; it involves neither a coherently ordered set of propositional statements nor a series of deduced lower-order generalizations. As Katz and Kahn (49) explain, "Open-systems theory is rather a framework, a meta-theory, a model in the broadest sense of that over-used term. Open-systems theory is an approach and a conceptual language for understanding and describing many kinds and levels of phenomena." (See also 63.) It is, in short, a particular way of thinking about and organizing data concerning various phenomena in the world.

In this context, the central kernel of the theory, the notion of "system," serves to highlight those assumptions which inform GST as well as serving as a ground for family therapy. For purposes of the present discussion, a system will be defined as two or more persons who interact with each other in a patterned and stable manner through time despite fluctuation in their environment (41, 87).

This definition involves the following assumptions:

1. Causality within systems is non-linear, involving circular processes which reflect the reciprocity of social interaction through time; concomitantly, this holds (a) that it is impossible, in principle, to fruitfully isolate the behaviour of an individual from a social context that gives it meaning; and (b) insofar as all parts of the system are interconnected, a change in one part will, directly or indirectly, be associated with a change in all other parts.

2. There is no direct relationship between antecedent causes and final effects such that the whole is always greater than the sum of its parts. This means that systems will exhibit characteristics and/or properties at higher levels which are qualitatively different from those found at lower levels, characteristics which cannot, except under most unusual circumstances, be induced from the characteristics of the system's multiple lower-level components. From this it follows that, however complete one's a priori knowledge of the parts, it would be practically impossible to predict the final shape of the system.

3. Phenomena in systems are described and explained in terms of the stable patterns of interaction which evolve among their component parts. Systemic phenomena, then, are, by definition, "relational entities" (50)

characterized by "organized complexity." It follows that, from this perspective, the fundamental unit of analysis is not the individual but rather the system itself (12). Furthermore, the interactional patterns which characterize a given system need not and, indeed, typically are not cognitively available to the participants.

4. The explanation of systemic events is ahistorical but not atemporal; that is, while time is an integral part of the explanation of any event, there is assumed to be no direct or linear relationship between current and past states of the system. In part, this intersects with Assumption Number 1 above, in the sense that the effect of any initial event at a particular point in time is significantly affected by the reciprocal nature of interactional processes (i.e., causal diffusion). As such diffusion continues with the passage of time, any causal connection between distal and proximal states of the system diminishes to the vanishing point. It follows, then, that the current state of the system can only be explained in terms of ongoing interactional processes.

Clinical Practice Assumptions

The foregoing system assumptions permit the derivation of a series of further assumptions which serve to inform the nature and processes of intervention in family systems.

1. Individual behaviour seen as disordered or symptomatic—either by the individual, the family, or some category of institutional gatekeeper—is understood as a manifestation of interactional processes in family systems. A set of two or more individuals is said to be a family system if a patterned set of relationships exists among them and if they share a past history, a present reality, and an anticipated future (9). It is the interactional processes in such systems that are held to be responsible for family problem development, maintenance, and resolution;* concomitantly, it follows that (a) such behaviour can only be properly understood when seen within the context of family rules and prohibitions; (b) such behaviour is consistent with at least some of these family rules and prohibitions, that is, the behaviour is seen as both patterned and appropriate in some social context; and (c) such behaviour is in some sense functional for the larger family system insofar as it serves to maintain family stability (homeostasis) and/or to guard against the possibility of family dissolution (37).

2. The explanation of "disordered" behaviour is general in form and thus need not distinguish between the various forms or categories of behaviour used in traditional psychiatric taxonomies (i.e., DSM III); rather, family problems are conceptualized in terms of observed redundant interactional processes. It follows that (a) diagnosis, if such a term is to be used at

---

*Note that these criteria are neither biological (i.e., bloodties), residential (i.e., common habitation), nor legal (i.e., marital status).

all, is based on the interpretation and formulation of feedback following initial clinical intervention; (b) diagnostic formulations are not directed at uncovering the reason why family dysfunction has arisen; rather, it focusses on the form that dysfunction takes and upon the interactional processes serving to maintain it; and (c) such formulations are necessarily metaphorical in nature insofar as the definition of behaviour as disordered is arbitrary, depending upon the context in which it occurs, the perspective of the observer, and the way in which the sequence is "punctuated" (i.e., ordered).

3. The client's history is regarded as more or less irrelevant; since dysfunctional behaviour is maintained by ongoing interactional processes in the present, it is those current interactional processes that are the target of investigation and intervention.

4. In order to maintain stable interactional processes, family systems, by definition, must be extremely sensitive to fluctuations in the environment; the therapist is part of that environment. This means that what a practitioner sees in therapy will, in part, be a function of the family's reaction to the therapist. It follows then, that, for purposes of assessment and intervention, the therapist must be seen as part of the system and, consequently, must also be part of the ongoing therapeutic process.

5. The primary aim of family therapy is not individual transformation; rather, it is an attempt to shift the balance of dysfunctional patterns of interaction among family members in order that new forms of relating become possible. Such shifts in the family organization are held to be coterminous with problem-resolution. It follows that, while insight may be associated with family reorganization, this is neither a necessary nor a sufficient condition for therapeutic change. Indeed, to the extent that interactional processes are typically not cognitively available to the participants, it is typically the case that insight will be a consequence rather than a cause of change.

6. While family members are typically unaware of the interactional processes underlying their behaviour, this is not to say that members have no conceptual scheme to explain their behaviour to each other. Rather, all families create interactional realities in which behaviour is invested with meaning (i.e., second-order reality) and in which such meanings subsequently serve as a guide to behaviour (84). This view of family meaning systems is consistent with W.I. Thomas' now-famous dictum (80) that "that which a person perceives to be real, is real in its consequences." Taken together with Numbers 1 and 2, above, this suggests that (a) family systems operate at two levels, that of interaction and meaning; (b) these two levels interact such that they may be congruent or discrepant, synchronic or asynchronic; (c) patterns at the level of interaction will be isomorphic at the level of meaning; (d) to be effective, therapeutic intervention must take account of and be consistent with both levels of family reality; (e) a dysfunctional process will be said to have undergone change if, and only if, altered

interactional sequences are observed at *both* the level of interaction and the level of meaning.

7. Given wide public exposure to traditional psychiatric procedures, clients often believe that family intervention is a long, slow process. While this may in fact be so in some cases, there is no a priori justification for this assumption; rather, the opposing assumption is more in keeping with clinical experience, namely, that family reorganization may occur quickly.

8. To the extent that family systems work to maintain stability (homeostasis) in their interactional patterns, some resistance to therapeutic destabilization is to be expected. Whereas clients cognitively come to therapy in order to gain relief from pain and to seek solutions to life problems, interactionally they typically do so in order *not* to change. Resistance, then, is to be seen as a "normal" property of family systems and not as an indicator of deep-seated psychological problems; indeed, under circumstances to be specified in Phase Four below, family resistance can offer the therapist immense leverage in helping families change.

9. Finally, in accord with Number 4 above, it is the therapist, rather than the client, who is in charge of the therapeutic process; this means that, as much as possible, therapeutic intervention should be a planned and highly predictable process. Consequently, it is the therapist, and not the client, who is ultimately responsible for either therapeutic success or failure. Although in interaction with the client, it is the former who takes credit for failure, while it is the latter who gets credit for success.

Phase One: Family Assessment

The first phase of a therapeutic process involves the initial assessment of the family in order: (a) to decide whether or not they exhibit dysfunctional patterns of interaction, either at the level of behaviour, affect, and/or meaning; (b) to determine the extent to which such dysfunctional processes are serious enough to warrant therapeutic intervention; (c) to identify and clearly define one or more resolvable family problems; (d) to specify the interactional mechanisms which serve to maintain the problem, together with the persons, familial or extrafamilial, who actively participate in them; (e) to state in operational terms the goals of therapeutic intervention—such statements should take the form of an hypothesis that explicitly indicates the predicted consequences of a particular therapeutic intervention; and (f), finally, to decide whether or not a therapeutic contract is in order and what form it should take.*

With these objectives in mind, family assessment essentially involves two components. The first of these is the target information on the basis of which a formulation of the family's problem will be developed. Generally,

---

*For a more elaborated discussion of assessment objectives, see Garfield (33) and Steinfeld (76).

three categories of information are sought: (1) demographic information pertaining to the family constellation, for example, their gender, age, occupation, religion, ethnicity, income, and so on; (2) substantive information, which includes the examination of their past treatment history, pertinent medical facts (e.g., the use of drugs for pleasure or medicinal purposes), the identity of the "patient," information concerning a series of sensitive topics such as the use of physical violence (e.g., child abuse), a recent death in the family, the level of sexual functioning, a retarded family member, and so forth; and (3) interactional data pertaining to family rules, alignments, and coalitions, sub-system functioning (e.g., marital, parental, sibling), meaning systems (second-order realities), hierarchy and sequences or patterns of behaviour, and cultural differences.

Irrespective of the type of information in question, relevance is determined by the extent to which the data shed light on the processes which appear to maintain the problem and which may, in turn, be important in effecting therapeutic change.

Furthermore, it can be safely assumed that there will be some discrepancy between what the client wishes the therapist to know and what the therapist needs to know in order to develop the formulation that will serve as an intervention guide (75). Consequently, it is important that the therapist be in charge of the assessment process. This will include: (a) deciding who to have attend the first interview; while there is at present no scientific basis upon which to decide who to include in treatment (36), our own bias is to include the entire family, especially the often-reluctant father (32, 24, 48);* (b) deciding where it is to be conducted; while interactional processes tend to be stable independent of setting, family systems are nevertheless sensitive to the "demand characteristics" (59) of the situation; furthermore, different institutional contexts (e.g., in-patient vs. out-patient) place different treatment constraints on the practitioner (14, 54, 40); (c) deciding on the duration of the interview; while the 50-minute hour is the tradition in many clinical settings, it has been our experience that a fixed-time interview is generally counterindicated; rather, the length of the interview should reflect the nature of the problem, the composition of the family system, the level of anxiety, and so on; (d) the therapist's initial refusal to argue with family members, offer them early interpretations of their behaviour, give them premature advice, or attempt to get them to "see" things differently; (e) the therapist's ability to offer the client-family members hope by communicating to them that there are alternatives to their present situation; (f) the therapist's capacity to join, confirm, and respect all members of the client system; (g) the therapist's skill in inducing client-families to divulge information pertinent to the development of a

---

*For a discussion of techniques involving resistant family members in treatment, read Bauman (6), Starr (75), Fisher (29), and Teismann (79).

case formulation, even in areas experienced as stressful or taboo; conversely this involves avoiding a common therapeutic trap, namely, accepting second-hand messages from a member regarding the thoughts, feelings, or intentions of an absent member (75), accepting the client's description and explanation of family interactional processes, or allowing clients to respond to questions with yes/no responses; and finally (h) the therapist's ability to keep track of content while primarily attending to the interactional processes.

This need to collect pertinent information brings us to the second component of assessment, namely, the data-collecting techniques by means of which such information can be obtained. Although a large number of techniques are available for this purpose (57, 19), the following procedures are typically adequate for most purposes. These include:

1. *Directing the content of information*: as noted above, client preferences, areas of stress or taboo areas of avoidance mean that the therapist will obtain a skewed or distorted "picture" of the family; to prevent this, the therapist must obtain information in areas other than those offered by the client system. Directing the content of information is one way of getting access to such information; it involves stopping the existing content flow and then "positively" introducing the desired content.

2. *Directing the flow of communication*: assuming that only limited data can be obtained from verbal descriptions of the client system and, further, that the relationship between two or more family members is maintaining dysfunctional behaviour, additional data can be obtained by having family members transact in the presence of the therapist (56); to facilitate an "enactment," the therapist directs certain family members to interact with each other under specified conditions and prescribes the flow of content. For example, a therapist may direct a husband to "talk to your wife about establishing some rules for your son." The transaction that results allows the therapist to observe the participants' method of verbal and non-verbal signalling as well as their range of tolerable transactions in the present (56).

3. *Manipulation of physical space*: the physical arrangement of family members in relation to each other is frequently a metaphorical statement concerning other, more salient interactional processes; as such, physical arrangements can provide significant information. They can also be misleading, as members unwittingly arrange themselves in such a way as to appear as they would like to be seen. One way of testing the validity of such information involves extending the enactment technique to include the manipulation of the physical space; such manipulation requires that the therapist give an appropriate pretext for the placement of one family member in relation to another.

4. *Highlighting differences*: the fact that so much of what transpires interactionally in families is not cognitively available to their members

means that discrepancies, whether of content or sequence, can occur unnoticed. Discrepancies of content can take either of the following forms: a logical inconsistency in the content of a family member's report or a contradiction between a member's verbal report (e.g., "I love You") and non-verbal behaviour (e.g., clinched fist). Discrepancies of sequence involve a contradiction between what is reported and what is observed interactionally; thus, a husband may tell the therapist that he loves his wife but may then act towards her in a critical and bullying manner (45). In either event, highlighting differences involves calling these discrepancies to the client's attention (18, 73); the client's response to this information may, in turn, provide important new information for the therapist.

5. *Gossip technique*: clinical experience suggests that family members know far more about how their family works than the therapist can ever know (40). One method for obtaining interactional data, then, is simply to ask one family member to "gossip about the relationship between two other members" (71). For example, a therapist might ask mother, "What happens when there is a disagreement between father and your son?" It should be noted that this technique should not be used with young children, because the therapist may find him or herself "triangulating" the child, that is, making the child a medium through which parents interact, with destructive consequences.

6. *Probing*: perhaps the single most commonly used technique, probing involves asking family members direct questions about content in order to (a) recover missing information, (b) elicit information regarding interactional processes (e.g., who is involved and under what circumstances), and (c) clarify and make specific any information that seems vague, ambiguous, or devoid of detail.

In order to illustrate the use of these techniques, the following example is taken from the case files of the senior author:

> A family came to see the senior author with regard to a fourteen-year-old adolescent. The presenting problem was that the adolescent girl was depressed, refused to talk to anyone in the family, and was repeatedly disobedient. The family consisted of four members: mother, father, eldest daughter, age nineteen, and the identified patient.
>
> The therapist began by using the probing technique, asking each member of the family why they had come to therapy. This revealed that family members would be reluctant to speak without first obtaining approval from mother. When asked a direct question each family member would first glance to mother, mother would make an effort to answer, while other members supplied supplementary information. It also quickly became clear that there were topics that were safe to talk about, while others could not be addressed. Furthermore, what answers were given tended to be short, guarded, and sketchy with respect to the amount of data provided.
>
> In order to gain further assessment information, the therapist then

utilized the gossip technique wherein each member of the family was asked to report about another dyad in the family. For example, "Mother, how do father and your daughter get along?" This elicited further diagnostic information other than that already provided solely by mother.

However, the therapist still had not seen the family negotiate directly with their fourteen-year-old daughter, the identified problem. Since the parents reported difficulties around daughter's disobedience, he utilized the technique of enactment. Specifically, he had them set a rule for their daughter. By "enacting" the problem he observed that whenever mother initiated a rule, father would negate it; similarly, father's efforts to develop a rule were reciprocally negated by mother.

Taken together, these assessment techniques allowed the collection of sufficient information to provide a clear picture of the interactional processes and family organization that were maintaining the problem.

Phase Two: Family Problem Formulation

The availability of assessment data allows a therapist to move to the second phase of the therapeutic process, namely, the development of a case formulation. For our purposes a formulation is a statement which (a) describes the problem in terms of the interactional processes which serve to maintain it and (b) indicates the kind of changes in the pattern that will be associated with problem resolution.

While family problem taxonomies remain at a primitive level (58), our own clinical experience is consistent with work presented by Haley (40) and Minuchin (56). It is our suggestion that the following dysfunctional family constellations account for the vast majority of clients seeking help.

1. In generic form, a common problem in intact families involves an intense parent-child relationship that excludes the other parent; this typically involves the following cyclic process; mother and son have an intense relationship; son misbehaves; father is called in to solve the problem; mother attacks father's solution or may threaten to leave the marital relationship; father withdraws; mother and son continue their close relationship until son again misbehaves and the entire cycle then repeats. A common variation on this theme involves mother and grand-mother struggling for control of a child while excluding father. Whoever is involved, this family constellation results in an intense symptom-producing relationship between an adult and child. It is dysfunctional for two reasons: first, it permits a violation of hierarchy in which a child is awarded more authority than appropriate; second, it makes a boundary about the marital subsystem so weak that it allows a child to break it (56). With these processes in mind, the goals of therapy will be to (a) block the child's intrusive efforts; (b) strengthen the boundary around the parental sub-system; and (c) encourage the parents to form a coalition characterized by consensus concerning control and discipline of the child.

2. Another common problem in intact families involves chronic boundary problems or "triangulation"; generically, this occurs when stress in one subsystem is negotiated through another family member, typically when parents use a child as a means of deflecting spouse conflict. Here, the goals of therapy are (a) to block the child's efforts at intrusion, the therapist taking full responsibilities for the child's symptoms as a way to promote child autonomy and spouse interaction; (b) to define the spouse relationship in positive terms in order to increase the level of marital affiliation, the therapist joining with the now-excluded child; and (c) to restructure the parental relationship in a coalition against the child.

3. A third common family constellation involves a dysfunctional relationship between mother, grandmother, and child. In this instance, mother is a single parent (because of death or divorce) and appears incompetent in the presence of her own mother. In this context, the child's misbehaviour acts to mobilize the mother and prevents her from withdrawing in the presence of grandmother. Such a family arrangement is dysfunctional for two reasons: first, the boundary around the mother-child system is sufficiently diffuse as to allow grandmother to intrude, thus weakening mother's parental authority; second, the relationship between mother and grandmother has become one of competition rather than one of complementarity and mutual support. Accordingly, the goals of therapy involve (a) blocking grandmother's effort at intrusion in the mother-child relationship; (b) helping mother and grandmother join in an alliance as parental executives; and (c) acting to clarify the boundaries about mother and grandmother.

4. A fourth family constellation involves a single parent, typically a mother, with several children, one of which has moved into the position of a parental child: a child who behaves as if he or she had parental authority over the remaining siblings as well as toward the parent. The arrangement clearly involves the violation of hierarchy. Consequently, the major goals of treatment are to (a) return the parental child to the sibling subsystem, while allowing this child to retain a position of leadership within that subsystem; and (b) to clarify the boundary between mother and child, such that the child's leadership position will apply only in the absence of the mother thus allowing the other children direct access to their mother whenever she is present.

5. A fifth family constellation concerns the transitional situation involving the temporary loss of a member, typically a parent, caused, for example, by illness or employment. In this situation, mother and children form a coalition in which father is excluded from parenting and in which children frequently intrude upon spouse transactions. The primary problem here centres on the boundary around the parental subsystem in which parental transactions need to be renegotiated. Here, the goals of therapy are (a) to exclude the children from spouse transactions by blocking mother-

child interaction; and (b) to strengthen the boundary around the parental subsystem, thus permitting father to resume parenting his children.

6. A sixth family constellation also revolves around the issue of transition, that is, a need for family reorganization following divorce. Problems arise when one parent leaves and the remaining parent fails to adjust appropriately by remaining committed to a now-obsolete set of rules and prohibitions. The most common form of this occurs when one or both parents refuse to permit the other to maintain a separate and autonomous relationship with the children, countermanding their instructions, contradicting their rules of discipline, and so on. The primary problem here concerns a lack of clarity about the new boundary that is formed between the former spouses. The goals of therapy are (a) to strengthen and clarify this boundary by seeing mother and father, separately, with the children; and (b) to block any and all efforts of the children to intrude into the marital relationship, thus forcing the spouses to deal directly with any of their disagreements rather than through the children.

7. The final problem-family constellation concerns an increasingly common phenomenon, the blended family, that is, one in which one or both marital partners have previously been divorced and bring with them their children from that former relationship. Problems typically arise over the issue of parenting; one or both spouses have failed to make the transition to the new situation and they refuse to give the other spouse the parenting authority over their children, thus placing the other spouse in the disengaged position. The problem here concerns the clarity of the boundary around the parental subsystem. Accordingly, the goals of therapy are (a) to block the interaction between the over-involved spouse and his or her children; and (b) to encourage the spouses to negotiate their relationship around the issue of parenting in order to allow the excluded parent to "borrow" power from his or her partner. The result is a temporary transitional arrangement which gradually becomes permanent.*

Having tentatively established that the family in question falls into one of the foregoing family constellations, the therapist is now in a position to construct a formulation of the case as a guide to initiating subsequent therapeutic intervention. At this stage, such a formulation can only be a rough approximation, which has yet to be verified empirically. Consequently, it is important that it be stated in the form of a falsifiable hypothesis (72). This is critical for several reasons: first, it forces the therapist to be as clear, specific, and operational as possible; second, it allows the therapist to freely acknowledge the probability that he or she may be wrong; third, it introduces the possibility that the therapist's commitment to a given formulation will cause interaction with the family in such a way as to elicit confirming data while preventing the emergence

---

*For a more elaborate discussion of the blended family see Wolpert-Zur and Bross (88), Chapter 4 in this volume.

of disconfirming information; finally, it forces the therapist to be sensitive in tracking the feedback that results from his or her effort at intervention in search of data which either confirms, elaborates, or disconfirms the formulation.

While the primary place of hypothesis-testing is centred on the case formulation, it is worth noting that this should also reflect a style of operation that should pervade all aspects of the therapeutic encounter. For example, as one probes for assessment data, the specifics of an interactional sequence should be stated in the form of an hypothesis which can then be confirmed by the client's response, direct or indirect, to the therapist's questions. The same is true with any phase of the therapeutic process.

To clarify the way in which assessment data are used to develop a case formulation in the form of a hypothesis, the following case example (15) is offered.

> The X family was referred to the senior author by a public health nurse. Following an initial telephone contact, the mother, Mrs X., explained that Paul, age 11, was having problems at school which "affects his character and school work." Mrs. X., who had been separated from her husband four and a half years prior to this contact, believed that Paul had not accepted the loss of his father, which would be the purpose of the therapy.
>
> He next met the family during the initial interview. At that time, the mother reported that since she and her husband had separated, Paul had become disrespectful and "bossy" within the family, frustrating his mother by telling everyone what to do and usurping her parental authority. She added that Paul's demands placed severe constraints on her time and energy.
>
> As she was telling him this, Mrs. X. came across as an overly protective mother. Based on her report that she was a single parent and that her son was being disrespectful and bossy, the therapist *hypothesized* that Mrs. X. had failed to make a transitional shift; her anxiety, as a manoeuvre to protect her children, would be the key to the solution of this family's difficulty. In contrast with her former husband who had been a strict and harsh disciplinarian, Mrs. X. was afforded the role of being soft and protective of her children. She continued to maintain her protective posture, feeling badly about her children's loss of their father. Consequently, she placed herself in an ineffectual position vis-à-vis her eldest son, Paul. At the same time, Paul was undergoing his own transitional shift, fulfilling more of the parental functioning in order to help his mother. However, his inappropriate attempts at parenting had caused heightened conflict between mother and son.
>
> The therapist's *hypothesis*, that this family had not made the appropriate transitional shift, helped establish his primary therapeutic goals. This was to mobilize Mrs. X.'s helplessness into a position of strength in order for her to set clear parental limits for Paul. Towards that end, he would shift the power from the child to the mother, breaking the dysfunctional repetitive sequence of events which in fact was perpetuat-

ing the problem. In doing so, he would be helping the single parent family overcome a transitional shift in which they had been previously "stuck.".

Phase Three: The Maintenance of Therapeutic Contact

Whether long- or short-term, the therapeutic process takes time. During that time, the client's family must be sufficiently motivated to continue with therapy. Similarly, the client must maintain a frame of mind that allows him or her to be open to change.

Both these ends are achieved by means of supportive operations designed to (a) reduce the psychological distance between the therapist and the client-family; (b) validate the client; (c) provide encouragement and approval of the client's actions; and (d) convey respect and understanding.

The use of such operations is not confined to any phase of therapy, although they are listed together here for convenience as Phase Three; rather, they must occur throughout the therapeutic process; without them, it has been our experience that all attempts at obtaining data and implementing change strategies have failed.

While a range of techniques may be used to provide therapeutic support, we have found five operations to be especially pertinent and useful.

1. *Attentive listening*: in order to establish and maintain emotional contact with client families, it is crucial that the therapist communicate to them, by his or her body posture, facial expression, verbal responses, vocal qualities, and so on, that he or she is interested in and receptive to what the client has to communicate (64). Called "attentive listening," this technique represents a generic category which encompasses all of the support operations listed below.

2. *Empathy*: based on the work of Rogers (65), Truax (82), Carkhuff (18), and Carkhuff and Truax (19), empathy is a technique designed to make the client and family feel that the therapist has understood what they have to communicate. Basically, it involves two components: a verbal component in which the therapist communicates his or her understanding in a language attuned to the client's feelings, and a non-verbal component, in which the therapist's behaviour, in terms of voice, tempo, mood, or body position, matches that of the client.

3. *Reinforcing strengths*: reduction of the psychological distance between therapist and client will occur when the therapist can identify and communicate a client's particular strengths. In many instances, this may be quite direct, as the therapist, for example, comments on the valiant efforts of one spouse to help his or her partner with some difficulty. However, it may also involve the process of "reframing" (84, 56), in which areas perceived as dysfunctional by family members are reinterpreted by the therapist in positive terms. Thus, a husband who is perceived by other

members as neglecting his family by spending twelve hours a day at work may be described as a "dedicated provider."

4. *Imitation*: imitative operations are those in which the therapist's behaviour, either verbal or non-verbal, approximates that of the client. This may include adopting the client's language, clichés, and voice tempo; joining the client's mood; matching the client's breathing rate or mirroring the client's body posture. While these operations are, by nature, quite subtle, they may often profoundly enhance the therapist-client relationship.

5. *Respecting differentiation*: finally, the therapist must honour and respect any prominent differences between therapist and client; they include variables such as age, sex, culture, ethnicity, race, language, specialized expertise, and so on. Such respect is easily conveyed by acknowledging these differences and enquiring about them.

These supportive techniques are crucial to the objectives of the therapeutic relationship and frequently make the difference between a successful and unsuccessful outcome. To emphasize the point, consider the following metaphorical story of the "Watermelon Hunter" (70).

> Once upon a time there was a man who strayed from his own country into the world known as the land of fools. He soon saw a number of people flying in terror from a field where they had been trying to reap wheat. "There is a monster in that field," they told him. He looked and saw that it was a watermelon.
>
> He offered to kill the "monster" for them. When he had cut the melon from the stalk, he took a slice and began to eat it. People became even more terrified of him than they had been of the melon. They drove him away with pitchforks, crying, "He will kill us next, unless we get rid of him."
>
> It so happened that, at another time, another man also strayed into the land of fools and the same thing started to happen to him. But instead of offering to help them with the "monster," he agreed with them that it must be dangerous and, by tiptoeing away from it with them, he gained their confidence. He spent a long time with them in their homes until he could teach them, little by little, the basic facts that would enable them not only to lose their fear of melons, but even to cultivate them themselves.

Phase Four: Intervention

The primary purpose of family therapy is to help change problem-maintaining patterns of interaction. While assessment, case formulation, and supportive manoeuvres all contribute to this end in their own right, these techniques serve to support intervention strategies which are specifically planned to induce change. For analytic purposes, each strategic manoeuvre involves three distinct components: task selection, task construction, and task delivery.

The selection of a therapeutic task is made on the basis of (a) the particular family in question; (b) the case formulation; and (c) the therapist's preferential style. In general, two broad categories of techniques may be distinguished (40). "Digital" tasks are simple, direct tasks which necessarily involve some quantitative (i.e., numerical) component such as "Count the number of temper tantrums your child has each day." Conversely, "analogic" tasks are more complex, indirect, tending to be metaphorical in nature. For example, in order to communicate the need for discipline, a therapist may tell a story to a "parental child" concerning a naughty child and the consequences of that child's behaviour. The use of fables, poems, written passages, and stories serves the same function. In practice, of course, many therapeutic tasks include some mix of the digital and the analogic.

In this context, the importance of the therapist's preferred style of working is illustrated by the following example.

> While supervising a therapist, it became evident to the senior author that when stress occurred in the client family, the therapist would enter to defuse the stressful situation. This would prevent further data collection and ultimately the therapist felt "stuck." The instruction, then, to the therapist was to select tasks that were more suited to her style. For example, while using the gossip technique, instead of allowing the enactment to occur in the session, she would encourage members to report about what would happen, thus allowing her to collect data, and at the same time, not get involved in a stress-provoking situation.

Having selected a general task category, the specific task will vary as a function of the level of client-family resistance, that is, the extent to which they appear committed to a problem-maintaining interactional pattern. Two broad task categories can here be distinguished. Positive-co-operative tasks are those in which the client-family members agree to perform a specific task, which the therapist expects they will in fact perform. Conversely, negative-co-operative tasks are those in which the client-family agrees to perform a specific task but which the therapist expects the family will ultimately reject or not perform. Typically, the determination of resistance will precede task selection. However, this need not occur in all cases. A client-family may appear ready to co-operate but, for a variety of ostensibly plausible reasons, may consistently fail to complete the tasks assigned, or perform them in such a way as to nullify their intended effect. Such feedback will clearly suggest that the initial impression was wrong and that, in fact, the client-family is resistant. Accordingly, alternative tasks, more suited to such families, will need to be constructed.

With respect to client-families that are judged co-operative, construction of positive-co-operative tasks will include the following techniques:

1. *Clarification*: processing and labelling of a communication sequence of events in the family which occurs unwittingly; for example, the therapist may comment "Dad, did you realize that you cut off mother whenever she speaks?"

2. *Staging a failure*: construction of a task that the therapist knows or suspects the family cannot accomplish; this is done in order to obtain another treatment goal.

3. *Task prescription*: a directive indicating some activity or piece of work that two or more family members are to perform. The technique of enactment is an example and is used here to change the context and sequence of behaviour rather than for data collection.

4. *Blocking*: the therapist interrupts an ongoing interactional process; this procedure creates psychological stress by blocking the usual flow of communication.

5. *Reframing*: the therapist gives the client-family a message which is intended to change the conceptual or emotional meaning; it typically applies to a given situation or interactional process (85). Thus, a husband who continually criticizes his wife's physical appearance may be described by the therapist as "sensitive and concerned about his wife's appearance." In so doing, the therapist attempts to lift the problems out of the symptom "frame" and into another context that fits the facts equally well or better; this changes its entire meaning and does not imply that the problem is unchangeable. If successful, the therapist's alternative definition of the problem makes it difficult for the client-family to return to the previous meaning, with its associated pain and anxiety.

By contrast, with respect to clients judged resistant, the construction of negative-co-operative tasks will include the following techniques:

1. *Paradox*: this technique is especially powerful insofar as it uses resistance (66) as a means of inducing change (61). Such tasks typically direct the client to increase the frequency with which a "problem" transaction occurs to such a point that the client is induced to "resist" the therapist by ceasing the behaviour altogether. The prescription is paradoxical, insofar as it occurs within a therapeutic context defined by necessity for change (2, 3). Consequently, the client-family is instructed to change, but doesn't change. If properly applied, their "solution" to this paradox is to "win" by rejecting the therapist and moving towards the treatment goal.*
It should be noted that an accurate use of pretext together with effective task delivery is crucial to the success of this technique. Indeed, the construction of an appropriate pretext, to what are considered by family members to be nonsensical suggestions, and the manner in which such suggestions are delivered, is often more difficult than deciding which problem behaviour needs to be encouraged.**

---

*For further elaboration, see Fisher et al. (29), Dell (23), Harris (42), Jessee and L'Abate (44), Bergman (11), Madanes (52), Weeks and L'Abate (86), Beck (8), and Bross and Gove, Chapter 6 in this volume.

**For further elaboration, see Bross and Benjamin, Chapter 3 in this volume.

2. *Supporting resistance*: there are occasions when a client-family will openly refuse to comply with the therapist's directive. The therapist can directly challenge such resistance at the risk of having the client-family drop out of therapy. Alternatively, the therapist can reverse his or her previous position and agree with the client-family's communication and reasoning. This creates a transactional situation in which the client-family is induced to consider alternative ways of thinking and behaving, while perceiving the therapist to be open and flexible. To be successful, the therapist's consistency in supporting resistance must be complete, often to the client's dismay.

3. *Confusion*: for a client-family that tends to intellectualize everything, task prescription typically proves fruitless, as the client shoots down each suggestion with a variety of reasons why it cannot work, as impractical, garbled, analytically indefensible, and so forth. The confusion technique is designed to neutralize such resistance by producing intellectual confusion through "complex pseudo-logical explanations, through ponderous, complicated, and therefore confusing references to trivial facts" (84, 27, 38). Out of this welter of information is intended to emerge a piece of therapeutically useful meaning which can be grasped and held onto with tenacity. Use of this technique requires superior clarity of purpose on the part of the therapist.

4. *Illusion of alternatives*: as its name suggests, this technique is used to give the client-family the impression that there exist at least two choices with respect to a given problem. In fact, such choices are illusory because they exist within a limited set of alternatives ("You can go to bed now, or in ten minutes from now. You choose.") both of which achieve the therapeutic goal. The technique is especially appropriate with resistant client-families because it appears to respond to their refusal to perform one task by offering them others, thus passing by real and potential client resistance (84).

Finally, given the selection and construction of a task, the successful outcome still depends upon its being delivered properly. This means that the task be (a) feasible, that is, something that the client-family can reasonably be expected to accomplish (64); (b) desirable, that is, that accomplishment of the task be associated with positive consequences (64); (c) clear, that is, well-understood (40); and (d) believable, that is, be logically consistent with a client's understanding of the situation and the therapist's intentions.

Towards these ends, the following considerations have proven useful:

1. Give a task using the family's own language;

2. Provide an appropriate pretext for the task;

3. Frame the task in such a way that it is within the therapist's authority to make a given prescription;

4. Consciously select the appropriate physical setting in which to give the client-family the task selected (e.g., home versus office);

5. Consider whether some means other than a verbal message may be best suited to the situation in question (e.g., the postal system);
6. Describe the task in such a way that it cannot be misunderstood by the client-family (e.g., either verbally or in writing or both).

Two brief examples of task delivery will illustrate its importance. Given a father who has been uninvolved in the discipline of his children, the therapist may instruct him to completely take over all child discipline in his home. As a directive, however, this may be neither feasible, because it conflicts with his hours of work, nor desirable, as the individual perceives the probability of his success as nil, and thus bound to fail. Alternatively, it may be more appropriate to ask the father to take responsibility for child discipline one evening a week.

Extending the above example, in addition to this task, the therapist may frame the task in the following manner, "Would you like to discipline your children one evening this week if it is possible for you to take time out of your schedule?" This gives the father the illusion of choice; whatever he decides, his involvement with child discipline is assured. As stated, however, the task is suggested rather than prescribed and it creates ambiguity. Accordingly, it would be strengthened by being restated as follows, "Father, you are to select an evening this week when you *will* engage in disciplining the children without the help of your wife."

Phase Five: Evaluation and the Notion of Therapist Error

As noted above, while intervention may be used as a means of data collection, the primary purpose is to change problem-maintaining patterns of interaction. In this sense, three outcomes of intervention are possible: the intervention is successful, only partially successful, or completely unsuccessful.

1. With respect to the *first outcome*, a successful outcome is one in which a dysfunctional interactional pattern changes at *both* the level of behaviour and of meaning. Assessment of change involves neither the therapist's judgment alone nor the client's objective report alone. Rather, it is a matter of empirical evidence—behavioural sequences and ways of attributing meaning that were observed to occur regularly prior to intervention, no longer occur following intervention. Depending on the context of the case, a successful outcome of a specific intervention would suggest that (a) the treatment plan was correct; (b) the selection, instruction, and delivery of the task was appropriate; and (c) either remaining elements of the treatment plan be implemented or case termination be considered.

2. With regard to the *second outcome*, partial success, assessment is problematic for two reasons:
(a) The change process takes time; just as problem-maintaining interactional processes may take some time to evolve, so the impact of a

specific intervention may take some time to work through the client-family system. In accord with this reasoning, Selvini-Palazzoli and her colleagues (71), for example, may wait several months between sessions in order to provide time for their intricately designed interventions to have their desired effect. Consequently, what is deemed only a partial success at Time One, may be seen as a complete success at Time Two. The appropriate time frame, then, is crucial in coming to a conclusion regarding outcome.

(b) Reading the feedback that the family offers following an intervention may be a complex task. That some aspect of dysfunctional interactional process has undergone change clearly suggests that the intervention in question was not without impact. The question becomes: "Which parts were effective and which parts were not?" In simple, "positive-co-operative" tasks this may be easy to deduce. In more complex, multi-facetted tasks this may be more difficult.

For example, while the family's meaning system may undergo change, its patterns of interaction may not. A husband comes to therapy denying there is any problem, while his wife complains bitterly of being lonely and frustrated. Following intervention, the husband acknowledges the problem and promises to listen to his wife in the future; he suggests that things are better now but during this monologue his wife has tears in her eyes. Alternatively, while the family's interactional pattern may change, its view of the situation may not. Given a sexually dysfunctional relationship, intervention may restore functioning, only to leave both partners complaining of continuing dissatisfaction.

Furthermore, there is an extraordinary consideration here, namely, that insofar as the therapist is in charge of the therapeutic process, he or she takes responsibility for all failure. Clearly, a task that is only partially completed, is a task that is partially a failure. It follows that while partial successes may be extremely valuable for the new information they provide, they may not be distinguished either analytically or clinically from complete failures.

3. This brings us to the *third possible outcome*, failure. A failed intervention is simply one that is associated with no change in dysfunctional family processes at *any* level. This outcome may be interpreted in one of two ways: as a result of client resistance, or of therapist error. With respect to the former, two considerations are especially pertinent:

(a) First, therapists are only human and so may become inordinately attached to a given case formulation, a preferred intervention style or technique, an experientially validated association between certain family constellations and certain intervention processes, and so on. Consequently, there is the ever-present danger, especially among experienced practitioners, that they will be over-inclusive in their use of the category label "resistant." Indeed, too often, in our experience, the label is virtually unquestionable for the simple reason that it is founded on a pernicious tautology: families are resistant because they have not responded to my interventions by changing in a particular direction; they have not changed in a particular direction because they are resistant.

(b) Second, to a significant degree, resistance and error tend to shade into each other. Predicated on the notion that the practitioner is responsible for the course of therapy, and noting that level of resistance is part and parcel of task selection, construction, and delivery, it follows that intervention failure provides at least prima facie evidence of therapist error. This is not to suggest that our clinical knowledge is so complete that therapist error is the only explanation for intervention failure; the "tough stability" (5) of schizophrenic families, for example, is well-known. Nor is it to disregard the fact that the "fit" between the therapist and client—in style, language, culture, class, and so on—is seldom perfect. Nor is it to deny that certain therapist errors are only "errors" in a nominal sense; they may be the only way to gather certain kinds of data that will subsequently be invaluable in guiding the course and insuring the success of future interventions (see above, Phase Four). Rather, it is intended to call attention to several salient features of the family therapy literature in general and the therapeutic process more specifically:

(1) The therapeutic encounter is fundamentally an interactional process involving two or more active participants each of whom *necessarily* affects the other at least in some respects (cf. Framo (31); Walsh (83)). Consequently, a significant proportion of client behaviour will occur in reaction to the therapist's behaviour and is thus not merely a reflection of intrafamilial interaction.

(2) Family therapists, like all professionals, may vary widely in their levels of expertise, acumen, creativity, flexibility, and so on. This varies not only from therapist to therapist, but even within each therapist's self from day to day, as factors such as the demand characteristics of the situation, fatigue, marital and financial difficulties, physical ill health, age, and so forth come into play.

(3) An unknown but probably significant proportion of intervention failures can be traced to therapist error. Logically, three levels of error may be distinguished: (a) "beneficial" errors in which the therapist employs intervention for the purpose either of data collection or case formulation verification; (b) "neutral" errors resulting from Number 2 above, but which are benign in the sense that they neither help nor hinder the client-family; and (c) "destructive" errors resulting, again, from Number 2 above, but which "harms the client-family by causing it unnecessary distress, further stabilizing existing problem-maintaining interactional processes, or

causing the real and/or perceived level of functioning in the client-family to deteriorate."

(4) While practitioners, both "beginners" and "old hands," routinely acknowledge to each other that they make "mistakes," the notion of therapist error is formally contained neither in existing models of practice nor in that portion of the family therapy literature concerned with training (cf. Harvey (43), Tomm and Wright (81), and Beal (7)).

(5) To be adequate, any comprehensive model of family therapy practice must have, built into it, some notion of therapist error.

In accord with the above consideration, in what follows below we present our own tentative typology of therapist error.* This is grounded upon the notion that the therapeutic process contains a finite number of "choice points" or "decision nodes." At each of these, the therapist is confronted with the need to select among two or more alternative courses of action. Assuming that in any given instance some choices are better than others (i.e., more efficient with respect to desired ends), the therapist will be said to have made an error if the outcome is judged either "neutral" or "destructive," as in Number 3 above. Interventions that are not intended to produce change, but which yield valuable data, and are thus "positive," as in Number 3 above, will be said to involve an "error strategy," that is, they are not errors in the proper sense.

Inspection of the recursive model in Figure 1.1 reveals that there are five major decision nodes with respect to intervention; these correspond to the five major categories into which our typology is divided. Each of these error types is listed and briefly discussed below, followed by an illustrative example.

1. *Assessment error:* as noted above (Phase One), assessment involves the collection of pertinent information concerning a client-family; consequently, assessment error essentially involves errors in information. Thus, information may be incomplete, either because the wrong combination of assessment techniques has been employed; such techniques have been employed incorrectly: the family's portrayal of itself has been too readily accepted, or all appropriate information targets have not been "hit"; or the family may have tacitly refused to discuss "sensitive" information (e.g., family secrets, see 46); for similar reasons information may be distorted, vague, or misleading (e.g., family myths, see 69, 45).

2. *Formulation error:* the development of the case formulation involves the integration and organization of available data into a coherent

---

*For an elaborated discussion of this typology, see Benjamin and Bross (10), Chapter 3 in this volume.

whole which permits the derivation of falsifiable hypotheses. This end involves a high level of professional judgment, with few hard-and-fast guidelines to employ. As such, it is probably the hardest aspect of the therapeutic process to master and is thus correspondingly vulnerable to error. Because the case formulation will determine the interventions to be employed, a particular formulation which later proves inaccurate or at least incomplete will almost certainly render the therapist's efforts ineffective. Consequently, it is essential to understand the treatment process as a hypothesis-testing encounter.

3. *Tactical error*: tactical or strategic manoeuvres refer to the therapist's use of interventions, either singly or in combination, aimed at producing change. As noted above, the selection, construction, and delivery of therapeutic tasks is technically complex and thus affords the therapist, especially the "beginner," with an array of opportunities for error. Without attempting a comprehensive list, such errors include: (a) selecting a digital task when an analogic one would have been more appropriate; (b) constructing a positive-co-operative task when a negative-co-operative task was called for; (c) constructing a task using a disengaged style when an enmeshed style was called for; (d) constructing a task without giving sufficient attention to the creation of an appropriate pretext; (e) constructing a task perceived as either unbelievable, undesirable, or not feasible by the client-family; (f) delivering the task in language far too sophisticated for the client-family; and so on.

4. *Support error*: supportive operations are needed throughout the therapeutic process in order to permit the therapist to get close to, and be trusted by the client-family. Failing this, it is unlikely that the client-family will be responsive to anything the therapist has to offer, however sincere or brilliant. Support errors, then, occur when the therapist is unable to establish that relationship of trust, whether because he or she is insufficiently attentive, fails to be sympathetic or to respect differences, does not reinforce strengths, and so on.

5. *Evaluation error*: finally, once a therapeutic intervention has been made, the therapist's evaluation of the feedback from this effort will determine his or her subsequent course of treatment. Additional interventions may be required, or the case may be terminated; either alternative is subject to error. The therapist may have traced the feedback inaccurately and so concluded that termination is appropriate, when in fact all treatment objectives have not been met. Similarly, misreading of available data may cause the therapist to incorrectly re-apply the same intervention when an alternative intervention would have been more appropriate, or, conversely, to switch altogether when a small refinement of the same intervention would have sufficed.

These various errors may occur singly or in some combination. However they occur, they will delay the family's search for relief from their problem, which may in turn encourage client drop-out. As an illustration of two such outcomes, consider the following case vignettes about the J family.

> The parents of the J family brought their daughter, Joan, age sixteen, to a social worker. They complained that she was disobedient, disrespectful, and sexually promiscuous. As the consultant on the case, the senior author observed the initial interview on the basis of which he concluded that the parents had lost total parental authority over this girl; to resolve their problem they would have to become effective parents again.
>
> While it was not yet completely clear at this point why Mr. and Mrs. J. had ceased to parent effectively, it was clear that this was significantly related to their prior contact with several mental health consultants. Their first contact was with the local mental health clinic. Having completed his assessment, the therapist commented that the parents were too strict with the girl and suggested that they should "loosen up." After taking the therapist's advice, Mr. and Mrs. J. were dismayed that their daughter was getting progressively worse; she would stay out later and later, had gotten into drugs, and was arrested by the police. In this instance, it was our opinion that there was an assessment error made by the therapist which in turn resulted in an inappropriate task.
>
> Dissatisfied with the advice of the first therapist, the J's went to see a psychiatrist in another mental health centre. This therapist told them that there was nothing emotionally wrong with their daughter except that she was being spoiled rotten by them; he indicated that Mr. and Mrs. J. had to become firm and strict with her. Specifically, he suggested that in order to regain their parental authority over Joan, the J's should kick her out of the house to teach her a lesson. In this instance, it was our opinion that the therapist had made an accurate assessment. However, his task selection was clearly undesirable with respect to this family who felt very close to their daughter. The J's left that therapist without any resolution; however, they did agree that being more strict with Joan was what they had felt like doing all along.
>
> Finally, following the assessment at our clinic, we concluded that the previous therapist's assessment had been correct; however, our task selection and construction were somewhat different. We directed the parents to engage in a variety of tasks all of which would encourage them to set firm rules and limits for Joan, while paying no attention to Joan's protests. These included: grounding her, setting curfews, curtailing generous allowances, and going out to get her if she failed to return home. The results were almost immediate: the dysfunctional family situation reversed itself as Joan came to accept her parent's authority and behaved in accord with the rules they set down.

Phase Six: Termination

Having begun, every therapeutic encounter must eventually come to an end. Case termination may occur in any one of six ways:

1. Termination may result from the recognition of health, that is, the

recognition that no problem exists. Brief assessment is usually sufficient to reveal that there is really nothing wrong with the client-family, but rather that they have erroneously concluded that some problem they face *must* be "sick." Typically, this conclusion derives from ignorance of the range of healthy solutions to a given problem, while the anxiety associated with such ignorance can easily be overcome by giving the family some factual information. While comparatively rare, such cases are very significant because they point out the need to approach every therapeutic encounter with a presumption of health. Conversely, they also reveal that the presumption of illness is founded upon a pernicious tautology—the family can only have come to therapy because they are sick; the proof of their illness is the fact that they have come to therapy—which can cause unnecessary pain, anxiety, and expense to client-families.

2. Even though a problem exists and is serious enough to warrant treatment, intervention may be contraindicated. There is, however, little consensus among practitioners concerning the criteria for case termination and referral, in this context. Martin (55), for example, offers the following list of criteria: (a) a therapist who is neither enthusiastic nor convinced of the superiority of this method with respect to a given case; (b) a lack of motivation on the part of one or more significant family members; (c) a marital relationship so filled with violent feelings and sexual problems that exposing the children to them would destroy their normal development; (d) parental distress initiated by child behaviour indicative of individuality and autonomy; (e) a family system in which destructive secrets (e.g., child abuse) are not allowed to surface and so impede the therapeutic process; and (f) a "folie à deux" family in which it is crucial to separate the psychotic member in order that he or she may receive individual treatment. Alternatively, Clarkin et al. (20) present a different list. It is our preference to exclude *only* families in which one or more members are showing evidence of either an organic problem or a learning disability.

3. Termination automatically follows client withdrawal (i.e., dropout) of the treatment process. While such a withdrawal may be mutual, in response, for example, to recognizing the lack of "fit" between the therapist and the client, it is more often unilateral, related to the occurrence of one or more therapist errors. The client-family may have felt that the therapist was too aggressive or too passive, too quick or too slow, too distant or too close, and so on.

4. Termination may be initiated by the therapist, even against the opposition of the client-family (22), after intervention has failed to produce any significant movement in the case. Whatever the reason for such failure—whether it be client resistance or therapist error or both—it is incumbent upon the therapist to terminate appropriately, so that both therapist and client can move on to a new therapeutic encounter.

5. Termination may be initiated by the client following partial

success, that is, when only some of the therapist's objectives have been achieved. This may occur for a variety of reasons. Commonly, this is indicative of resistance as each therapeutic change becomes increasingly threatening to the client-family (35). Alternatively, however, it can also result from physical relocation, a change in family financial status, a shift in employment, and so forth. Whatever the reason, the best therapeutic manoeuvre in such situations is for the therapist to agree with the family's decision. It reduces the possibility of separation and anxiety and at least leaves the door open for the family to resume treatment at a later time, even with another therapist.

6. Finally, termination is a logical and welcome outcome of therapeutic success, that is, in which all treatment goals have been achieved. This is clearly the type of termination sought after by all therapists and clients alike. Accordingly, it must be done properly and with care. This will involve (a) solidifying gains by giving the family the responsibility for all changes; (b) encouraging the maintenance of change by predicting failure, thus mobilizing family resistance to this prediction; and (c) contracting for a follow-up session—three to six months is a suggested interval—in order to empirically verify the durability of change (21).

To illustrate two of the above types of termination, consider the following case vignettes.

> Mr. and Mrs. M. brought their son, Peter, age six, into treatment, complaining that he was "uncontrollable." After a series of four treatment sessions, Mr. and Mrs. M. had gradually learned how to discipline Peter, who was showing a marked improvement. At this juncture, the senior author commented to Mr. and Mrs. M. how amazed he was at how quickly they had understood what needed to be changed, and how surprised he was that they "somehow" intuitively grasped what he was saying and so had accomplished the desired task with their child. Further, he noted that he wasn't certain how this had been accomplished and so cautioned that they might be expected to slip up in the future. However, he concluded, he was sure they would know how to recover; having identified their errors by themselves the first time, they would certainly be able to do so again. Accordingly, they were to continue what they were doing and carry on with their lives.
>
> The comments to the M family were intended to maintain their improvement by rejecting my notion of potential failure.

By contrast, case termination with the Y family involved a different outcome.

> The senior author had worked with the Y's for close to seven months without any significant change. The problem concerned a single mother with a sixteen-year-old daughter who had become involved with drugs. No matter what positive-co-operative strategies were attempted, the Y's only partially succeeded. A series of negative-co-operative tasks were then employed with similar results.

In this kind of situation, prudent therapists will recognize that either they are not "clicking" with the family or they do not really understand the interactional processes maintaining problem behaviour. Having come to this conclusion, the therapist must recognize that he or she is wasting the client's time as well as his or her own, and should acknowledge failure. Consequently, the only course of action open to the therapist is to make a referral to another practitioner who may be more helpful to the family in question; in our view, to do anything else (e.g., continue to work with the family) would be unethical.

Conclusion

The foregoing material describes and explains a recursive model of family therapy practice. The model is scarcely definitive; like a living organism, it continues to grow and develop as we gain further clinical experience and as new data emerge in the literature. Furthermore, it is no substitute for experience under the tutelage of a skilled supervisor. Rather, we developed the model in order to (a) clarify the assumptive base of family therapy; (b) provide a brief but comprehensive overview of the multiple stages of the therapeutic process; (c) indicate the recursive nature of the connection between and among therapy phases; (d) highlight the notion of therapist error; and (e) underline some of the logical and ethical traps into which the therapist, "beginner" or "old timer," may fall.

In the course of doing the work necessary to the construction of this model, we were forced, again and again, to confront and rethink our own assumptions, preferences, and prejudices about the nature, course, and objectives of family therapy. If we have imposed the same constraints on you, as you have read this paper, our purpose will have been served.

References

1. Ackerman, N.W. *The Psychodynamics of Family Life.* N.Y.: Basic Books, 1958.
2. Andolfi, M. "Resistance to change in families with a schizophrenic member." In A.S. Gurman, ed. *Questions and Answers in the Practice of Family Therapy.* N.Y.: Brunner/Mazel, 1981.
3. Andolfi, M., Menghi, P., Nicolo, A.M., and Saccu, C. "Interaction in ridi systems; A model of intervention in families with a schizophrenic member." In M. Andolfi and I. Zwerling, eds. *Dimensions of Family Therapy.* N.Y.: Guilford, 1980.
4. Bandler, R., and Grinder, J. *The Structure of Magic.* Vol. 1. Palo Alto, Cal.: *Science and Behaviour,* 1975.
5. Bateson, G. "The group dynamics of schizophrenia." In L. Appleby, J.M. Scher, and J. Cumming, eds. *Chronic Schizophrenia: Explorations in Theory and Treatment.* Glencoe, Ill.: The Free Press, 1960.
6. Bauman, M.H. "Involving resistant family members in therapy." In A.S. Gurman, ed. *Questions and Answers in the Practice of Family Therapy.* N.Y.: Brunner/Mazel, 1981.
7. Beal, E.W. "Current trends in the training of family therapists." *American Journal of Psychiatry.* 133 (1976): 137-141.

8. Beck. M.J. "Management of treatment-destructive resistance in family therapy." In A.S. Gurman, ed. *Questions and Answers in the Practice of Family Therapy.* N.Y.: Brunner/Mazel, 1981.

9. Bell, J.E. *Family Therapy.* N.Y.: Jason Aronson, 1975.

10. Benjamin, M., and Bross, A. "Family Therapy: A Typology of Therapist Error." In A. Bross, ed. *Family Therapy: A Recursive Model of Strategic Practice.* Toronto: Methuen, 1982.

11. Bergman, J.S. "The use of paradox in a community home for the chronically disturbed and retarded." *Family Process.* 19 (1980): 65-72.

12. Bertalanffy, L. Von. *General Systems Theory.* N.Y.: Braziller, 1968.

13. Bowen, M. *Family Therapy in Clinical Practice.* N.Y.: Jason Aronson, 1978.

14. Boyd, J.H. "Family therapy goals in short-term inpatient hospitals." In A.S. Gurman, ed. *Questions and Answers in the Practice of Family Therapy.* N.Y.: Brunner/Mazel, 1981.

15. Bross, A. "Strategic Family Therapy . . . Feedback and Response." *Journal of Systemic and Strategic Therapy.* I (1981): 9-13. Chapter 10 in this book.

16. Bross, A. "Subtext, Context, Pretext in Family Therapy." Unpublished paper. Toronto, 1980.

17. Bross, A., and Gove. P. "Paradox: A common element in individual and family psychotherapy." In A. Bross, ed. *Family Therapy: A Recursive Model of Strategic Practice.* Toronto: Methuen, 1982.

18. Carkhuff, R. "Training in the counselling and therapeutic process: requiem or reveille?" *Journal of Counselling Psychology.* 1966.

19. Carkhuff, R., and Truax, C. "Training in counselling and psychotherapy: An evaluation of an integrated didactic and experiential approach." *Journal of Consulting Psychology.* 29 (1965).

20. Clarkin, J.F., Francis, A.J., and Moodis, J.L. "Selection Criteria for family therapy." *Family Process.* 18 (1979): 391-404.

21. Comrinck-Graham, L. "Termination in family therapy." in A.S. Gurman, ed. *Questions and Answers in the Practice of Family Therapy.* N.Y: Brunner/Mazel, 1981.

22. Davis, D.I. "Couples who do not want to terminate therapy." In A.S. Gurman, ed. *Questions and Answers in the Practice of Family Therapy.* N.Y.: Brunner/Mazel, 1981.

23. Dell, P.F. "Some irreverent thoughts on paradox." *Family Process.* 20 (1981): 37-41.

24. Doherty, W.J. "Involving the reluctant father in family therapy." In A.S. Gurman, ed. *Questions and Answers in the Practice of Family Therapy.* N.Y.: Brunner/Mazel, 1981.

25. Erickson, M.H., and Rossi, E.L. *Experiencing Hypnosis: Therapeutic Approaches to Altered States.* N.Y.: Irvington, 1981.

26. Erickson, M.H., and Rossi, E.L. *Hypnotherapy: An Exploratory Casebook.* N.Y.: Irvington, 1979.

27. Erickson, M.H., Rossi, E.L., and Rossi, S.I. *Hypnotic Realities: The Induction of Clinical Hypnosis and Forms of Indirect Suggestion.* N.Y.: Irvington, 1976.

28. Fisher, L. "Helping parents get resistant adolescents into family therapy." In A.S. Gurman, ed. *Questions and Answers in the Practice of Family Therapy.* N.Y.: Brunner/Mazel, 1981.

29. Fisher, L., Anderson, A., and Jones, J.E. "Types of paradoxical intervention and indications/contraindications for use in clinical practice." *Family Process.* 20 (1981): 25-36.
30. Flomenhaft, K., and Carter, R.E. "Family Therapy Training: Program and Outcome." *Family Process.* 16 (1977): 211-218.
31. Framo, J.L. "Personal Reflections of a Family Therapist." In J.G. Howells, ed. *Advances in Family Psychiatry.* Vol. 1. N.Y.: International University Press, 1979.
32. Gaines, T., Jr. "Engaging the Father in Family Therapy." In A.S. Gurman, ed. *Questions and Answers in the Practice of Family Therapy.* N.Y.: Brunner/Mazel, 1981.
33. Garfield, R. "Convening the Family: Guidelines for the Initial Contact with a Family Member." In A.S. Gurman, ed. *Questions and Answers in the Practice of Family Therapy.* N.Y.: Brunner/Mazel, 1981.
34. Grinder, J., and Bandler, R. *The Structure of Magic.* Vol. 2. Palo Alto, Cal.: *Science and Behavior,* 1976.
35. Grosman, P., Bross, A., and Benjamin, M. "The Systemic Treatment of Hysterical Paralysis: A Case Report." In A. Bross, ed. *Family Therapy: A Recursive Model of Strategic Practice.* Toronto: Methuen, 1982.
36. Gurman, A.S., and Kniskern, D.P. "Family Therapy Outcome Research: Knowns and Unknowns." In A.S. Gurman and D.P. Kniskern, eds. *Handbook of Family Therapy.* N.Y.: Brunner/Mazel, 1981.
37. Haley, J. "The Family of the Schizophrenic: A Model System." *Journal of Nervous and Mental Disease.* 129 (1959): 357-374.
38. Haley, J. *Uncommon Therapy: The Psychiatric Techniques of Milton H. Erickson.* N.Y.: Ballantine, 1973.
39. Haley, J. "Why a Mental Health Clinic Should Avoid Family Therapy." *Journal of Marriage and Family Counseling.* 1 (1975): 3-13.
40. Haley, J. *Problem-Solving Therapy.* San Francisco: Jossey-Bass, 1976.
41. Hall, A.D., and Fagen, R.E. "The Definition of System." *General Systems Yearbook.* 1 (1956): 18-28.
42. Harris, L. "Analysis of a Paradoxical Logic: A Case Study." *Family Process.* 19 (1980): 19-34.
43. Harvey, M.A. "On Becoming a Family Therapist: The First Three Years." *International Journal of Family Therapy.* 2 (1980): 263-274.
44. Jessee, E., and L'Abate, L. "The Use of Paradox with Children in an Inpatient Setting." *Family Process.* 19 (1980): 59-64.
45. Kaplan, S.J. "Utilizing Myth/Game Systems with Couples in Conflict." In A.S. Gurman, ed. *Questions and Answers in the Practice of Family Therapy.* N.Y.: Brunner/Mazel, 1981.
46. Karpel, M.A. "Family Secrets." *Family Process.* 19 (1980): 295-306.
47. Kaslow, F.W. "History of Family Therapy in the United States: A Kaleidoscopic Overview." *Marriage and Family Review.* 3 (1980): 77-111.
48. Kaslow, F.W. "Involving the Peripheral Father in Family Therapy." In A.S. Gurman, ed. *Questions and Answers in the Practice of Family Therapy.* N.Y.: Brunner/Mazel, 1981.
49. Katz, D., and Kahn, R.L. *The Social Psychology of Organization.* N.Y.: Wiley, 1966.

50. Laszlo, E. *Introduction to Systems Philosophy.* N.Y.: Harper and Row, 1972.
51. Lieberman, R.P. "Behavioral Methods in Group and Family Therapy." *Seminars in Psychiatry.* 4 (1972): 145-156.
52. Madanes, C. "Protection, Paradox, and Pretending." *Family Process.* 19 (1980): 73-85.
53. Madanes, C., and Haley, J. "Dimensions of Family Therapy." *Journal of Nervous Mental Disease.* 165 (1977): 85-98.
54. Mandelbaum, A. "Developing a Family Therapy Program in a Psychoanalytically Oriented Setting." In A.S. Gurman, ed. *Questions and Answers in the Practice of Family Therapy.* N.Y.: Brunner/Mazel, 1981.
55. Martin, P.A. "No Treatment is the Treatment of Choice." In A.S. Gurman, ed. *Questions and Answers in the Practice of Family Therapy.* N.Y.: Brunner/Mazel, 1981.
56. Minuchin, S. *Families and Family Therapy.* Cambridge, Mass.: Harvard University Press, 1974.
57. Minuchin, S., and Fishman, C. *Techniques of Family Therapy.* Harvard University Press, Cambridge, Mass., 1981.
58. Ohlson, D.H., Sprenkle, D.H., and Russel, C. "Circumplex Model of Family Systems." *Family Process.* 18 (1979): 3-28.
59. Orne, M.T. "On the Social Psychology of the Psychological Experiment: With Particular Reference to Demand Characteristics and Their Implications." *American Psychologist.* 17 (1962): 776-783.
60. Papp, P. *Family Therapy.* N.Y.: Gardner, 1977.
61. Papp, P. "Paradoxical Strategies and Countertransference." In A.S. Gurman, ed. *Questions and Answers in the Practice of Family Therapy.* N.Y.: Brunner/Mazel, 1981.
62. Patterson, G.P. *Families: Applications of Social Learning to Family Life.* Champaign, Ill.: Research Press, 1971.
63. Rapoport, A. "The Search for Simplicity." In E. Laszlo, ed. *The Relevance of General Systems Theory.* N.Y.: Braziller, 1972.
64. Reid, W.J., and Epstein, L. *Task-Centered Casework.* N.Y.: Columbia University Press, 1972.
65. Rogers, C. "The Necessary and Sufficient Conditions of Therapeutic Personality Change." *Journal of Consulting Psychology.* 21 (1957): 95-103.
66. Saposnek, D.T. "Aikido: A Model for Brief Strategic Therapy." *Family Process.* 19 (1980): 227-238.
67. Satir, V.M. "Conjoint Family Therapy: A Guide to Theory and Technique." Rev. ed. Palo Alto, Cal.: *Science and Behavior,* 1967.
68. Satir, V.M. "Peoplemaking." Palo Alto, Cal.: *Science and Behavior.* 1972.
69. Sederer, L.I., and Sederer, N. "A Family Myth: Sex Therapy Gone Awry." *Family Process.* 18 (1979): 315-321.
70. Shah, S. *The Way of the Surf.* N.Y.: Dutton, 1970.
71. Selvini-Palazzoli, M.S., Cecchin, C., Prata, G., and Boscolo, L. *Paradox and Counterparadox: A New Model in the Therapy of the Family in Schizophrenic Transactions.* N.Y.: Jason Aronson, 1978.
72. Selvini-Palazzoli, M.S. "Hypothesizing-Circularity-Neutrality: Three Guidelines for the Conductor of the Session." *Family Process.* 19 (1980): 3-12.
73. Spooner, S., and Stone, S. "Maintenance of Specific Counselling Skills Over Time." *Journal of Consulting Psychology.* 24 (1977).

74. Stanton, M.D. "Who Should Get Credit for Change which Occurs in Therapy?" In A.S. Gurman, ed. *Questions and Answers in the Practice of Family Therapy*. N.Y.: Brunner/Mazel, 1981.
75. Starr, S. "Dealing with Common Resistances to Attending the First Family Therapy Session." In A.S. Gurman, ed. *Questions and Answers in the Practice of Family Therapy*. N.Y.: Brunner/Mazel, 1981.
76. Steinfeld, G.J. "Establishing Treatment Contracts in Family Therapy." In A.S. Gurman, ed. *Questions and Answers in the Practice of Family Therapy*. N.Y.: Brunner/Mazel, 1981.
77. Straus, M.A. "A General Systems Theory Approach to a Theory of Violence Between Family Members." *Social Science Information*. 12 (1973): 105-125.
78. Stuart, R.B. "An Operant Interpersonal Program for Couples." In D.H.L. Olson, ed. *Treating Relationships*. Lake Mills, Iowa: Graphic, 1976.
79. Teismann, M.W. "Convening Strategies in Family Therapy." *Family Process*. 19 (1980): 393-400.
80. Thomas, W.I. Cited in Aldrich, H.E. *Organizations and Environments*. Englewood Cliffs, N.J.: Prentice-Hall, 1979.
81. Tomm, K.M., and Wright, L.M. "Training in Family Therapy: Perceptual, Conceptual, and Executive Skills." *Family Process*. 18 (1979): 227-250.
82. Truax, C.B. "A Scale for Rating of Accurate Empathy: The Therapeutic Relationship and its Report." In C. Rogers, et al., eds. *The Therapeutic Relationship and its Report*. Madison, Wis.: University of Wisconsin Press, 1967.
83. Walsh, F. "Preventing Burnout in Therapeutic Work with Severely Dysfunctional Families." In A.S. Gurman, ed. *Questions and Answers in the Practice of Family Therapy*. N.Y.: Brunner/Mazel, 1981.
84. Watzlawick, P. *The Language of Change*. N.Y.: Basic, 1978.
85. Watzlawick, P., Weakland, J., and Fisch, R. *Change: Principles of Problem Formation and Problem Resolution*. N.Y.: Norton, 1974.
86. Weeks, G., and L'Abate, L. "A Bibliography of Paradoxical Methods in Psychotherapy of Family Systems." *Family Process*. 18 (1978): 96-98.
87. Weiss, P.A. "The Living System: Determinism Stratified." In A. Koestler and J.R. Smythies, eds. *Beyond Reductionism*. N.Y.: Macmillan, 1969.
88. Wolpert-Zur, A., and Bross, A. "The Formation of the Reconstituted Family System: Processes, Problems, and Treatment Goals." In A. Bross, ed. *Family Therapy: A Recursive Model of Strategic Practice*. Toronto: Methuen, 1982.
89. Zuk, G.H. *Family Therapy: A Triadic-Based Approach*. N.Y.: Behavioral Publications, 1971.

2

General Systems Theory, Family Systems Theories, and Family Therapy: Towards an Integrated Model of Family Process

Michael Benjamin

The family therapy literature contains a number of different models of family process. All, however, are excessively narrow, focussing only on a restricted range of patterns and processes. In an effort to develop a more comprehensive integrated model, General Systems Theory and four family systems theories are reviewed and evaluated, and pertinent concepts are either highlighted or derived. The result is a recursive model of family process centred on five multi-dimensional constructs: meaning, affect, communication, interaction, and level of demand. This yields a picture of family life that is more fluid, contingent, and changeable than that found in existing models. In closing, I examine the clinical implications of the model and indicate its connection to Bross and Benjamin's recursive model of strategic practice.

1. Introduction

No model of clinical intervention, including our own (29), exists in a theoretical vacuum. Rather, it is rationalized by its grounding in some body of theory which explains how families work (12), how they go wrong (63), and how they change (74).

While a multiplicity of explanatory models in the family therapy literature is available, no single model deals adequately with all three areas. More specifically, dissatisfaction with current family models rests on at least six points.

1. Existing models, explicitly or implicitly, tend to create an artificial polarization around different aspects of family process. Thus, structural theories (e.g., 98) tend to emphasize spatial processes while communication theories (e.g., 150) focus on temporal processes (139). However, just as Einstein recognized that space and time were different aspects of the same phenomenon in the physical world (e.g., 36), so space and time are interrelated phenomena in family life. Differences between these theories, then, are more artificial than real, and are reminiscent of the efforts of twelve blind men to describe an elephant by touch alone: each comes to recognize one facet of the beast, but none comes to know it totally.

2. The emphasis of family theorists on pattern, consistency, redundancy, and so forth tend seriously to underestimate the role of chance, randomness, or variety (13, 31) as an important impetus to change (95, 144, 39). This is not to suggest that either a patterned or variable interaction sequence is more important than the other, but that both need to be taken into account.

3. In a related fashion, time, both in the short and long term, has been given rather limited attention. In the short term, the timing or staging of events and/or experiences require attention if one is to understand their impact or lack of it (74). The family that has just lost its home to fire is likely to respond quite differently to the unanticipated lay-off of the breadwinner than one that is not in crisis (51). Similarly, in the long term, developmental processes have been given relatively scanty attention. While most theories acknowledge the importance of developmental processes (4, 23, 138), they tend to limit their concern to the observation that the onset of symptoms tends to be associated with developmental transition periods, especially the loss or addition of members (60, 57, 133). While the observation is an important one, it is hardly equivalent to a thoughtful conceptualization of the processes involved (e.g., 35, 139).

4. The principal concern of family theorists with interactional process has meant that individual choice has been largely, or wholly, ignored (56, 81, 162). To some extent, this is understandable. The focus on interactional pattern in the family has been intended to counteract the traditional focus on the individual patient, seen in social isolation. The traditional focus has tended (1) to reify the dualistic distinction between mind and body, subject and object (41); (2) to ignore the larger ecosystemic context of which the individual is but a part (10, 58, 83); and, (3) to deny that the "self" is quintessentially a social product (12, 13, 27). None of this, however, is inconsistent with the notion that the individual is a system in his or her own right (23), and acts dynamically to shape his or her environment rather than merely responding to it (21). In this sense, while the individual, together with other family members, may be caught up in an interactional process over which they have relatively little control (59, 72), it is also possible that they may, through a self-reflexive and creative act, transcend that system (85). Thus, the explanation of family process requires that some attention be paid to individual variation and choice in all family members.

5. While all family theorists routinely acknowledge a debt to general systems theory (GST), few indicate what is meant by the term, and even fewer make any effort to spell out the epistemological base or basic concepts of GST. This is, no doubt, related to the fact that available models claim varying degrees of allegiance to GST, some explicitly systemic (e.g., 150), others only moderately so (e.g., 98), and still others conceptually committed as much to psychoanalysis as to GST (e.g., 1, 25). Even so, with the exception

of Steinglass (139), one is hard-pressed to find even a moderately complete statement of GST in the family therapy literature. Consequently, of the many family therapists of my acquaintance, most have only a vague notion of what GST is all about. Therefore, some explanation of GST is essential, if for no other reason than to be clear about how one is diverging from it.

6. Finally, with few exceptions (e.g., 80), the bulk of the family theory literature and certainly most family theorists are primarily concerned with clinical as opposed to non-clinical families. On the one hand, this is only reasonable. The focus of most writing in the area has traditionally been concerned with therapeutic intervention with symptomatic families, hence the long-standing concern with the characteristics of such families (e.g., 101, 120, 136). On the other hand, it makes no sense at all. With the possible exception of the most severely disturbed families, all families change over time and with circumstances, and all families face "difficulties" which may become "problems" (149, 151). Even so, most families either manage to overcome their "problems" or learn to live with them without the need of clinical assistance (23, 160). Furthermore, even the most disturbed family is not completely maladaptive, having a variety of entirely conventional areas of family life. Thus, the "clinical" family is not an absolute status, but rather typically represents a temporary part of the shifts and changes that are part and parcel of the family's life cycle. It follows that for theoretical purposes it is just as important to know why a family goes "right" as why it goes "wrong."

Collectively, these remarks suggest the need for a new model of family dynamics which is simultaneously recursive (i.e., systemic), multi-dimensional, and integrative. In the present chapter, I attempt to sketch such a model in relatively broad terms. The model in question is necessarily broad and rudimentary for three reasons: first, our own ideas about family life continue to change and develop as our own clinical experience and theoretical expertise grow; second, the knowledge base for many of the issues noted above remains extremely scanty; and, finally, "the extraordinary complexity of a family at any given moment, much less over a lifetime, makes it impossible to attempt more here." (60)

Accordingly, in what follows below, I first present an exploration of the epistemological base and major concepts of GST. Next, I critically examine four major conceptual models of family process: communicational, strategic, structural, and developmental models. Selecting ideas from both general and family systems theories, I go on to present my own integrative process model of family dynamics. Finally, I conclude by examining the clinical implications of the model in question and indicate its connection to the recursive model of strategic practice (29).

2.1 General Systems Theory

Reading the current family therapy or family theory literature, one seldom runs across a reference to GST that pre-dates World War II. By implication, this suggests that GST in particular and the systemic perspective in general are relatively recent ideas. While reasonable, such a conclusion would be in error. As Buckley (31, p. 36) explains, "Modern systems theory, though seemingly springing de novo out of the last war effort, can be seen as a combination of a broad shift in scientific perspective striving for dominance over the past few centuries."

Following Buckley (31), this shift in perspective may be examined in terms of five overlapping phases.

1. Phase One extended from the 17th to the 19th centuries and centred on a mechanical model of man. According to this model, an analogy was drawn between human behaviour and mechanical processes, with the interplay of forces resulting in the social equilibrium that tended to remain unchanging or static.

2. Phase Two extends from the latter half of the 19th century into the 20th century and emphasized an organic model of man. Essentially, proponents of this model drew an analogy between a human social group and a biological organism. In extreme form, this led theorists to search for the analogue in human groups for organ systems such as the heart, the brain, the liver, and so on. In more general terms, however, the idea of the mutual dependence of parts was employed, with some fluctuation in essential variables acknowledged.

3. Phase Three encompassed approximately the last half of the 19th century and the first third of the 20th century. The focus here was on a process model of social interaction. Such a perspective allowed that the interaction among individuals in social groups tended toward a temporary equilibrium in relation to external and internal conditions. As these conditions changed, the groups in question shifted their structure to accommodate or adapt to these changed conditions. The process model, then, conceptualized groups as inherently unstable systems having both structure-maintaining and structure-elaborating components. While not systematically developed, these ideas were clearly precursors of modern systems theory.

4. Phase Four extends from approximately 1925 to 1950 and includes a range of theorists who systematically explored and elaborated many of the basic concepts that we now know collectively as GST. Important among these are four men: Bertalanffy, Bateson, Cannon, and Weiner. Bertalanffy, now recognized as the "father" of GST, was the first (in 1928) to develop "a series of concepts intended to develop an 'organismic' approach to biological problems." (21, 139) This approach particularly emphasized the "coordination of parts and processes" and sought to discover "the laws of biological systems (at all levels of organization)." (22, p. 152) Bateson, studying the Iatmul of New Guinea in the 1930's developed the idea of symmetrical and complementary schizmogenesis (8). This referred to self-reinforcing circular processes (i.e., escalation) involving either similar or different behaviours on the part of interacting individuals. What is

important about this formulation is that the end result, whatever it is, necessarily involves a mutual causal process in which both or all parties participated, but which was controlled by none of them unilaterally. Cannon (34) coined the term "homeostasis" in reference to biological systems in order to emphasize their dynamic, processual capacity to maintain physiological processes within relatively fixed limits despite continual fluctuation. Finally, Weiner (153, 152) explored the principles of cybernetics, the most central of which was the notion of feedback control of goal-directed systems.

5. Phase Five: These ideas were formally pulled together and integrated into what has now come to be called general systems theory by Bertalanffy in 1950 (20). Thus began the fifth and current phase of this work. In the next two subsections, I briefly review the major ideas of GST as they stand today, first examining its epistemological base, and then reviewing its basic concepts. With respect to the latter, I include a number of ideas developed primarily by Norman W. Bell and the author*—subsequently referred to as "B & B"—which serve to elaborate and clarify these concepts as they apply specifically to the family.

2.2 General Systems Theory: Ecosystemic Epistemology

All theories constitute multi-level conceptual structures. At the most concrete level stand the "facts" which the theory seeks to explain. Most laymen and even some professionals (e.g., 53) hold that the "facts" have an independent existence, apart from. In reality, theory necessarily precedes the "facts," for as Harris (68, p. 202) explains "Theoretical conceptions permeate the entire process of thinking; and facts always involve interpretation, so that no sharp distinction can be drawn between theory and observation."

Similarly, at a still higher level of abstraction, theory cannot exist independent of some epistemological base, that is, the implicit assumptions, premises, presuppositions, and rules for understanding and knowing things about the world (9, 12), as exemplified by how one extracts, orders, and analyzes observed data (7). As Bateson (11) explains, "All descriptions are based on theories of how to make descriptions. You cannot claim to have no epistemology. Those who so claim have nothing but a bad epistemology. Every description is based upon, or contains implicitly, a theory of how to describe."

While this statement is applicable to all theories, it is especially pertinent to GST which, as noted in Bross and Benjamin (29), is not a

---

*While developed jointly, responsibility for the presentation and elaboration of the ideas in question rests solely with the author.

"theory" in the proper sense, but rather an approach or perspective for understanding various phenomena in the world. In this sense, the epistemological base of GST may technically be referred to as a "meta-epistemology" and may be differentiated from traditional approaches by its position with respect to entitivity and causality.

Entitivity refers to those beliefs in terms of which an observer defines what things or "entities" in the world are to be regarded as real, and thus to be accorded objective status. In this context, the social and behavioural sciences in general, and psychology and psychiatry in particular, have typically understood the world to consist of discrete entities in the form of individuals (12, 59). Accordingly, the social group, including the family, has been regarded as an abstraction to be understood in terms of the sum of the attributes of its constituent members (148).

This choice of the individual as a unit of analysis has meant that individuals are to be examined one at a time (i.e., atomism), and are to be seen in isolation from their social surround (anti-contextualism) (83). It has meant, furthermore, that the study of social groups such as the family is necessarily reductionistic, an approach which rests on

> . . . the notion of a whole which (is) completely equal to the sum of its parts; which (can) be run in reverse; and which . . . behave(s) in exactly identical fashion no matter how often these parts (are) disassembled and put together again, and irrespective of the sequences in which the disassembly or reassembly . . . take(s) place. It implies consequently that the parts (are) never significantly modified by each other nor by their own past, and that each part once placed in its appropriate position with its appropriate momentum, . . . stay(s) exactly there and continue(s) to fulfill its completely and uniquely determined function. (Deutsch, 1951, in 154)

Not only is such a view inappropriate in the light of current knowledge about social interaction (143), but it is impractical. As Ashby (5) explains, reductionism as applied to complex systems "gives us only a vast number of separate parts or items of information, the results of whose interaction no one can predict. If one takes such a system to pieces, we find that we cannot reassemble it."

In light of these difficulties, the shift from the traditional to the GST approach involves a shift from discrete to relational entities (88). This is not to suggest that the family system, for example, is suddenly to be seen as somehow more real than the individuals which make it up; the individual (as system), the family, the ecosystem, and so on are all regarded as arbitrary organizational abstractions useful in terms of the purposes, concerns, and priorities of the observer (163). Rather, what is important is that the unit of analysis selected should be seen as having gained its objective status from the pattern of interaction among its lower-order elements and from the interaction of the whole in relation to some larger system of which it is a part. In other words, the focus on relational entities serves to emphasize the dynamic interaction between parts of the whole rather than on the parts themselves.

This perspective rests on the notion that the whole is necessarily greater than the sum of its parts (i.e., non-summativity, 22). This holds that the characteristics of the whole emerge out of the interaction among the lower-order elements of which it is constituted and the interaction between the whole and the larger ecosystem within which it is embedded and of which it is, in turn, a part. Thus, the attributes of the whole are qualitatively different from either the properties of the parts or the larger context, nor can they be induced from the behaviour of these intra- or suprasystem parts (143). It is in light of these characteristics of relational entities that GST is highly sensitive to wholes or "total circuits" (13), the interaction among elements, complexity, and context (83).

Turning next to causality, this refers generically to the belief that events do not spring out of nothing, but rather are a product of (i.e., caused by) the lawful (i.e., orderly, non-arbitrary) connection between two or more things in the world (i.e., individuals, processes, etc., 32). From a traditional perspective, causality is conceptualized in linear terms which "portray the deterministic, cause-and-effect world in which the outcome of any set of events can be analyzed and predicted if only one knows beforehand the quantified characteristics of the objects involved. The world described by this epistemology is one in which change is . . . continuous and reversible." (41)

When applied to mechanical systems, this view clearly has some utility. With respect to living (i.e., family) systems, however, linear causality neglects the relational nature of the entities in question. Reciprocal interaction among system elements and between the system and objects in its environment means that the organization which characterizes some initial state of the system will necessarily change in response to ongoing events and processes. As the number of such events and processes accumulates with the passage of time, any causal connection between past and present states of the system diminish to the vanishing point (5). Thus, the notion of a continuous, linear relationship between antecedent "causes" and final effects is precluded in principle. Rather, knowledge of the current state of a system necessarily involves scrutiny of ongoing interactional patterns. Since a pattern reflects the qualitative state of the system, change within complex systems is necessarily discontinuous and irreversible (41, 73, 74). Such discontinuity is embodied in the twin notions of equifinality and multifinality.* This suggests, in reference to the former, that many different initial states of a system may have the same end state. Conversely, this implies, in terms of the latter, that a single initial state may have many different end states.

---

*This is sometimes also referred to as "equipotentiality."

In accord, then, with the relational nature of the entities in question, causality is more appropriately conceptualized in circular or recursive terms in which "the designation of variable A as coming first and variable B as determined by it is recognized as dependent on where one chooses to break the continuity of process. One might just as well start with variable B as a determinant of subsequent changes in variable A." (39) Circular causality, then, involves simultaneous, mutual causal processes whose locus is in the "space" between interacting system members rather than within them, either in their past or the present (44, 150).

This concern with recursiveness, embodied in the idea of the "space between people," explains the interest of the proponents of GST with pattern, process, transaction, and context. It cannot be over-emphasized, however, that such concepts tend to be foreign to most people in our culture, in which thought is dominantly linear in structure (12). Such linearity is especially evident in our conception of time as "monochronic," that is, sequential and segmented, and our use of language, which tends to involve the sequential and decontextualized presentation of ideas (65). Since such usage of both time and language are not "merely" a representation of reality, but rather serve to define it (126, 158), our tendency is to think that linearity is the *only* natural and reasonable way to understand the world. This helps explain why the ecosystemic epistemology has received an uneven reception in the social and behavioural sciences (139).

2.3 General Systems Theory: Basic Concepts
Following Steinglass (139), the basic concepts of GST can be grouped under four major categories: organization, control, information, and time.

2.31 Organization
Rapoport and Horvath (115) differentiate things in the world in terms of three levels of organizational complexity. At the simplest level, "chaotic complexity" involves a large number of components whose interaction can be described in stochastic (i.e., probabilistic) terms. At the intermediate level, "organized simplicity" refers to a complex set of relatively static components whose relations are linear, sequential, and additive. At the highest level, "organized complexity" refers to living systems, including the family, in which a second component interacts in an organized, consistent, and predictable manner. This organized assemblage of components is virtually synonymous with our definition of system, namely, any set of two or more elements which interact in a patterned and stable manner through time despite fluctuation in their environment (66, 155).

Stability or consistency of organization, however, does not specify the nature of that organization. Even complex systems tend to vary in terms of their degree of systematicness or organization (31). Thus, complex family systems may range from the under-organized (3), in which there is a loose coupling between members, to the over-organized (6, 100), in which there is an extremely tight coupling between members, with some intermediate level of organization optimal under most conditions (9, 13).

Whatever the degree of organization at any given point in time, this is unlikely to endure over the long term, as complex systems tend to be negentropic (31), that is, they tend to become increasingly complex, either in terms of increasing elaboration and differentiation (e.g., additional members, task specialization) or in terms of increasing simplification (e.g., encoding, ritualization). (B & B) Furthermore, no degree of organization is likely to be optimal under all conceivable circumstances. Accordingly, the extent to which a given organizational structure is deemed "optimal" will be a function of the extent to which the system in question is able to successfully solve the problems posed by those circumstances without endangering the continuity and integrity of the system.

Pattern

A major aspect of organization is that the connection between elements is patterned, that is, involves redundant interactional sequences (55, 150). This suggests that no single element or subgroup of elements can ever have unilateral control over the whole (9), nor can they act independently of at least some of the other elements (97). Conversely, all parts of the system are interconnected, either directly or indirectly. Consequently, a change in any one element will ultimately affect all other elements, with the time required for that initial change to reverberate through the entire system being one index of the degree of organization of the total system (9). This is not to suggest that all system elements are necessarily equal in their impact on the system. Rather, an element or set of elements may act as a "leading part," a change in the value of which has a greater impact on the system than a similar change in any of the remaining elements (66).

Further, the contingent nature of patterned interaction necessarily implies some limitation on the range of all possible behaviours of the participant elements (58). That such patterns display some degree of organization, however, implies that the behaviour of the participants exhibits some degrees of freedom. Indeed, such freedom is embodied in the notion of macro-determinacy (143), which holds that while a system is determinant (i.e., predictable) at the level of the whole (i.e., system or subsystem), it is not determinant for the lower-level components (i.e., individuals). Thus, the notion of pattern implies freedom within constraint; while a pattern may set limits on the tolerable range of a given behaviour, it does not determine the specific behaviours within that range. This characteristic of interactional patterning is one reason why members in even the most over-organized families retain some sense of free will and individual choice.

Another reason for the perception of freedom relates to the fact that many, if not most, of the patterns in question persist unnoticed by the participants. This is so on at least four grounds. (1) The Central Nervous System is organized in such a way that it provides the individual with news of the consequences of perception, omitting news of the process by which this information is acquired (12). Consequently, family members tend to focus on the behaviour of the self and/or the other, rather than the interactional processes by which these behaviours are shaped. (2) The external environment rarely makes demands on the family that are sufficiently significant to make evident the patterning of responses to them (106). (3) In monitoring complex real-life situations, it is difficult for participants to clearly and consistently differentiate between those response patterns governed by the family itself as opposed to those associated with environmental influences (e.g., the presence of non-significant others, social circumstances, legal standards, etc., 106). Finally, (4) interactional patterns remain largely opaque because of the extremely subtle way in which they are constructed, maintained, elaborated, and changed. As Berger and Kelner (18) explain in reference to the marital subsystem:

> It cannot be sufficiently strongly emphasized that this process (of constructing reality) is typically unapprehended, almost automatic in character. The participants of the marriage drama do *not* set out deliberately to re-create their world. Each continues to live in a world that is taken-for-granted—and keeps a taken-for-granted character even as it is metamorphosed. . . . Reconstructed present and reinterpreted past are perceived as a continuum, extending forward into a commonly projected future. The dramatic change that has occurred (following marriage) remains, in bulk, unapprehended and unarticulated. And where it forces itself upon the individual's attention, it is retrojected into the past, explained as having always been there, though perhaps in a hidden way.

As a consequence of these combined processes, interactional patterns in family systems tend to be extremely powerful forces shaping, to one extent or another, the behaviour, perception, and feelings of all the participants. Indeed, so powerful are such patterns that even when family members become explicitly aware of their existence (i.e., gain insight), they may still be unable to break free of their pervasive influence (59, 150).

Given the primal importance of such patterns for understanding (family) systems, it seems only reasonable to consider what forms these patterns take and whether they are simply arbitrary arrangements or move in some direction. With respect to the latter, living systems, including the family, are conceptualized as purposive or goal-directed systems (31), meaning that they involve "a purposive pattern of moves towards a target or goal made by two or more people who are systematically bound in a social-biological arrangement." (81, p. 18) Ultimately, the goal of all such systems is survival, that is, adaptations in response to environmental demands that serve to support the continued operation of the system (66; see below, Section 2.32). Over the short term, this involves either the preservation or the transformation of existing interactional patterns (55). In this sense, the notion of goal refers to an inference based on the observation of the interactional patterns of a given system over time.

With respect to the former, a range of specific patterns has been identified in the family therapy literature, most of them associated with clinical families. However, two generic patterns transcend the clinical/ non-clinical dimension, namely, relations referred to as either symmetrical or complementary (8). Bateson (9) describes a symmetrical relationship as follows: "If, in a binary relationship, the behaviour of A and B are regarded (by A and B) as similar and are linked so that more of a given behaviour of A stimulates more of it in B, and vice versa, then the relationship is "symmetrical" in regard to these behaviours." An example of such a pattern are those married couples who engage in repetitive arguments, without resolution (40, 23). Bateson (9) describes a complementary relationship as follows: "If . . . the behaviour of A and B are dissimilar but mutually fit together . . . and their behaviours are linked so that more of A's behaviour stimulates more of B's fitting behaviour, then the relationship is "complementary" in regard to these behaviours." An example of such a pattern is a couple in which one partner is "dominant" and the other "submissive" (74), although these terms tend to under-emphasize the necessary involvement of both participants if the pattern is to be sustained. These patterns may either occur in pure form or may oscillate from one to the other, that is, Lederer and Jackson's (90) "parallel" type. Furthermore, such patterns are not restricted to dyadic or "binary" relationships, but rather to systems of varying size (9).

Finally, a word about concepts that are all too often applied to social systems such as the family, but which are non-systemic. Such notions as role, motive, need, and so on, while used in formulations allegedly systemic (e.g., 144, 70), all share two features which indicate that they are inappropriate for inclusion in any truly systemic formulation: linearity and stasis. Roles, motives, and needs can only be held or experienced by one individual, and thus are inappropriate for describing the relational character of family systems (79). Similarly, they may exist independent of interactional processes, and thus are not useful in explaining either how families stay the same or change (12).*

Level

Another aspect of organization is the notion of level of complexity. According to this view, the universe is organized in terms of a series of levels

---

*The notion of "need" has the additional difficulty that it leads to infinite regress in terms of where they come from, how they arise, and how they change. In traditional terms, answers to these questions invariably point to the far past, either in the life of the individual or, indeed, of the human species.

of increasing complexity, with each level exhibiting systemic properties (isomorphy) logically related to those above and below it (88). The nature of that relationship is hierarchical. Like a series of nested Russian dolls, each system is simultaneously a whole, composed of lower-order elements or subsystems (intrasystemic hierarchy), and a part of one or more higher-order suprasystems (intersystemic hierarchy) (21, 130). Such simultaneity of membership is referred to as a system's "holon property" (84).

With respect to the family, at least four levels of complexity may be distinguished, one intersystemic and three intrasystemic. At the intersystemic level, the family is a subsystem with respect to several suprasystems at once, including the extended family, peer system, the school, the work place, the law, the religious community, and so on (139). Given that characteristic patterns of interaction are likely to vary across these systems, it follows that the participation of family members in them is likely to result in a high level of behavioural variation between members across systems (132, 140, 141). In this sense, the notion of the "self" as a discrete entity is seriously misleading and is, at this level, more appropriately conceptualized as "an organization that is developed and maintained only in and through a continuously ongoing symbolic interchange with other persons." (31, p. 44; see 9)

Moreover, insofar as all of the systems involved are goal-directed, the relevant suprasystems may have goals which are congruent or discrepant in terms of the family system (74). Generally, goal congruence tends to be supportive of system operation (e.g., 77) while goal discrepancy may be inimical to it (15). This relationship between system goals and system functioning, however, highlights the central importance of context in the effort to describe family processes from a systemic perspective (see also Section 2.32). Thus, words such as "supportive" and "inimical" have meaning only in context. The capacity of the family to deal effectively with its daily interpersonal and environmental problems may threaten the ability of some higher-order systems (e.g., the extended family) to do the same; what is "supportive" in one context becomes "inimical" in another.

At the intrasystemic level, the family consists of a number of different subsystems, most notably the parental or "executive" subsystem and the child or sibling subsystem (98). Typically, the relationship between these subsystems is such that the former has influence over the latter. This is often conceptualized in terms of some notion of "power" (4, 58), with the family organized in terms of a hierarchy of power levels (61). As Keeney (83) notes, however, this is a linear metaphor, implying that while parents have power over children, children have no reciprocal capacity, a conception (of unilateral control) clearly inconsistent with the ecosystemic epistemology of relational entities. A more adequate metaphor is that of the parental subsystem as "leading part," thus emphasizing, on the one hand, that the parental subsystem has more impact on the family system than does the child subsystem, while, on the other hand, recognizing that both parent and child subsystems remain subject to the constraints of interactional patterns which characterize their family system (see Bateson, 1974 in 83).

At the next intrasystemic level, family systems and subsystems may be described in terms of their operation at four additional levels (B & B). These are:

1. *Meaning*: those habitual assumptions, premises, and presuppositions about the nature of the social world which, in part, determine how family members will perceive, understand, and interact, both with each other and with people outside the family system (18, 69, 119).

2. *Affect*: the limits of affective expression together with feelings of affiliation, attachment, and commitment; it is thus closely related to the dimension of closeness and distance (81, see also 26).

3. *Communication*: the range of verbal expressions and non-verbal behaviours which convey information (10) and effect behaviour (i.e., pragmatic communication, 150), that is, convey information that is relevant to those to whom it is sent. In the absence of relevance, behaviour which conveys information is "noise" and remains important in the examination of communicational clarity.

4. *Interaction*: the range of behaviours in a family which indicate who is relating to whom and in what way. This includes such things as who spends time interacting with whom, how much time is involved, and what kinds of topics and issues such relating involves. It is thus closely related to the dimension of separateness (i.e., aggression, hostility) and connectedness (i.e., intimacy, 23) as well as a shifting pattern of family alignments and splits (161, see also 62, 92).

These levels are clearly arbitrary in nature, since most interaction in families encompasses all of these levels simultaneously. Nevertheless, they are both legitimate and useful in the sense that they speak to the problems observers have in attempting to understand the incredible complexity of family life. As used here, each of these levels is conceptualized as analytically distinct and separate, as having systemic properties (i.e., they arise out of the patterned interaction among family members), and as interacting in much the same way that families interact with suprasystems at the intersystemic level. In accord with this analogy, interactional processes at these various levels may be synchronous (e.g., "open" at both affect and communication levels) or asynchronous (e.g., "open" at the level of communication but "closed" at the level of affect), with the degree and extent of synchrony supportive of, or threatening to the operation of family systems (B & B). Once again, these terms only have meaning in context. Asynchrony, for example, may serve as a source of interpersonal conflict, thus initially reducing the system's capacity to deal effectively with its daily intra- and extrasystemic problems and so may be inimical to family functioning. If it is persistent, however, it may precipitate a crisis that results in the transformation of family organization and thus may be supportive of family functioning. Consequently, what is supportive in one context may be inimical in another and vice versa. Consequently, descriptions of synchrony or asynchrony must necessarily include some reference to context.

Finally, at the most concrete intrasystemic level, two levels of communication may be differentiated (15). The "report" level conveys information, that is, the content of the message. The "command" level operates at a higher level of abstraction and serves to qualify report-level statements, indicating how messages are to be interpreted and thus defining the relationship between the participants in the relationship. Information at report and command levels may be congruent or discrepant, with positive and negative consequences, respectively, for the operation of the family system (14, 58).

Boundary

A final aspect of system organization is that of boundary. Patterning in the interaction among family members necessarily means that they interact with each other in ways that are both qualitatively and quantitatively different from the way they relate to people outside the system (132). In this sense, family members are bounded or constrained by the nature of their mutual relationship (139).

The bounded nature of family systems serves simultaneously to delimit the extent of the system in question (who is in) and to differentiate it from all other systems (who is out). The implication here, that family boundaries always have two "sides," suggests a parallel between a boundary and a physical structure and, indeed, such was its intent when used originally to describe biological systems (22). With respect to family systems, however, the imagery associated with most of the concepts used to elaborate the notion of boundary, like "sides," is seriously misleading. As intended here, they are to be understood as convenient metaphors for describing one aspect of the organization of family systems.

With this understanding, another aspect of boundary, namely, permeability, begins to make sense. Family boundaries necessarily vary, both across family systems as well as within families over time. With respect to the former, family systems vary in terms of their degree of permeability, that is, the extent to which family members and non-members can move freely into and out of the family (21). In part, such variation relates to the degree of system organization, with over-organized systems having relatively impermeable boundaries (with reference to non-family members) and under-organized systems having extremely permeable boundaries (98). In part, such boundaries may also be determined by the environment, particularly cultural (112), ethnic (135), and occupational (2, 142) systems.

With reference to the latter, family systems have a biologically based built-in trajectory of change. In all families, members eventually die and, in most (see 146), children are born, grow up, and eventually leave to form new family systems. Consequently, family boundaries tend to ebb and flow through time, expanding and becoming more permeable with the addition of members and showing the reverse tendency with loss of members (51).

These aspects of family boundaries are intersystemic in nature. However, boundaries also apply at the intrasystemic level. The first of these relates to the various subsystems which comprise the whole. Subsystem boundaries operate simultaneously to connect and segregate, symbolizing the special characteristics of certain relationships (e.g., marital dyads), while differentiating them from other family subsystems. Across family systems, subsystem boundaries may vary considerably in terms of their degree of permeability, while similar variability may be observed within any given family system through time. Furthermore, assuming that there is an optimal balance between separateness and connectedness, Minuchin (98) has argued that optimal family functioning is associated with clear boundaries between subsystems. By this, he means that the interactional processes that define who participates in any given subsystem, and how, are defined well enough to permit each subsystem to operate without interference, while remaining in sufficient contact with other systems so that subsystem cohesion is not in danger. Thus, evidence that subsystem boundaries are unclear—in the sense that they are either excessively rigid or diffused—is thought to be associated with family dysfunctioning.

Finally, the second aspect of intrasystemic boundaries concerns the levels of meaning, affect, communication, and interaction in which behaviours within family systems occur (B & B). At the level of system, families are likely to vary considerably in terms of the degree of permeability found at each of these bounded levels. Furthermore, the levels in question may be synchronous or asynchronous with respect to permeability. Thus, a family system that is relatively permeable at the level of interaction may be equally "open" at the level of meaning, affect, and communication. But such co-variation need not always be the case, for permeability at the level of interaction and communication may be associated with impermeability at the level of meaning and affect.

At the level of subsystem, boundaries at the levels of meaning, affect, communication, and interaction may vary considerably, both in terms of clarity and congruence (B & B). Although relations at the level of interaction may respect generational lines of cleavage, they may not do so with respect to the level of affect. Subsystem boundaries that are clear at the level of communication may be less clear at the level of meaning. Furthermore, boundaries at the levels in question may be either synchronous or asynchronous within and/or between subsystems. Within the marital subsystem, for example, relatively open communication may coincide with relatively free affective expression. Conversely, a relatively restricted meaning system may be associated with relative permeability at the level of interaction. Similar examples may easily be envisaged with respect to the interaction between family subsystems. This yields a picture of family boundaries that is more complex and fluid than that found in most formulations in the literature (e.g., 98) and also requires rather more information to display; that is, one needs to specify the degree of separateness and connectedness at certain levels, among certain groups, over certain periods of time (B & B).

2.32 Control

Implicit in the foregoing are twin images of the family as system. One pictures the family as maintaining stable patterns of interaction over the short term despite rapid, random variation, both in the environment and among family members. The other shows the family as an adaptive system that undergoes orderly or controlled change in response to important fluctuations either within the system and/or in the environment. Still a third picture is suggested by recent statistics concerning divorce and separation (e.g., 103), namely, family dissolution or, more correctly, uncontrolled change. All three images suggest the operation in family systems of complex mechanisms that either maintain stability or promote change— mechanisms, moreover, which themselves sometimes malfunction.

Feedback

First developed in a study of physiological processes (22) and later elaborated through the cybernetic study of servo-mechanisms (e.g., the thermostat, 152), the concept of feedback is central to any GST formulation. Unfortunately, its very popularity has resulted in its being vulgarized (31) to variously mean "response" ("John, would you read my paper and give me some feedback?"), "reinforcement," or simply any form of reciprocal interaction (pseudo-feedback).

In fact, the feedback loop generally refers to the operation of a system such that its output behaviour is reintroduced as input. This is then compared with some reference value or goal state, with information about a difference, and then is used to direct subsequent output behaviour (111). In other words, true feedback necessarily involves some comparative operation in goal-directed (telenomic) systems.

In this context, two types of feedback are differentiated. Negative feedback tends to reduce deviation from the system's goal state and thus serves to maintain patterns within specified limits (78). In contrast, positive feedback, often triggered by some minor random event, tends to amplify or increase the deviation from the goal state and thus serves to alter the prevailing pattern (95).* If such deviation persists for only a short time and

---

*To avoid confusion with the notion of "positive and negative reinforcement," Kantor and Lehr (81, p. 14) prefer the terms "constancy-feedback loops" and "variety-feedback loops."

then ceases at some predetermined limit of tolerance, a "short-term runaway" (71) or "irresistible run" (74) is said to have occurred, with any associated change only temporary. If such deviation cannot be controlled and persists over an extended period, then a "runaway" is said to occur (156), leading either to the radical reorganization of the system (73) or its dissolution (153).

With regard to the family, Steinglass (139) offers the following example of a negative-feedback loop in an alcoholic family:

> Each time the husband decreases his alcohol intake, behaviour on the wife's part, such as stocking the liquor cabinet or becoming increasingly argumentative, increases the likelihood of her husband's drinking. Conversely, an increase in the husband's drinking might be followed by his wife's suggestion that they return to a therapy group, or threats to leave him, or hiding money with which to buy alcohol.

Failure of the wife in this example to engage in these last behaviours, thus encouraging her husband to increase his drinking, would transform this from an example of negative feedback to one of positive feedback.

The simplicity of this example is somewhat misleading and so requires four qualifications: (1) As noted above, family systems are multi-levelled organizations, such that both positive- and negative-feedback loops may occur simultaneously at different levels, or they may oscillate back and forth, either within or between levels (74). (2) Description of a given feedback loop as either positive or negative is a function of context (15). With respect to the above example, what is negative looping for the couple in question may represent positive looping for the extended family of which they are a part, or vice versa. A similar analysis would apply to the interaction either between family subsystems or between one subsystem and the family system as a whole. For example, the interaction between mother and son may involve positive feedback—with potentially disastrous consequences for the son if this results in psychiatric (e.g., schizophrenia) or legal (e.g., delinquency) labelling—while the same behaviour may involve negative feedback for the system as a whole (61, 147). (3) To the extent that the relationship between levels within family systems may be asynchronous, such asynchrony may represent a positive-feedback loop for the system in question, inducing interaction processes to move beyond their prevailing limits (B & B). (4) Finally, looping necessarily occurs in time, such that the description of a given loop as positive or negative is relative to the time frame in use. What appears to be positive feedback over the short term will typically be transformed into negative feedback over the long term.

Homeostasis
Over the short term, family interaction patterns, including behavioural measures such as speech-interaction rate and physiological measures such

as free fatty-acid production (i.e., one type of response to stress), show remarkable stability, varying only within relatively restricted limits (48, 49, 101, 118). This process, initially based on the study of physiological systems, is called homeostasis (34) or morphostasis (31). This is not a final, static resting point, but is defined as a central tendency around which a (family) system varies, based on the operation of negative feedback (78, 79).

Thus, while family systems vary considerably in terms of the degree of interactional variation they will tolerate, all exhibit some homeostatic limits (150). While these limits themselves exhibit homeostatic properties, showing minor fluctuations (i.e., calibration) in response to changing circumstances either within the family or the environment (10), they nevertheless remain relatively stable through time.

Such homeostatic stability is crucial to the viability of family systems, for it allows them to respond adaptively to changing internal or external conditions without continuously facing the threat of family dissolution. Conversely, however, homeostatic processes can get out of control, as families persist in maintaining prevailing interactional patterns (i.e., perseverance) even when changing internal and/or external conditions makes such persistence maladaptive (72, 151), with symptomatic behaviour or even family dissolution possible outcomes.

Heterostasis

As noted above, families have a built-in trajectory of change and, moreover, must necessarily undergo some degree of organizational alteration (homeostatic transformation) in response to radical internal (e.g., suicide, murder) or external (e.g., war, depression, loss of employment) disruptions. This suggests that the notion of homeostasis is inadequate to deal with the full range of (family) system phenomena. As Deutsch (43) explains, "Homeostasis is not a broad enough concept to describe either the internal restructuring of learning systems or the combinatorial finding of the solutions. It is too narrow a concept because it is change rather than stability which we must account for."

The solution would appear to be the extension of homeostasis to recognize the fact of change. In this regard, Mace (93) states the case most eloquently.

> The first extension would cover the case in which what is maintained or restored is not so much an internal state of the organism as some relation of the organism to its environment. This would take care of the fact of adaptation and adjustment, including adaptation to the social environment . . . the second extension would cover the case in which the goal and/or norm is some state or relation which has never previously been experienced. There is clearly no reason to suppose that every process of the homeostatic type consists in the maintenance or restoration of a norm. There is no reason whatever to suppose that the process always begins in a state of equilibrium which is then disturbed . . . there are, at any rate,

many cases in which we require the concept of homeostasis to be extended so that it may apply not only to the restoration of an equilibrium but also to the discovery of new equilibria.

More recently, nearly identical sentiments have been expressed in the family literature (see 73, 74, 134).

The result is the notion of heterostasis (128) or morphogenesis (31) which refers to those processes which, based on the operation of positive-feedback loops or cycles, tend to elaborate or change a system's prevailing organizational state (95).

In this context, four issues are particularly important: the degree of change, the form of change, the triggers for change, and the level of change.

With respect to the degree of change, Buckley (31, p. 58) differentiates between "1) Temporarily adjusting the system to extend contingencies; 2) directing the system towards more congenial environments; and 3) permanently reorganizing aspects of the system itself to deal more effectively with the environment." This is closely related to Ashby's (6) "bi-modal model of feedback" in which he discriminates between "first-order change," namely, small changes in response to minor fluctuations,* and "second-order change," namely, systemic reorganization in response to dramatic fluctuations. Both category schemes, however, assume that (1) following change, the system will be as viable as, if not more viable than, it was prior to the change; and (2) change will involve the establishment of a new homeostatic level. While this is certainly often the case, these assumptions do not apply universally insofar as there is a variety of examples of systems which go into "runaway," with system dissolution the result (e.g., divorce, family murder). An additional category would, therefore, seem to be required which might be called "failed second-order change."

With respect to the form of change, Ashby (6) identifies three types.** (1) A "full-function" involves a continuous, progressive movement. (2) A "step-function" involves a period of relative stability followed by sudden, discontinuous change whenever some part or set of parts reaches a "critical state" (i.e., passes a threshold of tolerance). (3) Finally, a "part-function" operates much like a step-function except that change from one level of organization to another tends to be gradual and continuous. While these distinctions were based on the study of non-living systems, available clinical data support their validity with respect to family systems (73, 51, 150). It should be noted, however, that few changes in family systems are truly abrupt (i.e., totally unexpected). Rather, change occurs as a continuous process that sets the stage for some "marker event" in time (51). The distinction between the "event marker" (e.g., birth, death, divorce,

---

*Watzlawick et al. (150) refer to this as "calibration."
**A fourth type, a "null-function," indicates the absence of change.

marriage, etc.) and a change process helps explain why family theorists speak of discontinuous change (e.g., 73) whereas family members typically experience family life as a continuous stream of events, both minor and major (18).

With respect to triggering mechanisms, day-to-day activity of the full-function variety is typically associated with first-order change (150). Conversely, major changes, for example, of the step-function type, are generally associated with crises induced by developmental transition (60, 151) or gross environmental change (144). While this may often be the case, there is no necessary relationship between the magnitude of the change and the degree of perturbation. Quite apart from much individual variation in stress responsiveness (160), Maruyama (95) explicitly notes that major change may arise out of "an insignificant or accidental initial kick," while Bateson (13, p. 98) observes that "The ongoing process of change feeds on the random." Consequently, major change can often be associated with relatively minor events, particularly those associated with children, who act as an important source of variety (27).

While the full array of variables determining the system's response to such triggers is not clearly understood, two variables stand out as being of critical importance. The first concerns the timing of such events, with periods of instability especially susceptible to radical reorganization (51, 74). The second concerns the family's number and range of available patterns of interaction, its degree of "requisite variety" (31). In general, the greater the number and range of such patterns, the less likely is system operation to be seriously disrupted by such events and the more likely is change to be orderly and in the appropriate direction in relation to environmental demand (107, 108, 125).

Finally, with respect to the level of change, reorganization may occur at different rates and at different degrees of intensity at the various levels at which family systems operate. In turn, such a symmetry may act as the impetus for further change. Widdich (159), for example, found that, after the experience of discrepancy, the re-evaluation of family-shared meanings may produce a transformation of the family meaning system. Once this shift in perception had occurred, family members came to see their life together in a new way, including a reinterpretation of the past. Suddenly, things that were not problematic before now became problematic, and vice versa. Furthermore, returning to the example of a child as a source of variety, the level at which an "initial kick" to the system may determine how what is outside gets in and what is inside gets transformed and integrated into the family system. The unanticipated discovery of a child's masturbatory activity, increasingly "cool" responses to a parent's display of affection, the casual report of a totally different disciplinary regime in the home of a friend, may all have quite different consequences for the subsequent organization of the family system.

2.33 Information

In systems terms, all living systems are described as "open" in the sense that they are continuously engaging in some exchange with their environment (21). In biological systems, this involves the exchange of energy. In social (family) systems, the commodity of exchange is information conveyed among people by communication (31).

Information is defined by Bateson (9, 12) as a "transformation of a difference which makes a difference." Events in the world only become known to the extent that they are accessible through our sensory apparatus which transforms the event into a series of physio-chemical nerve impulses. The information being so transformed is "news of a difference," that is, a change in the ratio between things (e.g., a ringing telephone that was previously silent), the sensory apparatus achieving this report by scanning static differences. Note that this ratio of difference is dimensionless—it refers to the relationship between things or states of things rather than the things themselves—and it assumes the availability of energy ahead of the stimulus-event making possible the perception of non-existent events (e.g., an expected telephone call that does *not* arrive). Thus, news of a difference refers as much to quiescence as to activity. Finally, such news must be judged to be relevant or meaningful for the receiver before it can be said to have been communicated; news without relevance is "noise."

The importance of this formulation resides both in what it says about the nature of communication and what it says about the nature of communication within family systems. With respect to communication, the information exchange occurs within the context of negentropic systems. What is communicated is not merely a collection of bits of information, but also a set of rules for information receipt, encoding, storage, decoding, and transmission, together with rules for using and changing the rules (124). This helps explain how human meaning systems can achieve the magnitude of complexity they have. The power of such a system is evident in the magnitude of the multiplier-effect when relevant information is conveyed. While it takes almost no energy to shout "Fire!" in a crowded theatre, such information triggers the release of a great deal of energy (31).

With respect to family systems, prolonged, intense, and intimate interaction among members results in the construction of meaning systems that are, at least in part, unique to each family unit (18). This is exemplified by the "restricted language code" in use in family systems (19): words and sentences are shortened and collapsed; vocabulary and individual words merge; idiosyncratic variation across families is the rule. Such meaning systems, moreover, are stabilized and changed by the same feedback processes as are all other aspects of systems. Consequently, they too are subject to the amplified effect of minor events and as such are susceptible to "sudden" reframing in which meaning systems undergo radical reorganization (see 129). The consequences of an unanticipated discovery—of the lipstick-stained handkerchief of one's spouse, of a teenage daughter using the pill, of a past criminal act by a parent, and so on—is a case in point.

2.34 Time

A final aspect of (family) systems is the often neglected insight that all system operations occur in real time, that is, they take time and occur through time. As used throughout the foregoing sections, time has been equated with context and process. It is processual in the sense that inter-action patterns necessarily shift and change—evolve—through time. Similarly, it is contextual in the sense that the system's organization over the short term may take on an entirely different complexion when viewed over the long term.

An implication of this perspective is that time and space are equivalent terms in the sense that the spatial arrangement or structure of a system merely represents its organization at *one point in time*. In other words, "structure" is merely a convenient way of referring to "a dynamically stable arrangement of interacting system components as seen at one point in time," and does not suggest that "space" is in any sense different from "organization and time."

The point is important, as it is often misunderstood. Steinglass (139, p. 317), for example, treats time and space as conceptually distinct dimensions, with "patterning observed along a spatial dimension . . . called structure" and "patterning along a temporal dimension . . . referred to as process." From a systems perspective, this is fundamentally misleading, for, as Bateson (12, pp. 42ff.) explains, "Spatial and physical metaphors in the scientific discussion of communicational and mental matters . . . always promote false epistemology." What is false here is that such metaphors tend, first, to confuse the notion of "system" with "the structure or organization its components may take on at any particular *time*" (31, p. 5); and, second, to identify a particular homeostatic state with "the particular structure of the system" (31, p. 15). In fact, as noted in foregoing sections, the notion of homeostasis is properly equated with constant variation rather than stasis. Consequently, the tendency to equate space with structure necessarily promotes an image of (family) systems that is both static and linear, and, as such, is non-systemic.

2.35 Conclusion

In the foregoing, we have presented a brief and at times unelaborated review of the epistemology and basic concepts of GST. My intentions in so doing have been twofold. First, my concern has been to present a succinct statement of GST in response to the scarcity of such statements in the family therapy literature. Their absence has made it relatively difficult for inter-ested practitioners to compare and contrast available models of family process in terms of the degree to which they are consistent with or diverge from GST (see 139).

Second, this review seemed to be a useful way of identifying those characteristics that a model of family process should exhibit if it is to be consistent with the premises and principles of GST. In general, seven such characteristics seem to be in order:

1. *Process:* Such a model must be sensitive to the fluidity and complexity of family life that derives from the continuous interaction among family members; in particular, this includes the necessity of viewing family systems from a relational and circular perspective.

2. *Context:* It must attend to the multiplicity of contexts in which family interaction simultaneously occurs, including both intersystemic and intrasystemic processes.

3. *Level:* It must include some conceptualization of family systems as multi-level organizations, with feedback loops operating both on and between the levels in question.

4. *Stability:* It must account for the regularity, orderliness, and patterning which provides the base for the coherence and continuity of family systems.

5. *Change:* It must also account for the ways in which families change, both in terms of increased and decreased capacity to effectively solve intrafamilial and/or environmental problems; in particular, it will note the contextual nature of change such that statements about system functioning will be couched in terms of the "fit" between systems/subsystems, and the environment.

6. *Chance:* It must entail some concern for the operation of situationally random events as an indispensable source of variety.

7. *Time:* Finally, it must recognize that all family processes exist in real time.

3.1 Family System Models:
Review and Evaluation

With GST as backdrop, I now turn to an examination of the four models of family process dominant in the family therapy literature: communicational, strategic, structural, and developmental. In each case, my concern will be (1) to briefly identify the model's major concepts and formulations; and (2) to critically evaluate the model in order to select those aspects of it that I regard as useful for inclusion in my own model. This focus on theory will preclude examination of the clinical aspects of the models in question. Furthermore, since each of these models claims some degree of allegiance to GST, some overlap between this section and the preceding one is inevitable.

3.2 Communication Model

The communication model is generally associated with a small series of authors centred (now or at some time in the past) at the Mental Research

Institute in Palo Alto, California (23), including the work of Jackson (78, 79, see 55), Haley (58, 59), Watzlawick (150), and Bateson (10) from which most of this section is derived. As its name suggests, its proponents focus on the explication of communication processes (especially its pragmatic aspects) as the primary vehicle for understanding family life (117) and, moreover, their work tends to be the most thoroughly systemic of all the models under consideration (139).

Basic Concepts

While extremely broad and general, the model essentially resolves into three primary concepts which are combined to yield two formulations.

1. Rule—Interaction among family members is not random. Over time, the full range of possible interaction sequences becomes restricted. Covert agreement arises concerning what categories of behaviour are acceptable or not and, moreover, the tolerable range of variation within acceptable categories. Consequently, interpersonal interaction comes increasingly to exhibit redundant interaction sequences. As inferred by an observer, such sequences are called "rules." Rules give coherence and order to family life, and, as such, all family systems are said to be rule-governed.

Once in place, however, rules need not be considered as set in concrete, but as open to negotiation, albeit covert, and thus can be modified as circumstances require. Changing rules, however, is a rule-governed activity. Accordingly, in addition to rules, family systems also have meta-rules, that is, rules about how to change the rules. In this respect, families are thought to vary in terms of the number and range of meta-rules, with the relative scarcity of meta-rules typically associated with family dysfunction.

2. Level—Family communication involves multiple channels, that is, occurs simultaneously at different levels or is of several different classes. Generally two levels—report (digital: verbal) and command (analogic: non-verbal) (123, 58)—are distinguished, although Raush et al. (117) extends this formulation to identify a third (meta-communication) and fourth (inference about communication) level. The relationship between levels may be congruent (in our terms, synchronous) or disjunctive (in our terms, asynchronous). Four types of disjunction are recognized and each is thought to have negative consequences for family functioning:

1. *Binding:* A dysfunction between report and command; in the absence of punitive consequences, this is a "simple bind" (74, p. 168); in the presence of such consequences, this is a "double-bind."

2. *Disqualification:* Communication in which the way the message is sent or qualified invalidates the communication.

3. *Disconfirmation:* Communication in which the receiver behaves in such a way as to deny both the content of the message and the other's right to send the message.

4. *Punctuation:* Differential ordering of the messages between sender and receiver such that each blames the other for the conflict and/or the confusion associated with such disjunction.

3. Axioms—The regularities of family communication are codified in the form of a set of five axioms, the violation of which is thought to be associated with various forms of communication disorder:

Axiom 1: One cannot *not* communicate; violation of this axiom takes the form of denial of communication, rejection of communication, disqualification, and symptomatic behaviour as a form of communication.

Axiom 2: Every communication has aspects of content and report; violation here is associated with confusion between levels, disagreement within levels, disqualification, and imperviousness to corrective feedback.

Axiom 3: The nature of the relationship is contingent on the mutual punctuation of communication; dysfunction with regard to this axiom includes discrepant punctuation and self-fulfilling negative prophecies.

Axiom 4: Human beings communicate in both digital and analogic terms; violation here centres on errors in translation between these two modes, including, for example, the inability to terminate an unpleasant interaction sequence occurring at the analogic level.

Axiom 5: All communication is either symmetrical or complementary; dysfunction associated with this axiom includes symmetrical escalation and rigid complementarity.

4. Formulation 1: The Functional Family—Within this model, superior family functioning is primarily associated with flexibility and balance. This is associated with a range of characteristics, including: the presence of family meta-rules, the ability to acknowledge and conceptualize problems in non-escalatory (i.e., solvable) terms, easy alternation between symmetrical and complementary interaction modes, communication that is clear and congruent, and a balance between separation and togetherness. Put slightly differently, functional families are characterized by (1) a large number and wide range of patterns of interpersonal communication; (2) communicational clarity; and (3) the relative absence of communicational disjunction. As problems arise, a mix of selected interactional patterns is brought to bear on them, such that even if they are not immediately solvable, the family system is not immobilized by them. While family reorganization, that is, discovery and/or development of new patterns of interaction, is acknowledged as an alternative possibility, this is generally not stressed.

5. Formulation 2: The Dysfunctional Family—In contrast to their functional counterparts, dysfunctional families are characterized by rigidity and imbalance. This includes (1) a small number and narrow range of patterns of interpersonal communication; (2) a tendency to resist change, seemingly at all costs; (3) communication which is confused and mystifying; (4) communicational disjunction; and (5) as the consequence of these

characteristics, symptomatic behaviour on the part of one or more family members. On one hand, such symptoms symbolize the dysfunctional nature of family interaction, while, on the other hand, they serve a homeostatic function, acting to bring such systems back into balance.

Evaluation

More than any other group, proponents of this model are responsible for the popularity and the effectiveness of family therapy as an intervention modality. Their contribution to our understanding of family process has been profoundly significant. Consequently, my concern is not with what they include—communicational clarity and dysfunction, the number and range of available interactional patterns, and homeostasis—but with what they exclude.

Four such omissions may briefly be listed:

1. They fail to distinguish between communication and affect, with the latter regarded as merely a facet of the former. As Raush et al. (117) quite correctly note, proponents of this model do not recognize that affective processes act as a major contextual frame for communication acts and, as such, affect is a relational concept. As they put it, "Nowhere is love mentioned. If power was once the 'dirty word' of intimacy, so now it is with love."

2. Although proponents of the model acknowledge the existence of developmental processes, they give such processes rather scanty attention (139).

3. Similarly they attend not at all to the interface between family processes and the extrafamilial environment (117).

4. Finally, a fundamental assertion of the model is the linear relationship between communicational deviance and symptomatic behaviour. The difficulty with this formulation is that it is based exclusively on the examination of seriously dysfunctional clinical families. When non-clinical families are examined, however, the finding does not hold. Raush et al. (116), for example, found no evidence that pathological communication leads to an "unhappy" marriage, either as defined by the partners themselves or by other measures used to evaluate the quality of their relationship. Similarly, Kantor and Lehr (81), Cuber and Haroff (40), Lederer and Jackson (90), Udry (145), and Landis (87) have all reported that there is no necessary correlation between levels of marital adjustment and marital stability, with some poorly adjusted marriages exhibiting extraordinary staying power (see 91). Rather, Raush et al. (116) argue that dysfunctional communication inhibits the growth and development of the partners in their relationship and limits their capacity to adjust to changing circumstances.

3.3 Strategic Model

The strategic and communication models share many concepts and assumptions in common and, indeed, many of the same authors (58, 60, 61,

64, 149, 151, 109, 94). Indeed, its name derives more from the therapeutic strategies of its proponents than from its conceptual structure. Nevertheless, it may usefully be distinguished from the communication model (138) by its emphasis on four concepts and its particular formulation of family dysfunction.

1. *Coalition Structure:* All societies recognize a particular family-coalition structure as culturally appropriate. In North America, this includes inter-generational cleavage, in which marital and sibling sub-systems remain separate and distinct. Violation of this arrangement is associated with family dysfunction. Specifically, "perverse triangles" arise when there is a coalition between two people of different generations (either parent and child or grandparent and child) at the expense of a third. Such an arrangement interferes with the proper functioning of the family system, resulting in communicational dysfunction and confusion between levels of organization. The child, caught in the middle, may find himself being punished for choosing sides, or even for failing to choose sides. In this impossible situation, unable to see any way out (see below, #2), the development of symptomatic behaviour may be the child's way of attempting to break out of the situation.

2. *Reality:* The proponents of this model distinguish between two levels of reality for family members. One concerns the concrete facts of a particular situation, "first-order reality." The other refers to the meanings attributed to and the premises about the facts of the situation, "second-order reality." These two levels of reality may or may not be congruent. The family's premises about the facts may be regarded as "more real" than reality, with inappropriate responses to the facts as the result (see below, #3). In the terms used in Section 2.3, what this is saying is that asynchrony between meaning and interaction systems operates as positive feedback which takes the form of mishandling a minor "difficulty," thus transforming it into a major "problem."

3. *Change:* Distortion in "second-order reality" results in the tendency for family systems to mishandle difficulties. This may take any one of several different forms: (a) the existence of a real difficulty requiring some responses is denied and thus the problem is ignored; (b) efforts at change may be initiated in regard to a difficulty which is either unchangeable or non-existent; (c) simplistic solutions may be applied to complex problems; or (d) families may persist in using a problem-solving strategy which has already proven manifestly unsuccessful. In all of these cases, efforts at finding a solution merely cause the real problem to recede so that the intended solution becomes the immediate problem with which the family is confronted. A "vicious circle" is thus created in which the more they try, the more they fail, the more they get "stuck" in a dysfunctional interaction pattern of their own creation.

4. *Developmental stage:* The family life cycle is divided into a sequen-

tial series of stages that are biologically grounded and involve images of birth, maturation, death, and renewal. Each of these stages is associated with an array of tasks the completion of which, together with processes of aging, move the family along to the next stage. The shift or transition between stages is a stressful time insofar as some old patterns must be discarded and new ones developed in their place. For functional families, with a broad and varied response repertoire, such transitions are weathered without inordinate stress. For dysfunctional families, with a narrow and sparse response repertoire, such transitional periods are associated with stress of crisis proportions. Under these conditions, such families are unable to complete the required tasks, become "stuck" at a particular development stage, resulting in symptomatic behaviour often associated with such circumstances.

5. *Formulation:* Putting these concepts together yields the following formulation. Family systems characterized by distorted second-order reality mishandle the demands for change associated with, among other things, developmental transition periods. The intended solution—one of which may involve the establishment of a cross-generational coalition—subsequently becomes a problem, as the real difficulty recedes into the background. The problem in question places one or more family members in an impossible situation, with symptomatic behaviour an indication of the family's distress caused by the interaction patterns they have inadvertently become locked into.

Evaluation

The strengths of this model are manifold: it gives explicit recognition to developmental processes; it is one of the few to begin to explore the interaction between system levels (i.e., meaning and interaction, communication and interaction); it recognizes the contribution of the extended family; and, it takes seriously Maruyama's (95) notion that a small initial kick may, through deviance amplification, have highly significant consequences for the system. The result is a powerful and parsimonious theoretical model.

In this context, my concern is less with the model's concepts than with their explication. The notion of meaning is a case in point. While the distinction between meaning and interaction systems (to use my language) is an important one, the theoretical utility of the notion of "second-order reality" is limited because of a lack of explication. That every family "sees" reality in a particular way is neither new—W.I. Thomas developed the notion of the "definition of the situation" in 1928—nor does it tell us much about the family's view, apart from its congruence or disjunction with "factual reality." This contrasts sharply with Reiss (119), for example, who expands our understanding of family meaning systems by differentiating between configuration, co-ordination, and closure (see Section 4.2), three dimensions in terms of whose operations such systems may be studied.

A related difficulty concerns the implied connection between distortion of reality and family dysfunction. I suspect that this relationship is a methodological artifact of the focus on clinical populations. Given a sample of families who exhibit both dysfunctional behaviour and distortion of reality, it is only a small jump to suggest that one gives rise to the other. That there need be no necessary connection between the two, however, is supported by the recent findings of Oliveri and Reiss (106). Studying non-clinical families, the authors report wide variation on all three of the above-noted dimensions. In other words, while family meaning systems vary from open and flexible to closed and rigid, all of the families in question were asymptomatic.

Finally, the model's conception of family developmental process is problematic in several respects. In order to minimize redundancy, however, my critical remarks will be deferred to Section 3.5, when I examine the developmental model.

3.4 Structural Model

The structural model is less a model of family process than it is a model of family therapy (139). Nevertheless, through the work primarily of Minuchin (98, 100, 101, 99, 4), there has developed a number of concepts of theoretical interest.

1. *Structure/Function:* Behaviour in families is constrained by the interactional patterns through which members relate to each other in the present in order to fulfill system functions. A family's set of transactional patterns in the present constitutes its "structure." The inherent or generic needs towards which family transactions are directed constitute its "functions." Such functions exist, both at the level of system (e.g., the necessity of a marital subsystem) as well as at the level of three primary subsystems (e.g., marital, parent-child, sibling). In general, most family patterns centre around three dominant structural dimensions: boundary, alignment, and power.

2. *Boundary:* Those interactional patterns which determine who participates and how, both in the system per se and in its constituent subsystems, define a system's boundaries. Since each subsystem has certain functions that it must perform, it is essential that the boundaries around them be "clear," that is, that each subsystem be sufficiently free from interference that it may fulfill its functions but not so impermeable that interaction between subsystems cannot occur. This is a curvilinear dimension insofar as excessive (enmeshment) or insufficient (disengagement) interactions are regarded as dysfunctional, while an intermediate level (clear) is associated with good family functioning. The level of boundary clarity is perhaps the single most important indicator of family adjustment.

3. *Alignment:* This refers to the joining together or opposition of one member to another in relation to the completion of family functions. Like the proponents of the strategic model, proponents of the structural model

suggest that inter-generational cleavage is a rule in well-functioning families. Conversely, cross-generational alignment, which violates family hierarchy and undermines the authority of the executive (i.e., parental) subsystem (e.g., triangulation, detour), is dysfunctional.

4. *Power:* Defined as the relative influence of one member in relation to another, family systems are conceptualized as hierarchically structured power ladders. On this ladder, the parent or executive subsystem is thought to have the most power; this arrangement is necessary if the family is to function properly. Conversely, maladjustment is associated with a weak executive subsystem that lacks functional power.

5. *Transactional pattern:* This refers to the stable configuration of family members in their relationships with each other, and is thus similar to the notion of homeostasis. As Steinglass (139) notes, however, it is rather more diffuse, pointing more to the juxtaposition of behaviour and context "in space" than to the sequential ordering of their occurrence "in time." While statements about transaction may involve the observation of repetitive transactions, they typically describe the way family members fit together rather than how they transact over time. Indeed, the model seldom refers to the cycles, sequences, and runaways that are the mainstay of communicational and strategic models examined above (74).

6. *Formulation:* Taken together, the above concepts suggest the following formulation: a family system's functionality is described in terms of the adequacy of fit between its structural organization and its functional requirements in a given set of circumstances. In this context, dysfunction may involve one or more structural dimensions and is not specific to any symptom. Thus, poorness of fit typically refers to a family structure that is poorly defined and elaborated, inflexible and either poorly integrated or excessively cohesive.

Evaluation

On theoretical grounds, the model's attention to the effects of particular coalition structures and confusion of intersystemic boundaries are its special strengths. It remains problematic, however, in at least three respects:

1. Its focus on structure obscures the fact that all family processes take time and occur in time. Consequently, the model has serious difficulties in dealing with interactional processes over time (139). In turn, since alteration in family functioning also takes time, the model deals poorly with change (74).

2. As noted in Section 2.32, the idea that parents have power over their children obscures the relational character of parental influence.

3. Its focus on family functions tends to be arbitrary, static, and non-parsimonious. Neither logical nor empirical grounds are provided upon which a specific list of functions may be rationalized. Consequently, the list of needs provided reads more like a set of axioms than a set of hypotheses. Furthermore, the list is arbitrary, easily amenable to being shortened or

extended. In addition, the functions in question are not conceptualized as arising out of interaction, but rather are taken as given; families that meet these functional requirements, given their circumstances, are "healthy" and those that do not are "unhealthy." Finally, this formulation is non-parsimonious. As Ashby (6) suggests, systems whose components are densely connected function poorly because all must change before any one component can change. Accordingly, optimal functioning should be associated with an intermediate level of intrasystemic interaction, while poorly functioning systems should be characterized by interaction that is either too dense or too loose. This suggests that boundary clarity may be parsimoniously re-formulated as "degree of intrusion." This accounts for the observations of the model's proponents, while dispensing with the concept of "function."

Removal of the notion of function similarly calls for the reformulation of "fit." This is an important idea since it suggests that family functioning may be conceptualized in terms of context, both internal and external. A promising possibility, in accord with the stress literature, concerns the relationship between perceived demand and response capacity (39, 46, 89). Thus, "fit" would refer to the extent to which a family's response capacity was adequate to cope with its perception of the demands being made upon it. I will pursue this formulation further in the next subsection.

3.5 Developmental Model

The idea that a family moves through a developmental cycle is not a new one. Its origin, at least in the modern era, can be traced to the late 1940's with the work of Erikson (47) in psychiatry and Hill (70) and Duvall (45) in sociology (see 122). It did not enter the family therapy literature in any serious way, however, until the early 1970's (35).

Irrespective of when and by what route the developmental model arose, it has taken the same invariant form. The course of family life can be divided into a number of stages, ranging anywhere from five to twenty-four depending on the author examined. The family moves from stage to stage in a sequential, additive manner, that is, movement is always in a forward direction and the stages always proceed in a fixed order. Each stage is characterized by a certain set of tasks all or most of which must be completed before movement to the next stage is possible; these tasks fulfill certain fundamental family functions. While the functions in question vary across authors, the following list by Hill (70) is fairly typical: "1) Physical maintenance for family members through providing food, shelter, and clothing; 2) addition of family members through reproduction or adoption and releasing them when mature; 3) socialization of children for adult roles in the family and in other social groups; 4) maintenance of order within the family and between family members and outsiders; 5) maintenance of family morale and motivation to carry out tasks in the family and in other groups; 6) reduction and direction of goods and services necessary for maintaining the family unit." Finally, the transition between stages, insofar as it requires some degree of family reorganization, is deemed stressful, although most families manage the transition without undue disruption. Some transitional processes (e.g., divorce), however, may be sufficiently complex as to require additional developmental stages or substages.

The idea that family systems are not static, but rather move and change through time, is crucial to an adequate understanding of family life. From a systemic perspective, however, the model's handling of the processes involved is the least adequate of any of the models examined thus far. Its problems are multiple and serious.

1. The model is uni-directional. Stages progress in lockstep, ever forward, and, by implication at least, ever better—more mature, balanced, experienced, and so on. Development, then, is necessarily smooth and uninterrupted. There is never any sense of slippage, of goals attained and then lost. Note further that the transition from stage to stage applies to families as units; that subsystems and/or levels may progress at uneven rates is not considered.

2. Each stage is separate and distinct from every other; there is no interaction between them. Yet it is not uncommon for a family to span three generations and to include children from infancy to maturity (24, 104). This raises the possibility that at any one point in time, the family may be seen not as having achieved a certain stage of development, but rather as a configuration produced by the simultaneous interaction of several different stages.

3. From the perspective of the developmental model, the family system is de-contextualized. Stability and change are described in terms of a set of biologically based individual attributes (e.g., age) set in a closed system. But as I have indicated earlier, family systems are never closed and are thus continually being bombarded by events, experiences, and demands from their social (e.g., kin, neighbours, friends) and non-social (e.g., occupation, religion, law, politics) environments. Indeed, under some conditions, the impact of these systems may be more significant than concurrent processes within the family. At present, proponents of the developmental model pay such systems little or no attention.

4. The concepts of stage, function, and task are poorly explicated and are used in an arbitrary manner. Since no theoretical rationale is provided to explain the number of stages, the number of functions, or the number and mix of tasks, all three can be shortened or extended at will, with no loss in explanatory power. Put differently, theoretical ideas that exhibit such elasticity are unlikely to be especially fruitful.

5. Finally, proponents of the developmental model tend to focus primarily on the nuclear family, typically meaning an intact family with

two parents, a male breadwinner and a female housewife, and one or two children. As Ramey (114) and others (42, 131) note, however, the family as an institution has so changed in the last three decades, that only 13% of U.S. families in 1975 were nuclear families in the above sense. This suggests that the developmental model is neither well-suited to varying family forms nor to alternate life styles (139).

Taken together, these remarks suggest that a model that conceptualizes stability and change in terms of stages, tasks, and functions is unlikely to be fruitful and should be abandoned; it is too narrow, too rigid, too static. How then are we to conceptualize the important processes in question in a more generic manner?

Bodin's (23) reformulation of Haley (60) is a step in the right direction. Briefly, Bodin differentiates between two types of life-cycle markers: predictable and unpredictable, with the former further subdivided into expected and unexpected. Predictable events, the timing of which are expected, include marriage and birth. Predictable events, the timing of which may be expected or unexpected, include death and an adolescent's first date. Unpredictable events, the timing of which may or may not be expected, include divorce, a woman's decision to return to the workplace after childbearing, and family murder. Finally, unpredictable and unexpected events include "major illnesses, serious accidents, unusual failures, or triumphs in the course of school or career. Such events would also include non-accidental misfortunes such as robbery, rape, and (criminal) murder." (Bodin, p. 275) The salient dimension underlying both expectability and predictability is the degree of family preparedness. As Bodin (p. 275) explains, "The more prepared a person for what happens, the better able to cope he or she would probably be. If an event is both unexpected and unpredictable, it is likely that the opportunity to prepare for coping will be minimal and the perception of unwarrantedness and injustice will be maximal." This assertion is well-supported by empirical evidence (see 160).

Preparedness is related to two additional dimensions. The first of these concerns the rate and absolute magnitude of demand.* (160) In general, the greater the rate of change and the greater the absolute magnitude of the event in question, the greater will be the experience of demand. A series of minor events—a shift in residence, change of school, new job, an adolescent having problems making new friends—may collectively be experienced as high demand. Conversely, a single event of sufficient absolute magnitude— the premeditated murder of the breadwinner following a robbery—may have the same consequences. Both sources of demand, however, are subject to an important caveat, namely, that families vary widely in their interpre-

---

*The notion of "demand" is taken from Selye's (128) definition of stress: "The non-specific response of the body to any demand."

tation and response to such events (39, 106). As Hansen and Johnson (67) observe, "What for some families may be a crisis . . . may be more akin to a 're-genesis' for other families in which members accept disruption of habit and tradition not so much as unwelcome problems, but more as opportunities to re-negotiate their relationship." Level of demand, then, involves the perception of change events as mediated by the family's meaning system, which, in turn, mediates its perception of its response capacity.

A second dimension concerns the matter of timing (74, 139). A minor event occurring during a period of low demand may have no effect whatever. However, the same event occurring during the period of high demand may have consequences of a different order, approaching the level of crisis in some families. Thus, some appreciation of the "prevailing level of demand" at the point of change is crucial to understanding the consequences of the event. Note that the relationship of both preparedness and prevailing level of demand is multiplicative; a given level of demand is likely to have significantly more impact on the family if it is unprepared for it and already experiencing a high level of demand.

Still another related dimension is that of duration (67). Events that are perceived as high in demand may, if they are short-term, simply be endured until things change for the better with the passage of time (160). Such a response is not possible when the event or events in question are of a long-term nature (e.g., the death of a spouse) and thus may wear down a family's capacity to respond, leading, at least in some cases, to complete collapse. This dimension would also appear to have a multiplicative relationship to level of demand.

Finally, while change is typically associated with demand (85, 113), this is not a necessary part of all change (67). Rather, following Buckley (31) and Maruyama (95), change may be associated with increased variety, that is, the input of new information which may induce change by "pushing" the system, a subsystem, or a family member (cf. 81) to see things in a new way. A case in point concerns the happily married housewife who accidentally discovers her husband's lipstick-stained handkerchief and "suddenly" comes to view him, their relationship, and, indeed, their entire life together over the ten years of their marriage in a new way (see 76, 159). Such an increase in variety (1) may induce family reorganization during a period of low demand; (2) may provide a solution to a high-demand problem otherwise perceived as irremediable; or (3) may be a consequence of some previously unsuccessful solution (e.g., symptomatic behaviour) to a problem that has come to be perceived as high demand. In other words, a chance increase in variety is an independent dimension that may or may not interact with level of demand to induce change.

Taken together, the five dimensions noted above suggest a model of developmental process that is considerably more complex, variable, contingent, and changeable than the developmental model now dominant in the family therapy literature. Furthermore, it suggests a further elaboration of the notion of "fit" previously referred to. Specifically, a family's response capacity refers to its problem-solving style as embodied in its meaning system, its number and range of interaction patterns, and its access to increased variety. Conversely, its perceived level of demand refers to the rate and absolute magnitude of the change events to which it is exposed, modified by its prevailing level of demand at onset, its degree of preparedness, and the duration of the demand level in question. Fit, then, refers to the relationship between response capacity and demand, and thus is conceptualized as a transactional or processional construct which is necessarily in a constant state of flux. This implies, first, that the description of a family as "dysfunctional" is a statement about a system's highly variable process of "fit," hence the high proportion of "spontaneous remission" in response to neurotic disorder (86); and, second, that the purpose of therapeutic intervention is to adjust "fit," either by increasing the family's response capacity, decreasing its level of perceived demand, or both.

3.6 Summary

My purpose in examining the communication, strategic, structural, and developmental models was to abstract from them concepts of potential use in developing our own model of family process. The result has been to identify or derive a series of concepts—communication clarity and disjunction, coalition pattern, degree of intrusion, variety, degree of preparedness, level of demand, prevailing demand, and duration of demand—all of which, as will become apparent in the next section, play a prominent role in my effort at model building.

4.1 A Recursive Model of Family Process

The previous two sections provided an exploration and evaluation of GST and four prominent family system theories. Throughout, I have been at some pains to identify, reformulate, or derive concepts that I judge to be theoretically powerful or fruitful. In this section, I attempt to integrate these ideas into a single recursive model of family process.

Accordingly, in what follows below, I first list and briefly explicate the model's key constructs. Next, I present the model in diagrammatic form (see Figure 2.1) and, subsequently, explicate it verbally. Finally, I examine some of the model's implications.

4.2 Five Constructs

The heart of the model consists of five multi-dimensional constructs. These are listed below, together with (1) the dimensions of which it is constituted; (2) the shape of the dimension, that is, whether it is linear or curvilinear; and (3) its levels of measurement (i.e., nominal, ordinal, or interval). It will be apparent that of the constructs in question, four pertain to the levels at which I have suggested family systems operate, and one reflects my formulation of demand.

1. *Interaction:* Interaction refers to the repetitive interactional sequences of behaviour observed in family systems and, in particular, who relates to whom and the nature of their relationship. The construct dissolves into four dimensions: (a) the number of observed patterns; (b) their range; (c) the extent to which the family's coalition structure is culturally appropriate; and (d) the degree of intrusion, both among subsystems and between the family and its social and non-social environment. Of these, (a), (b), and (d) are linear, while (c) is curvilinear. One (a) achieves the interval level of measurement, while the remaining three ((b), (c), (d)) are ordinal. For purposes of simplicity, however, all dimensions in this construct (and all other constructs) are treated as either dichotomous (i.e., high or low) or, in the case of (c), as trichotomous (i.e., high, medium, low). "High" interaction refers to a high number and wide range of patterns, an appropriate coalition structure, and a moderate level of intrusion.

2. *Affect:* Affect refers to the feeling that family members have for each other, especially as these are made explicit through behaviour. This is composed of three dimensions: (a) the *rate* of affective expression; (b) the *range* of affective expression; (c) the *direction* of affective expression, as a ratio of positive to negative affect; and (d) the level of attachment. All dimensions are linear in shape and achieve either interval (a) or ordinal ((b), (c), (d)) levels of measurement. "High" affect refers to a high rate and wide range of affective expression, a high level of positive to negative affect, and a high level of attachment.

3. *Communication:* Communication refers to the range of verbal and non-verbal behaviours that convey information and effect behaviour. Two dimensions are identified here: (a) communicational clarity; and (b) the rate of disjunctive communication. All the dimensions are linear in shape and achieve either ordinal (a) or interval (b) levels of measurement. "High" communication refers to a high level of communicational clarity and a low level of communicational disjunction.

4. *Meaning:* Meaning refers to the assumptions that family members typically make about the nature of their social world. It involves Reiss's (119) three dimensions of (a) configuration: perception of the social world as orderly, and thus capable of mastery by the family; (b) co-ordination: belief that the environment regards the behaviour of individual members as a product of the family; and (c) closure: a temporal dimension in which families regard environmental events as either continually familiar or novel. All dimensions are linear in shape and achieve an ordinal level of measurement. "High" meaning refers to high configuration, high co-ordination, and delayed closure.

5. *Level of demand:* Level of demand refers to events and processes

either in the family and/or in the social or non-social environment that are perceived to require some family response. This involves four dimensions: (a) prevailing level of demand at any point in time prior to the onset of specified change events; (b) increased demand based on the number, rate, and absolute magnitude of change events during a specified time interval; (c) degree of preparedness; and (d) duration of demand. All dimensions are linear in shape and achieve either interval ((a), (b), (d)) or ordinal (c) levels of measurement. "High" demand refers to a high level of increased demand, a high prevailing demand, a low degree of preparedness, and long duration demand.

Finally, an additional point of clarification is in order. "Increased variety" refers to an increase in the chance availability of new information, either to the family as a whole or to any of its members.

4.3 A Theoretical Model:
Diagrammatic and Discursive Forms

The recursive model of family process is displayed in diagrammatic form in Figure 2.1, with diagramming conventions taken, in slightly modified form, from Burr et al. (33).

Pursuant to my concern with both stability and change, the following exposition of the model differentiates between two time periods: Time One during which the family system is asymptomatic, and Time Two which sees an increase in demand and the possible appearance of symptoms.

Time One

By definition, all family systems must cope with fluctuations both in their structure and in events in the outside world. As such, all systems, even at the best of times, face some level of demand. Determination of a given system's total prevailing demand involves simultaneous consideration of four aspects of the system: (1) its operation at the level of meaning, affect, communication, and interaction; (2) interaction among these levels; (3) the extent to which the levels in question are synchronous; and (4) external demand, either from the non-social environment (e.g., economic system) or the social (e.g., friend) and extended family systems. Across family systems, tremendous variation may occur in any or all of these components—total prevailing demand may thus vary from high to low—in the absence of symptomatic behaviour.

With respect to levels, we have seen in Sections 2 and 3 that non-clinical families may exhibit meaning and communication systems that vary from "high" to "low." It seems reasonable to predict similar variations in affect and interaction (see 157). Consider, for example, the level of interaction in anorexic families six months prior to symptom onset (cf. 101). While it is conceivable that "clear boundaries" would have been in evidence, with the appearance of enmeshment coincident with symptom

Figure 2.1
Recursive Model of Family Process

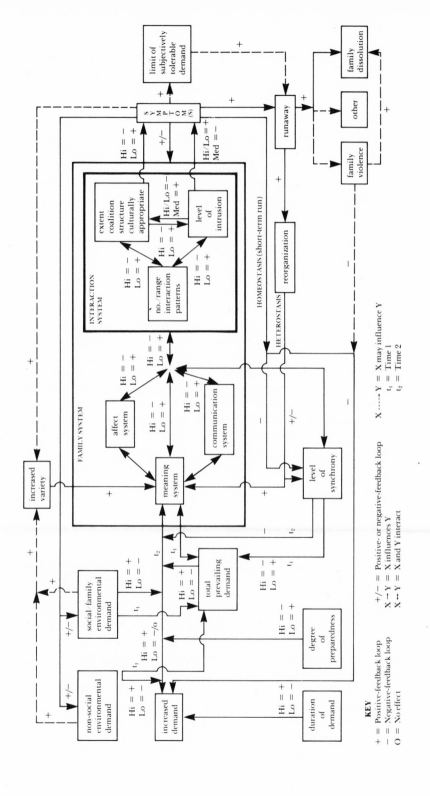

KEY

+ = Positive-feedback loop
− = Negative-feedback loop
O = No effect

+/− = Positive- or negative-feedback loop
X → Y = X influences Y
X ↔ Y = X and Y interact

X ‧‧‧‧ Y = X may influence Y
t_1 = Time 1
t_2 = Time 2

onset, it is also unlikely. Rather, it is more reasonable to expect enmeshment to have been present throughout, with some change in level of
demand associated with symptom onset. Similarly, one would expect that
affect systems, coalition structure, and the number and range of interaction
patterns would also exhibit wide variation in non-clinical families. One
qualification, however, would seem to be in order: following Colon (38), I
would anticipate that a certain minimal level of family organization would
be required in order for family systems to respond coherently to demand;
beyond that, under-organization would become so marked that even
minimal demand would overwhelm the system's capacity to respond.

With respect to the interaction between levels, I again anticipate high
variation across family systems. In effect, since each of these systems is
conceptualized as bounded, variation in interaction is analogous to variation in permeability. Relatively little data are available in this context. It is
unclear, for example, whether families which exhibit high communication
necessarily exhibit high affect. Similarly, it is uncertain whether an
increase in the number and/or range of interaction patterns must necessarily be matched by an increase in the meaning system. Anecdotal clinical
evidence, however, suggests that variation in the extent of the articulation
between levels can be expected across families.

With respect to synchrony, family systems vary in the extent to which
the relationship between levels is synchronous. That some systems can
sustain asynchrony over extended periods seems clear (e.g., 105). However,
following Newcomb (102), I assume that family systems also exhibit a
"strain towards symmetry." Consequently, the presence of asynchrony
would appear to represent a source of demand.

The preceding three aspects of family systems collectively constitute its
internal or intrasystemic source of prevailing demand. In practice, such
demand represents the incredibly diverse behaviours (e.g., conflict (see 137),
passion, involvement, and detachment) and events (e.g., birth, marriage,
school attendance) which comprise family life.

Such diversity, however, does not exhaust sources of prevailing
demand, for family exists in a larger social context—the worlds of politics
and economics, of work and leisure, of friends and kin. All of these constitute additional sources of demand as they interact with (rather than merely
have an impact upon) the family system. Nor do such demands merely
attend negative events (e.g., economic recession), but also include positive
ones (e.g., support from one's social network) (see 37, 110).

Finally, it is important to note that the level of prevailing demand is a
subjective matter, mediated by the perception, appraisal, and interpretation of the events in question (39). Consequently, there need be no 1-to-1
correlation between the number and magnitude of such events and
processes, and subjectively the experience-level of total prevailing demand.
Indeed, the meaning system, which mediates such perceptual processes,

may or may not be accurate (67, 160). Contrary to traditional belief in the importance of accurate "reality testing," misperception may actually be beneficial—especially in situations in which demand is irremediable—by fostering the illusion of competence and control.

In sum, then, (1) total prevailing demand represents an extraordinarily complex transactional process including both intra- and intersystemic components; and (2) asymptomatic families may vary widely, both in terms of prevailing demand (from high to low) as well as social organization (from typical to atypical).

Time Two

On the assumption of an increase in the level of demand, I explore the sources of that increase: the family's interactional response to it, including the appearance of symptomatic behaviour, and the alternative processes that such behaviour may set in motion. Accordingly, three processual phases will be delimited: (1) increase in demand; (2) response to demand; and (3) contingent consequences of symptomatic behaviour.* It must be emphasized that this tri-phasic distinction is purely a rhetorical device for simplifying the presentation of ideas. As represented in the model, demand, response, and consequences would occur simultaneously in a complex, contingent array of feedback loops.

1. Phase One: *Increased demand*—Superficially, increased demand refers simply to the number, rate, and absolute magnitude of change events, either within and/or outside the family, with demand and change linearly related: the higher the number, rate, and magnitude of change events, the greater the level of increased demand.

As noted in Section 3, however, the family's perception of demand is rather more complex, involving a set of additional contingencies and inter-action between demand level and meaning. With respect to the former, demand level is contingent on total prevailing demand, degree of prepared-ness, and duration of demand. High prevailing demand, low preparedness, and prolonged duration would each, separately and collectively, interact with demand level in a multiplicative manner. This means that even if the number and rate of change events were hypothetically low, their impact would be considerable under these conditions. Conversely, in their absence, both high number and rate of change would be mitigated considerably. The only caveat here refers to absolute magnitude in which a single event— for example, the criminal homicide of a parent—may be so significant that it would invariably be experienced as a significant increase in demand.

With respect to the latter, the experience of change events as involving high and low demand is mediated by the meaning system. I will examine

---

*Note that no mention is made of "outcome," which seems to me to be a static formulation for what are, in fact, many ongoing processes.

the contingent responses of the family's meaning system to increased demand in Phase Two. For the present, then, suffice it to say that increased demand perceived as "high" is likely to operate as a positive-feedback loop in relation to prevailing system processes, whereas an increase experienced as "low" is likely to have little or no effect on such processes.

2. Phase Two: *System response*—There is general agreement in the literature that the more flexible or adaptive the family system, the more it is likely to adequately cope with the increased demand, that is, without resort to symptomatic behaviour (see 107). While my own formulation is in keeping with this hypothesis, I suggest that "flexibility" is a complex construct, including *both* how a system functions at each of the four levels and the interaction between levels; furthermore, the presence of flexibility is no absolute guarantee of adequate functioning.

With respect to level, a family's response to increased demand will be contingent upon the extent to which the system in question is high or low at each of the four levels. With respect to meaning system, for example, Oliveri and Reiss (106) suggest that families "low" in meaning (i.e., low configuration, low co-ordination, early closure) would be significantly less likely to cope adequately with "high" demand—and thus significantly more likely to exhibit symptomatic behaviour—than those "high" in meaning (i.e., high configuration, high co-ordination, delayed closure). It is reasonable to believe that a similar conclusion would apply to families characterized by "low" affect, communication, and interaction. In general, then, I would predict that the "higher" the level in question and the more synchronous they are, the less likely to exhibit symptomatic behaviour are families with these attributes. Two important qualifications, however, are in order here. Note, first, that this statement is probabilistic and is thus likely to become increasingly asymptomatic as probabilities increase—in short, no family can be totally immune to symptomatic behaviour under conditions of high demand. Second, the "scope" conditions of the foregoing hypothesis concern the matter of absolute magnitude of demand—every family will break down given sufficiently high demand. This, however, suggests a secondary hypothesis, namely, that the "higher" the family on the levels in question, the less likely is symptomatic behaviour to become a stable feature of family structure and, conversely, the more likely is such behaviour to be a temporary anomaly. (I will return to this hypothesis again in discussing Phase Three.)

The foregoing hypothesis assumes independence between levels. As the model makes clear, this is, in principle, not the case. All levels interact, although the extent of interaction may vary across families. Data available with respect to such interactions remain rare, such that any statements I might make must be taken as speculative. The work of Oliveri and Reiss (106), however, is a welcome exception. This shows that "low" meaning tends to be associated with families who experience interpersonal isolation (i.e., low intrusion in my terms). Similarly, it has been reported above (Section 3.3) that (1) a direct relationship exists between culturally inappropriate coalition structures and dysjunctive communication, and (2) between "low" meaning and a restriction in the number and/or range of interactional patterns. Extrapolating from these few observations, I would speculate, first, that asynchrony between levels under conditions of high demand is likely to operate as positive feedback, "pushing" the system towards synchrony, either at the "high" or "low" end of the spectrum of functioning; and, second, that as synchrony towards the "low" end increases, the probability of symptomatic behaviour increases.

Ultimately, as pertinent data accumulate, it should be possible to explicate the formulation to predict the relationship between specific interactional configurations and specific symptoms or symptom clusters. While speculation about such correlations is available (see 23, 106, 147), no definitive or even systematic statement is yet possible.

3. Phase Three: *Symptomatic behaviour and its processual consequences*—The commonly accepted notion that symptomatic behaviour is a response to high demand implies that symptoms are an end point or outcome of a process. If the consequences of symptom onset were invariant, this would be a reasonable perspective. In fact, symptom onset may set in motion an array of alternate processes. Consequently, symptomatic behaviour may be more aptly described as a "process in motion," in the sense that it is a marker of an ongoing process that both recedes into the past and continues on into alternative possible futures.

One such alternative involves "homeostatic transformation" in which symptomatic behaviour becomes incorporated as a stable feature of the family's response repertoire through the process of error activation. This may occur either directly and/or indirectly. In the former instance, symptomatic behaviour reduces the level of demand by providing a "solution," however ineffective, to the family's problem. Triangulation, for example, which may diffuse or deflect symptom-threatening marital conflict, has become a classic case in point (see 98). In the latter instance, demand reduction may involve reduced asymmetry (see above, Phase One) or may operate through extrafamilial systems. Symptomatic behaviour which may act to destabilize the family system (i.e., positive feedback) may have the opposite effect (i.e., negative feedback) at the more inclusive suprasystem level.

However it is achieved, once homeostatic transformation has occurred, it will tend to endure through time, even though the circumstances that created the demand at onset have changed for the better. It is unclear, however, whether or not this is independent of the source of the problem. It may be that homeostatic transformation that "solves" intrafamilial problems may be much more resistant to change than problems which originate outside the family system. Symptomatic behaviour associated with economic depression, for example, may disappear spontaneously with increased affluence. Moreover, homeostatic stability of symptomatic behaviour may leave the family especially vulnerable to further destabilization and perhaps runaway should the level of demand increase in the future.

This brings me to the second major alternative facing a family system exhibiting symptomatic behaviour: runaway. Here, two divergent processes may be differentiated—heterostasis or full runaway—as functions of three factors: the level of experienced demand, the level of family functioning prior to symptom onset, and the availability of increased variety. Runaway will occur when symptom onset operates to amplify rather than dampen error. This will occur because some combination of the absolute intensity of demand, the restricted response capacity of the family system, and the "positive" input of extrafamilial suprasystems will have pushed the system to its limit of subjectively tolerable demand. Under such conditions, response patterns are typified by a subjective foreshortening of time, a diminished search for alternative responses, increasingly concrete and simplistic thought processes, diminished attention to events outside the focus of demand, impulsiveness, and a tendency to make decisions based on partial information (96). The collective result is the failure of error activation (16, 17).

In this context, heterostasis will tend to be associated with intense demand, a system operating at the "high" end of the functional spectrum, and, possibly, with increased access to variety, either because of the system itself or because of environmental input. In such systems, symptom onset will act as a "message" that (1) the system is in crisis; (2) established interactional patterns have failed under the circumstances at hand; and (3) a search for new patterns must be initiated immediately. While such a search pattern may occur in families at any point on the functional spectrum, it is more probable that families at the "high" rather than the "low" end will both initiate and successfully complete such a search. Furthermore, active searching increases the family's readiness to receive "new" information and therefore increases the probability that the family will discover it. Such discovery, while it may occur at the system level, may alternatively involve an individual member, who may, in effect, act as the conduit for increased variety, up to and including the decision "*not* to play the parts or make the moves assigned by a (family) strategy" (81, p. 20), thus potentially altering them. Under these conditions, heterostasis becomes probable, restructuring the family system and increasing its response repertoire. This would enable the family to handle the demand-inducing circumstances more effectively, thus reducing the level of experienced demand, altering the conditions under which symptomatic behaviour arose, and moving the family to a more complex and asymptomatic level of functioning. Given that heterostasis takes time, I would speculate that such families make up a disproportionately high number of those who exhibit "spontaneous remission" of symptoms (see 86).

Alternatively, full runaway will tend to be associated with intense demand, a system operating at the "low" end of the functional spectrum and, possibly, no access to variety. In such systems, the appearance of symptomatic behaviour will itself act to exacerbate the level of demand, thus increasing the rate of error amplification. Given a restricted level of functioning, such families are unlikely to undertake the search for increased variety and thus are unlikely to discover it, although the asymptomatic nature of this relationship must be noted. Furthermore, non-familial suprasystems are likely to be a further source of error amplification. In short, such families are likely to be simply overwhelmed with processes they neither understand nor can control, with family dissolution (e.g., divorce, family murder), non-lethal violence, or the expulsion of a member, just three among an array of possible consequences. Even at this point, however, homeostatic transformation remains possible if the processes in question operate to reduce level of demand, as has been reported anecdotally with respect to child abuse (see 30, 82).

These remarks with respect to runaway have, for the sake of simplicity, examined family systems at opposite ends of the functional spectrum. This is not to suggest that families at the "low" end will invariably exhibit runaway or that those at the "high" end will always exhibit heterostasis. Both are possible in either group. Rather, I am suggesting that as a population, these processes are simply more probable in the groups in question, an assertion that coincides with data concerning the structural (i.e., social class) distribution of a range of symptomatic behaviours (see 160).

4.4 Limits of the Model

The model in question is severely limited in at least two respects: the data base on which it is grounded and the restricted range of variables which it seeks to encompass. With respect to the former, this is a special problem for those attempting to develop system models of family process. As Broderick and Smith (28) explain, "The fact is that we know very little about the family as a system. Its system parameters have certainly not been specified and calibrated (let alone measured) in a degree to even approximate a level of precision required in much of the system literature." To add insult to injury, much of the available data pertain to clinical families that are, by definition, non-representative, both in terms of the presence of presenting symptoms and the fact of therapeutic selection, screening, evaluation, diagnosis (i.e., labelling), intervention, and follow-up (see 127). Consequently, many of the model's assertions must be seen as speculative, subject to confirmation or refutation by future research.

With respect to the latter, the inherent complexity of family systems means that any effort to include all possible variables considered relevant together with their interaction—assuming, for a moment, that this was possible—would produce a diagram so complex as to be completely useless. For this reason, the model in question deliberately excludes from consideration three major sets of variables:

1. A range of structural variables (e.g., class, education, race, family size, etc.) has been omitted, although their relationship to such things as response to demand (160) and level of organizational complexity (38) have been demonstrated.

2. I have ignored a range of institutional variables concerned with how families perceive and respond to symptomatic behaviour, how families come to the attention of official gatekeepers, consequences of formal labelling as part of the process of induction into the mental health system, and so forth (54, 75, 121, 127).

3. Finally, in the search for generic statements, I have not focussed in detail on the micro-processes at the levels of meaning, communication, affect, and interaction that are the bread and butter of most efforts to understand family dysfunction (101, 62).

The exclusion of these variable clusters is not to suggest that their integration into future versions of the model in question is neither possible nor desirable; quite the contrary. However, much work, both theoretical and empirical, is needed before this becomes a realistic possibility (cf. 52).

5. Implications

My concern in this chapter has been to draw a picture of family process which is more fluid, complex, variable, and subject to change than models currently available in the family therapy literature. Towards that end, the model presented in Section 4 includes concepts drawn from general and family systems theories, and focusses as much on "normal" family processes as those found in dysfunctional family systems.

This approach to model building together with the model itself suggests a number of implications for clinical practitioners. For illustrative purposes, I briefly examine three of these below.

1. It is generally assumed that (1) symptomatic behaviour represents a dysfunctional organization of family systems; (2) therapeutic reorganization of a system will be associated with symptom remission; and (3) once remission has occurred, symptoms will not recur. The present model suggests that the last assumption is likely to be in error. The multiple contingent nature of family processes means that no intervention, however successful, can be expected to endure over the long term. Shift in processes of levels of demand, response capacity, the availability of increased variety, all ensure that the interactional patterns that characterize the family immediately following intervention will not be those that define it in the future. Accordingly, symptomatic behaviour may reappear but for reasons entirely different from those underlying the initial symptom onset and possibly requiring entirely different intervention procedures. Conversely, asymptomatic functioning may endure indefinitely, but be unrelated to

any change associated with the initial intervention. Efforts to understand either process will need to attend, at least to some extent, to historical processes, although therapeutic intervention must remain focussed on the present.

2. Therapeutic assessment and intervention is generally focussed on intrasystemic processes. So long as this is the primary locus of demand, this is appropriate. Often, however, intersystemic processes confound the picture, acting either as additional sources of demand or, indeed, as the primary sources of demand camouflaged by intrasystemic processes that have arisen in response. (a) On the one hand, this would suggest that (1) assessment must automatically include intersystemic processes; (2) such processes become legitimate targets of intervention; (3) representatives of suprasystems be brought directly into the intervention process, where appropriate, because they are part of the system under treatment; (4) intervention in suprasystems and, indeed, in the interaction between such systems, may be more critical, in some cases, to family reorganization than intervention in the family system in question; (5) extensive knowledge of the structure and political context of such suprasystems is a prerequisite for successful strategic intervention; (6) the locus of intervention may require the therapist to abandon, in some cases, both the security of his or her own office "turf" as well as the regular office hours that typically go with it; and (7) where suprasystemic intervention is not possible, for whatever reason, intervention may focus, not on family reorganization per se, but rather on teaching family systems some strategic methods for handling these systems more effectively than has hitherto been the case. (b) On the other hand, failure to adapt this ecosystemic perspective may mean that (1) increased therapist error becomes inevitable; (2) a proportion of cases that do not respond to intervention and/or drop out, and which are explained by the catch-all of "resistance," will actually result from the therapist's use of an excessively narrow data base; and (3) in some cases, exclusively intrasystemic intervention may act to exacerbate family difficulties.

3. Finally, paradoxical interventions have been used successfully with a wide variety of problem families. Consequently, they have been the target of much clinical interest because of the apparently illogical interventions they make and the seemingly miraculous results they can achieve. As Fisher et al. (50) have noted, however, their successful use has been disproportionately associated with what I have called "heterostatic" as opposed to "runaway" families, that is, families at the "high" end of the functional spectrum, with access to increased variety. Accordingly, the authors conclude that paradox is contraindicated with what they refer to as "chaotic," "impulsive," or "childlike" families. In contrast, the model implies that (1) paradoxical interventions have their effect by inducing what might be called "controlled heterostasis," that is, escalating already high demand under the conditions of increased variety while preventing

runaway; (2) "runaway" families lack access to variety and may not function well enough to utilize such variety even when it is available; (3) increased functioning and increased variety would transform "runaway" families into "heterostatic families," thus making appropriate use of paradox. These remarks suggest that, rather than abandoning paradox in "runaway" families, intervention may be conceptualized in terms of a series of carefully planned stages, the first of these oriented towards improving functioning and introducing increased variety in the form of skills training, education in the rudiments of sexuality, conflict management, affective expression, child disciplinary techniques, and, generally, broadening their range of life experience. Once these goals have been achieved, paradox can then be effectively employed. In short, there need be no a priori contraindication to the use of paradox, with the exception, of course, that other techniques may be more effective in situ.

These implications of the model are fully consistent with our model of clinical practice (29). In both cases, the approach is fundamentally recursive, attempts to examine "total circuits," systematically accounts for a range of contingencies, is sensitive to both time and context, and acknowledges the dual roles of chance and individual choice. Further, in both cases, disruption of a given system at a point in time centres on the relationship between patterns of interaction and sources of demand, rather than on symptom clusters or intrapsychic processes. In this sense, the "family constellations" discussed in the clinical model represent a rhetorically convenient way of describing prevalent family arrangements rather than a theoretically grounded family typology; both clinical and theoretical models acknowledge, in principle, immense variation across family systems. Finally, these models intersect, with the present model providing the theoretical rationale for clinical intervention, while the clinical model offers an important source of empirical data which direct the course of the elaboration of theory.

6. Conclusion

In our view, theory and practice must necessarily be complementary. This chapter presents a theoretical model of family process that, while grounded in clinical data, seeks to move beyond the data. The model will be useful only so long as it helps inform the clinician's efforts to intervene therapeutically in troubled family systems and is, in turn, sensitive to the new information that clinical efforts will invariably uncover.

References

1. Ackerman, N.W. *The Psychodynamics of Family Life*. N.Y.: Basic, 1958.
2. Anderson, M. "Family, household and the industrial revolution." In M. Anderson, ed. *Sociology of the Family*. London: Penguin, 1971.
3. Aponte, H.J. "Underorganization in the poor family." In P.J. Guerin, ed.

Family Therapy: Theory and Practice. N.Y.: Gardner, 1976.

4. Aponte, H.J., and Vandeusen, J.M. "Structural family therapy." In A.S. Gurman and D.P. Kniskern, eds. *Handbook of Family Therapy*. N.Y.: Brunner/Mazel, 1981.

5. Ashby, W.R. "The effect of experience on a determinate synamic system." *Behavioral Science*. 1 (1956): 35-42.

6. Ashby, W.R. *Design for a Brain*. London: Chapman and Hall, 1969.

7. Auerswald, E. "Families, change, and the ecological perspective." In A. Ferber, M. Mendelsohn, and A. Napier, eds. *The Book of Family Therapy*. Boston: Houghton Mifflin, 1973.

8. Bateson, G. *Naven*. 2nd ed. Stanford, Cal.: Stanford University Press, 1958.

9. Bateson, G. "The cybernetics of "self": A theory of alcoholism." *Psychiatry*. 34 (1971): 1-18.

10. Bateson, G. *Steps to an Ecology of Mind*. N.Y.: Ballantine, 1972.

11. Bateson, G. "The thing of it is." In M. Katz, W. Marsh, and G. Thompson, eds. *Exploration of Planetary Culture at the Linisfarne Conference: Earth's Answer*. N.Y.: Harper and Row, 1977.

12. Bateson, G. "The birth of a matrix or double bind epistemology." In M.M. Berger, ed. *Beyond the Double Bind*. N.Y.: Brunner/Mazel, 1978.

13. Bateson, G. *Mind and Nature: A Necessary Unity*. N.Y.: Dutton, 1979.

14. Bateson, G., Jackson, D.D., Haley, J., and Weakland, J. "Toward a theory of schizophrenia." *Behavioral Science*. 1 (1956): 251-264.

15. Bell, N.W. "Extended family relations of disturbed and well families." *Family Process*. 1 (1962): 175-192.

16. Bell, N.W. "Metatheories of child abuse." in R. Volpe, M. Breton, and J. Mitton, eds. *The Maltreatment of the School-Aged Child*. Toronto: Lexington, 1980.

17. Benjamin, M. "Abused as a child, abusive as a parent: Practitioners beware." In R. Volpe, M. Breton, and J. Mitton, eds. *The Maltreatment of the School-Aged Child*. Toronto: Lexington, 1980.

18. Berger, P., and Kelner, H. "Marriage and the construction of reality." In H.D. Dreitzel, ed. *Recent Sociology, No. 2*. N.Y.: Macmillan, 1969.

19. Bernstein, B. *Class, Codes and Control: Theoretical Studies Toward a Sociology of Language*. Rev. ed. N.Y.: Schocken, 1974.

20. Bertalanffy, L. Von. "An outline of general system theory." *British Journal of Philosophy*. 1 (1950): 134-165.

21. Bertalanffy, L. Von. *General System Theory*. Rev. ed. N.Y.: Braziller, 1968.

22. Bertalanffy, L. Von. *Perspectives on General System Theory*. N.Y.: Braziller, 1975.

23. Bodin, A.M. "The interactional view: Family therapy approach of the Mental Research Institute." In A.S. Gurman and D.P. Kniskern, eds. *Handbook of Family Therapy*. N.Y.: Brunner/Mazel, 1981.

24. Bossard, J.S., and Boll, E. *The Large Family System*. Philadelphia: Univ. of Pennsylvania Press, 1956.

25. Bowen, M. *Family Therapy in Clinical Practice*. N.Y.: Jason Aronson, 1978.

26. Bowlby, J. *Attachment*. London: Penguin, 1969.

27. Bradt, J.O. "The family with young children." In E.A. Carter and M. McGoldrick, eds. *The Family Life Cycle: A Framework for Family Therapy*. N.Y.: Gardner, 1980.

28. Broderick, C., and Smith, J. "The general systems approach to the family." In W.R. Burr, R. Hill, F.I. Nye, and I.L. Reiss, eds. *Contemporary Theories About the Family*. N.Y.: Free Press, 1979.

29. Bross, A., and Benjamin, M. "Family therapy: A recursive model of strategic practice." In A. Bross, ed. *Family Therapy: A Recursive Model of Strategic Practice*. Toronto: Methuen, 1982.

30. Brown, J.A., and Daniels, R. "Some observations on abusive parenting." *Child Welfare*. 47 (1968): 89-94.

31. Buckley, W. *Sociology and Modern Systems Theory*. Englewood Cliffs, N.J.: Prentice-Hall, 1967.

32. Bunge, M. *Causality and Modern Science*. 3rd Rev. ed. N.Y.: Dover, 1979.

33. Burr, W.R., Hill, R., Nye, F.I., and Reiss, I.L. "Metatheory and diagramming conventions." In W.R. Burr, R. Hill, F.I. Nye, and I.L. Reiss, eds. *Contemporary Theories About the Family*. Vol. 1. N.Y.: Free Press, 1979.

34. Cannon, W.B. *The Wisdom of the Body*. Rev. ed. N.Y.: Norton, 1939.

35. Carter, E.A., and McGoldrick, M. "The family life cycle and family therapy: An overview." In E.A. Carter and M. McGoldrick, eds. *The Family Life Cycle: A Framework for Family Therapy*. N.Y.: Gardner, 1980.

36. Clark, R.W. *Einstein: The Life and Times*. N.Y.: World, 1971.

37. Cobb, S. "A model for life events and their consequences." In B.S. Dohrenwend and B.F. Dohrenwend, eds. *Stressful Life Events: Their Nature and Effects*. N.Y.: Wiley, 1974.

38. Colon, F. "The family life cycle of the multiproblem poor family." In E.A. Carter and M. McGoldrick, eds. *The Family Life Cycle: A Framework for Family Therapy*. N.Y.: Gardner, 1980.

39. Coyne, J.C., and Lazarus, R.S. "Cognitive style, stress perception, and coping." In I.L. Kutash, L.S. Schlesinger, et al., eds. *Handbook on Stress and Anxiety*. San Francisco: Jossey-Bass, 1980.

40. Cuber, J.F., and Haroff, P.B. "Five kinds of relationships." In G.F. Streib, ed. *The Changing Family: Adaptation and Diversity*. Boston, Mass.: Addison-Wesley, 1973.

41. Dell, P.F. "Researching the family theories of schizophrenia: An exercise in epistemological confusion." *Family Process*. 19 (1980): 321-325.

42. Delora, J.S., and Delora, J.R., eds. *Intimate Lifestyles: Marriage and its Alternatives*. Pacific Palisades, Cal.: Goodyear, 1972.

43. Deutsch, K. In R. Grinker, ed. *Toward a Unified Theory of Human Behavior*. N.Y.: Basic, 1956, pp. 161-162. In discussion of A.E. Emerson "Homeostasis and comparison of systems."

44. Dewey, J., and Bentley, A.F. *Knowing and the Known*. Boston: Beacon, 1949.

45. Duvall, E. *Marriage and Family Development*. 5th ed. Philadelphia: Lippincott, 1977.

46. Elder, G.H., Jr. *Children of the Great Depression*. Chicago: University of Chicago Press, 1974.

47. Erikson, E.H. *Childhood and Society*. 2nd ed. N.Y.: Norton, 1963.

48. Ferreira, A.J. "Family myth and homeostasis." *Archives of General Psychiatry*. 9 (1963): 457-463.

49. Ferreira, A.J., and Winter, W. "Stability of interactional variables in family decision-making." *Archives of General Psychiatry*. 14 (1966): 352-355.

50. Fisher, L., Anderson, A., and Jones, J.E. "Types of paradoxical intervention and indications/contraindications for use in clinical practice." *Family Process*. 20 (1981): 25-35.
51. Friedman, E.H. "Systems and ceremonies: A family view of rites of passage." In E.A. Carter and M. McGoldrick, eds. *The Family Life Cycle: A Framework for Family Therapy*. N.Y.: Gardner, 1980.
52. Gelles, R., and Straus, M.A. "Determinants of violence in the family: Toward a theoretical integration." In W.R. Burr, R. Hill, F.I. Nye, and I.L. Reiss, eds. *Contemporary Theories About the Family*. Vol. 1. N.Y.: Free Press, 1979.
53. Glaser, B.G., and Straus, A.L. *The Discovery of Grounded Theory: Strategies for Qualitative Research*. Chicago: Aldine, 1967.
54. Goffman, E. *Asylum*. N.Y.: Anchor, 1961.
55. Greenberg, G.S. "The family interactional perspective: A study and examination of the work of Don D. Jackson." *Family Process*. 16 (1977): 385-412.
56. Gurman, A.S. "Contemporary marital therapies: A critique and comparative analysis of psychoanalytic, behavioral and systems theory approaches." In T.J. Paolino, Jr. and B.S. McCrady, eds. *Marriage and Marital Therapy*. N.Y.: Brunner/Mazel, 1978.
57. Hadley, T.R., Jacob, T., Millones, J., Caplan, J., and Spitz, D. "The relationship between family developmental crisis and the appearance of symptoms in a family member." *Family Process*. 13 (1974): 207-214.
58. Haley, J. "The family of the schizophrenic: A model system." *Journal of Nervous and Mental Disease*. 129 (1959): 357-374.
59. Haley, J. *Strategies of Psychotherapy*. N.Y.: Grune & Stratton, 1963.
60. Haley, J. *Uncommon Therapy*. N.Y.: Ballantine, 1973.
61. Haley, J. *Problem-Solving Therapy*. San Francisco: Jossey-Bass, 1976.
62. Haley, J. "Toward a theory of pathological systems." In P. Watzlawick, and J. Weakland, eds. *The Interactional View*. N.Y.: Norton, 1977.
63. Haley, J. "Ideas which handicap therapists." In M.M. Berger, ed. *Beyond the Double Bind*. N.Y.: Brunner/Mazel, 1978.
64. Haley, J. *Leaving Home: The Therapy of Disturbed Young People*. N.Y.: McGraw-Hill, 1980.
65. Hall, E.T. *Beyond Culture*. N.Y.: Anchor, 1976.
66. Hall, A.D., and Fagen, R.E. "The definition of system." *General Systems Yearbook*. 1 (1956): 18-28.
67. Hansen, D.A., and Johnson, V.A. "Rethinking family stress theory: Definitional aspects." In W.R. Burr, R. Hill, F.I. Nye, and I.L. Reiss, eds. *Contemporary Theories About the Family*. Vol. 1. N.Y.: Free Press, 1979.
68. Harris, E. *Hypothesis and Perception*. London: George Allen & Unwin, 1970.
69. Hess, R.D., and Handel, G. *Family Worlds: A Psychosocial Approach to Family Life*. Chicago: University of Chicago Press, 1959.
70. Hill, R. "Modern systems theory and the family: A confrontation." *Social Science Information*. 10 (1970): 7-26.
71. Hoffman, L. "Deviation-amplifying process in natural groups." In J. Haley, ed. *Changing Families: A Family Therapy Reader*. N.Y.: Grune & Stratton, 1971.
72. Hoffman, L. "Breaking the homeostatic cycle." In P. Guerin, ed. *Family Therapy: Theory and Practice*. N.Y.: Gardner, 1976.

73. Hoffman, L. "The family life cycle and discontinuous change." In E.A. Carter and M. McGoldrick, eds. *The Family Life Cycle: A Framework for Family Therapy.* N.Y.: Gardner, 1980.
74. Hoffman, L. *Foundations of Family Therapy: A Conceptual Framework for Systems Change.* N.Y.: Basic, 1981.
75. Hollingshead, A.B., and Redlich, F.C. *Social Class and Mental Illness.* N.Y.: Wiley, 1958.
76. Hunt, M. *The Affair: A Portrait of Extramarital Love in Contemporary America.* N.Y.: World, 1969.
77. Irving, H.H. *The Family Myth.* Toronto: Copp Clark, 1972.
78. Jackson, D.D. "The question of family homeostasis." *Psychiatric Quarterly Supplement.* 31 (1957): 79-90.
79. Jackson, D.D. "The study of the family." *Family Process.* (1965, 4): 1-20.
80. Jackson, D.D. "The myth of normality." *Medical Opinion and Review.* 3 (1967): 28-33.
81. Kantor, D., and Lehr, W. *Inside the Family: Toward a Theory of Family Process.* N.Y.: Harper & Row, 1975.
82. Kaufman, I. "The physically abused child." In N.B. Ebeling & D.A. Hill, eds. *Child Abuse: Intervention and Treatment.* Acton, Mass.: Publication Science Group, 1975.
83. Keeney, B.P. "Ecosystemic epistemology: An alternative paradigm for diagnosis." *Family Process.* 18 (1979): 117-129.
84. Koestler, A. *The Ghost in the Machine.* London: Pan, 1967.
85. Koestler, A. *The Act of Creation.* London: Pan, 1969.
86. Lambert, M.J. "Spontaneous remission in adult neurotic disorder: A revision and summary." *Psychological Bulletin.* 83 (1976): 107-119.
87. Landis, J.T. "Social correlates of divorce and nondivorce among the unhappily married." *Marriage and Family Living.* 25 (1963): 178-180.
88. Laszlo, E. *Introduction to Systems Philosophy.* N.Y.: Braziller, 1972.
89. Lauer, R.H., and Lauer, J.C. "The experience of change: Tempo and stress." In G.K. Zollschan and W. Hirsch, eds. *Social Change: Exploration, Diagnosis, and Conjecture.* Cambridge, Mass.: Schenkman, 1976.
90. Lederer, W.J., and Jackson, D.D. *The Mirages of Marriage.* N.Y.: Norton, 1968.
91. Lewis, R.A., and Spanier, G.B. "Theorizing about the quality and stability of marriage." In W.R. Burr, R. Hill, F.I. Nye, and I.L. Reiss, eds. *Contemporary Theories About the Family.* Vol. 1. N.Y.: Free Press, 1979.
92. Lidz, T., Cornelison, A.R., Fleck, S., and Terry, D. "Schism and skew in the families of schizophrenics." *American Journal of Psychiatry.* 64 (1957): 241-248.
93. Mace, C.A. "Homeostasis, needs and values." *British Journal of Psychology.* 44 (1953): 200-210.
94. Madanes, C. *Strategic Family Therapy.* San Francisco: Jossey-Bass, 1981.
95. Maruyama, M. "The second cybernetic: Deviation-amplifying mutual causative processes." *American Scientist.* 51 (1963): 164-179.
96. McGrath, J.E., ed. *Social and Psychological Factors in Stress.* N.Y.: Holt, Rinehart & Winston, 1970.
97. Miller, J.G. "Living systems: Basic concepts." *Behavioral Science.* 10 (1965): 193-237.

98. Minuchin, S. *Families and Family Therapy*. Cambridge, Mass.: Harvard University Press, 1974.

99. Minuchin, S., and Fishman, H.C. *Family Therapy Techniques*. Cambridge, Mass.: Harvard University Press, 1981.

100. Minuchin, S., Montalvo, B., Guerney, B., Rosman, B.L., and Schumer, F. *Families of the Slums*. N.Y.: Basic, 1967.

101. Minuchin, S., Rosman, B.L., and Baker, L. *Psychosomatic Families: Anorexia Nervosa in Context*. Cambridge, Mass.: Harvard University Press, 1978.

102. Newcomb, T.M. "An approach to the study of communicative acts." *Psychological Review*. 60 (1953): 393-404.

103. Norton, A.J., and Glick, P.C. "Marital instability in America: Past, present and future." In G. Levinger and O. Moles, eds. *Divorce and Separation: Contexts, Causes, and Consequences*. N.Y.: Basic, 1979.

104. Nye, F.I., Carlson, J., and Garrett, G. "Family size, interaction, affect and stress." In J.S. DeLora & J.R. DeLora, eds. *Intimate Lifestyles: Marriage and its Alternatives*. Pacific Palisades, Cal.: Goodyear, 1972.

105. O'Keefe, G.J., Jr. "Coorientation variables in family study." *American Behavioral Scientist*. 16 (1973): 513-536.

106. Oliveri, M.E., and Reiss, D. "A theory-based empirical classification of family problem-solving behavior." *Family Process*. 20 (1981): 409-418.

107. Olson, D.H., Sprenkle, D., and Russel, C. "Circumplex model of marital and family system. I: Cohesion and adaptability dimensions, family types, and clinical applications." *Family Process*. 18 (1979): 3-28.

108. Olson, D.H., Russel, C., and Sprenkle, D. "Circumplex model of marital and family systems. II: Empirical studies and clinical intervention." In J.P. Vincent, ed. *Advances in Family Intervention, Assessment and Theory*. Greenwich, Conn.: JAI Press, 1979.

109. Palazzoli, M.S., Cecchin, G., Prata, G., and Boscolo, L. *Paradox and Counterparadox: A New Model in the Therapy of the Family in Schizophrenic Transaction*. Trans. E.V. Burt. N.Y.: Aronson, 1978.

110. Paykel, E.S., and Uhlenhuth, E.H. "Rating the magnitude of life stress." *Canadian Psychiatric Association Journal*. 17 (Sp. Suppl. 2): ss93-ss100.

111. Powers, W.T. "Feedback: Beyond behaviorism." *Science*. 179 (1973): 351-356.

112. Queen, S.A., and Haberstein, R.W. *The Family in Various Cultures*. Philadelphia: Lippincott, 1967.

113. Rabkin, R. "A critique of the clinical use of the double bind." In C. Sluzki and D. Ransom, eds. *Double Bind: The Communicational Approach to the Family*. N.Y.: Grune & Stratton: 1976.

114. Ramey, J. "Experimental family forms — the family of the future." *Marriage and Family Review*. 1 (1978): 1-9.

115. Rapoport, A., and Horvath, W.J. "Thoughts on organization theory." *General Systems Yearbook*. 4 (1959): 87-91.

116. Raush, H.L., Barry, W.A., Hertel, R.K., and Swain, M.A. *Communication, Conflict and Marriage*. San Francisco: Jossey-Bass, 1974.

117. Raush, H.L., Grief, A.C., and Nugent, J. "Communication in couples and families." In W.R. Burr, R. Hill, F.I. Nye, and I.L. Reiss, eds. *Contemporary Theories About the Family*. Vol. 1. N.Y.: Free Press, 1979.

118. Reiss, D. "The multiple family group as a small society: Family regulation of

interaction with nonmembers." *American Journal of Psychiatry.* 134 (1977): 21-24.

119. Reiss, D. *The Family's Construction of Reality.* Cambridge, Mass.: Harvard University Press, 1981.

120. Richardson, H.V. *Patients Have Families.* Cambridge, Mass.: Harvard University Press, 1945.

121. Rogler, L.H., and Hollingshead, A.B. *Trapped Families and Schizophrenia.* N.Y.: Wiley, 1965.

122. Rowe, G.P. "The developmental conceptual framework to the study of the family." In F.I. Nye and F.M. Berardo, eds. *Emerging Conceptual Frameworks in Family Analysis.* N.Y.: Praeger, 1981.

123. Ruesch, J. "Nonverbal language and therapy." *Psychiatry.* 18 (1955): 323-330.

124. Ruesch, J., and Bateson, G. *Communication: The Social Matrix of Psychiatry.* N.Y.: Norton, 1951.

125. Russell, C. "Circumplex model of family systems: III. Empirical evaluation with families." *Family Process.* 18 (1979): 29-45.

126. Sapir, E. *Selected Writings of Edward Sapir in Language, Culture and Personality.* Berkeley, Cal.: University of California Press, 1949.

127. Scheff, T.J. *Being Mentally Ill: A Sociological Theory.* Chicago: Aldine-Atherton, 1966.

128. Selye, H. "The stress concept today." In I.L. Kutash, L.B. Schlesinger, et al., eds. *Handbook on Stress and Anxiety.* San Francisco: Jossey-Bass, 1980.

129. Simmel, G. *Conflict and the Web of Group-Affiliations.* Trans. K.H. Wolff and R. Bendix. N.Y.: Free Press, 1955.

130. Simon, H.H. "The organization of complex systems." In H.H. Pattee, ed. *Hierarchy Theory: The Challenge of Complex Systems.* N.Y.: Braziller, 1973.

131. Skolnick, A.S., and Skolnick, J.H., eds. *Families in Transition.* 2nd ed. Boston: Little, Brown, 1977.

132. Skynner, H.C.R. *Systems of Family and Marital Psychotherapy.* N.Y.: Brunner/Mazel, 1976.

133. Solomon, M. "A developmental conceptual premise for family therapy." *Family Process.* 12 (1973): 179-188.

134. Speer, D.C. "Family systems: Morphostasis and morphogenesis, or 'Is homeostasis enough?'" *Family Process.* 9 (1971): 259-278.

135. Spiegel, J.P. "Ethnopsychiatric dimensions in family violence." In M.R. Green, ed. *Violence and the Family.* American Association for the Advancement of Science., Selected Symposium #47, Washington, D.C., 1980.

136. Spiegel, J.P., and Bell, N.W. "The family of the psychiatric patient." In S. Arieti, ed. *American Handbook of Psychiatry.* N.Y.: Basic, 1959.

137. Sprey, J. "The family as a system in conflict." *Journal of Marriage and Family.* 31 (1969): 699-706.

138. Stanton, M.D. "Strategic approaches to family therapy." In A.S. Gurman and D.P. Kniskern, eds. *Handbook of Family Therapy.* N.Y.: Brunner/Mazel, 1981.

139. Steinglass, P. "The conceptualization of marriage from a systems theory perspective." In T.J. Paolino Jr., and B.J. McCrady, eds. *Marriage and Marital Therapy.* N.Y.: Brunner/Mazel, 1978.

140. Steinmetz, S.K. "Occupation and physical punishment: A response to Straus."

Journal of Marriage and Family. 33 (1971): 664-666.
141. Straus, M.A. "Some social antecedents of physical punishment: A linkage theory interpretation." *Journal of Marriage and Family.* 33 (1971): 658-663.
142. Sussman, M.B. "The human meaning of social change." In A. Campbell and P.E. Converse, eds. *The Human Meaning of Social Change.* N.Y.: Russell Sage Foundation, 1972.
143. Sutherland, J.W. *A General Systems Philosophy for the Social and Behavioral Sciences.* N.Y.: Braziller, 1973.
144. Terkelson, K.G. "Towards a theory of the family life cycle." In E.A. Carter and M. McGoldrick, eds. *The Family Life Cycle: A Framework for Family Therapy.* N.Y.: Gardner, 1980.
145. Udry, J.R. *The Social Context of Marriage.* 3rd ed. Philadelphia: Lippincott, 1973.
146. Veevers, J.E. "The life style of voluntarily childless couples." In L.E. Larson, ed. *The Canadian Family in Comparative Perspective.* Toronto: Prentice-Hall, 1976.
147. Vogel, E.F., and Bell, N.W. "The emotionally disturbed child as the family scapegoat." In N.W. Bell and E.F. Vogel, eds. *A Modern Introduction to the Family.* N.Y.: Free Press, 1968.
148. Warringer, C.K. "Groups are real: A reaffirmation." In B.H. Stoodley, ed. *Society and Self.* Glencoe, N.Y.: Free Press, 1962.
149. Watzlawick, P. *The Language of Change: Elements of Therapeutic Communication.* N.Y.: Basic, 1978.
150. Watzlawick, P., Beavin, J.H., and Jackson, D.D. *Pragmatics of Human Communication.* N.Y.: Norton, 1967.
151. Watzlawick, P., Weakland, J., and Fisch, R. *Change: Problem Formulation and Problem Resolution.* N.Y.: Norton, 1974.
152. Weiner, N. *Cybernetics: Control and Communication in the Animal and the Machine.* 2nd ed. Boston: MIT Press, 1961.
153. Weiner, N. *The Human Use of Human Beings: Cybernetics and Society.* N.Y.: Avon, 1967.
154. Weinberg, G.M. *A Computer Approach to General Systems Theory.* N.Y.: Wiley-Interscience, 1972.
155. Weiss, P.A. "The living system: Determinism stratified." In A. Koestler and J.R. Smythies, eds. *Beyond Reductionism.* N.Y.: Macmillan, 1969.
156. Wender, P.H. "Vicious and virtuous circles: The role of deviation-amplifying feedback in the origin and perpetuation of behavior." *Psychiatry.* 31 (1968): 309-324.
157. Westley, W.A., and Epstein, N.B. *The Silent Majority.* San Francisco: Jossey-Bass, 1969.
158. Whorf, B.L. *Language, Thought and Reality.* N.Y.: Technology Press of MIT and Wiley, 1956.
159. Widdich, E. "Individual construction of meaning and communication problems in marriage." *Australian and New Zealand Journal of Sociology.* 10 (1974): 164-169.
160. Willis, T.A., and Langner, J.S. "Socioeconomic status and stress." In I.L. Kutash, L.S. Schlesinger, et al., eds. *Handbook on Stress and Anxiety.* San Francisco: Jossey-Bass, 1980.

161. Wynne, L.C. "The study of intrafamilial alignments and splits in exploratory family therapy." In N. Ackerman, F.L. Beatman, and S.N. Sherman, eds. *Exploring the Base of Family Therapy.* N.Y.: Family Service Association, 1961.
162. Wynne, L.C. "Discussion. In D.D. Jackson: The individual and larger context." *Family Process.* 6 (1967): 139-154.
163. Wynne, L.C. "Selection of problems to be investigated in family interaction research." In J.L. Framo, ed. *Family Interaction.* N.Y.: Springer, 1972.

PART 2
RELATED TOPICS

3

Family Therapy: A Typology of Therapist Error

Michael Benjamin and Allon Bross

On the assumption that the therapist rather than the client-family is responsible for the course and outcome of family therapy, we argue that unintended intervention failure is primarily attributable to therapist error. This suggests that a comprehensive understanding of the therapeutic process requires a systematic account of therapist error. Based on anecdotal evidence, we provide such an account in the form of a typology. This identifies 23 types of error divided into five generic categories. It also identifies errors typical of new therapists as opposed to those representative of experienced practitioners. We conclude by speculating that there are four primary reasons why the notion of therapist error has heretofore failed to receive systematic treatment in the family therapy literature.

Introduction

The history of psychotherapeutic modalities has traditionally been one of ebb and flow. With shifts in zeitgeist, norms, values, and technology, certain modalities have fallen out of favour and passed into history, while newer, more radical approaches have arisen.

Despite the vagaries of fashion, however, there appears to be a small number of modalities whose theoretical base and popular appeal seem broad enough to be accepted as a regular feature of the clinical practitioner's range of procedures. It is only when the battle for legitimacy is won that proponents of these stable modalities have the opportunity and the confidence to begin the arduous task of critically reconstructing their own model so that it begins to approximate the cumulative ideal of science.

This tri-phasic history of stable psychotherapeutic modalities—from the radical and revolutionary, to the legitimate and institutionalized, to the self-reflexive—serves to illuminate the history of family therapy.

Rooted in the work of communication theorists (43, 3, 37, 24) and innovative clinicians (1, 25), family therapy was initially perceived as a radical, indeed revolutionary, approach to clinical treatment (28, 14). Not surprisingly, then, its early years were filled with bitter rhetoric as its proponents vigorously defended its validity, even asserting its superiority over alternative, more traditional approaches (18).

With the passage of time, such zealous optimism began to cool as it became obvious that family therapy was not a clinical panacea. Schizophrenia, for example, which was the focus of much of the early clinical literature (49, 11), did not vanish overnight and continues to be a major clinical puzzle. Still, impressive results with a range of clinical conditions were reported (e.g., 37, 21, 35, 22, 46). With them have come a tremendous proliferation of written material and activities—books, journal articles, symposia, the nationwide establishment of training facilities (5), and the publication of handbooks documenting variations among family therapy "schools" (15). In short, over the course of approximately thirty years, family therapy has come to be widely regarded as one of a handful of legitimate and institutionalized psychotherapeutic modalities (31, 28).

Given this institutional base, proponents of family therapy have in recent years become self-reflexive, that is, have begun to examine their own theories and practices. By far the most prominent empirical aspect of this process has been the study of therapeutic outcome (16, 33, 48, 53). This is a necessary step in the evaluation of this treatment modality; it makes little sense to trumpet the superiority of family therapy over more "traditional" methods unless a superior outcome can be demonstrated. Still, it falls far short of the accumulative ideal of science for two reasons.

1. Existing outcome studies tend to treat family therapy as though it were a homogeneous modality (29). As we ourselves (6) and Gurman and Kniskern (15) note, family therapy is fractured into a plethora of models, schools, and approaches. By implication at least, each of these approaches to family therapy claims greater theoretical, if not empirical, adequacy in relation to its competitors. Clearly the only way that this debate—and the surfeit of choices that derives from it—can be resolved is by the analysis of empirical data. To date the outcome research fails to recognize these theoretical divisions and thus contributes little to this debate. Indeed, its atheoretical stance is more consistent with the effort to defend the legitimacy of family therapy per se, a position that we imply above is becoming increasingly obsolete.

2. Existing outcome research tends to contravene one of the primary assumptions of family therapy—the primacy of process over content—and consequently is static and has little explanatory power. In essence, such research employs a "black box" model of family therapy, focussing exclusively on input (e.g., family-problem type, therapist characteristics) and output (e.g., client satisfaction, therapist rating) variables (54). This necessarily excludes from consideration the variables pertaining to what happens during the course of therapy, that is, it neglects the therapeutic *process* per se (29). In turn, this renders futile any effort to explain *why* a given therapeutic modality is successful. This is not to suggest that client and therapist variables are not important, rather that these variable clusters alone are inadequate to the twin purposes of such studies: to indicate if a particular modality works and, if so, why.

These considerations suggest that if a self-reflexive phase of family therapy is to approximate the cumulative ideal of science, it must, in addition to narrowly defined outcome studies, begin to intensively examine the therapeutic process itself. Building on our recursive model of strategic family therapy (6), the present paper attempts to take a step in that direction by introducing the notion of therapist error. Specifically, the notion is derived and defined following an analysis of the notion of "outcome success." A typology of therapist error is then presented, followed by a speculative discussion of the reasons why the notion of "error" has heretofore not been used systematically in the literature.

Therapeutic Outcome and Therapist Error

During the course of treatment, every intervention is intended to alter some dysfunctional interactional pattern or subpattern. Such interventions may fail entirely, may be only partially successful, or may be completely successful.

For present purposes, a successful outcome is one in which the target pattern changes at the levels of meaning and of behaviour. Evaluation of change should depend neither on the therapist's subjective judgment nor on the client's subjective report; rather, it should be a matter of empirical evidence, that is, behavioural sequences and ways of attributing meaning that were observed regularly prior to intervention no longer occur following intervention. As a function of progress in the case, such an outcome suggests either that (a) the treatment plan was correct; (b) the intervention tasks were well chosen; (c) the next step in the treatment plan should be implemented; or (d) the case should be terminated.

Clearly, a successful outcome is the intended and desired end of all therapeutic interventions. Unfortunately, such is not always the case. Partial rather than complete success is one alternative. However, evaluation of this outcome is problematic for two reasons.

1. Some time may be required for the intervention in question to show the intended results. Just as dysfunctional interactional processes take time to evolve, so a varying amount of time may necessarily be required for these processes to reorganize. In accord with this logic, Palazzoli et al. (46), for example, may wait anywhere from several weeks to several months between therapy sessions to allow the necessary time for their intricately designed interventions to have their desired effect. It follows, then, that what seems only a partial success at one point in time may be considered a complete success later on. The appropriate time frame is crucial in determining the nature of therapeutic outcome.

2. The evaluation of outcome involves "reading" the feedback that the family offers following the intervention. As noted above, ideally this should be a straightforward matter. In practice, this task is often extremely complex and necessarily involves a large measure of the therapist's experiential subjective judgment. Since we are talking about partial success, this

would suggest that some aspects of a target pattern exhibit change to show that the intervention had some effect. The difficulty arises in attempting to identify those elements of the intervention that yielded change and those elements that did not. With respect to simple "positive-co-operative" tasks, this may be easy to infer; in more complex, multi-facetted "negative-co-operative" tasks, this may be considerably more difficult (6).

If, as noted above, a successful outcome involves change at both meaning and behavioural levels, then partial success may involve change in only one of these components. The family's meaning system, for example, may exhibit systematic change, but this may occur independently of behavioural interaction. During the course of family therapy, for example, a husband may deny that there is any problem in his marriage, while his wife complains bitterly that she is lonely, frustrated, and deeply resentful. Following intervention, the husband acknowledges the problem, promises to listen to his wife in the future, and suggests that things have become better between them. However, whenever his wife says something to him that is even remotely critical, he interrupts or disqualifies her and changes the subject. Conversely, the family's interactional process may exhibit change, but this may occur independently of their way of seeing their situation. For example, one component of family therapy may involve intervention designed to improve the sexual relationship between the marital partners. Such intervention may indeed resolve or improve sexual functioning only to leave both partners complaining bitterly of continuing mutual dissatisfaction.

Furthermore, apart from the difficulties involved in disentangling successful and unsuccessful intervention components, a superordinate consideration arises. As suggested in Bross and Benjamin (6), the therapist is in charge of all that occurs throughout the therapeutic process and, as such, is responsible for all failures. Clearly, a result that is only a partial success is also a result that is a partial failure. Clinically, such results may be extremely valuable for the new information they provide as a guide to further therapeutic intervention. For analytic purposes, however, they may not be distinguished from complete failures.

This points to the third category of outcome, that is, failure. For present purposes, a failed intervention is simply one that is associated with no change in dysfunctional family processes at either the level of behaviour or of meaning. Logically, this outcome is open to two possible interpretations: the result of client resistance or of therapist error. Of these options, the latter interpretation is resorted to quite rarely in the literature (20, 31); rather, reference is made to an "ineffective" intervention, thus making it a question of the therapist's role in the construction of that intervention. By contrast, client resistance is a major topic of discussion in the literature (15) and thus appears to be the interpretation of choice. This interpretation, however, is problematic in at least two respects:

1. As human beings, family therapists may have a variety of foibles. In clinical terms, this may include the tendency to become inordinately attached to a given case formulation, a preferred intervention style or technique, an experientially validated but spurious association between certain family constellations and specific intervention processes, or a tendency to interpret client resistance in linear terms (e.g., transference). Consequently, there is the ever-present danger—paradoxically, especially prominent among experienced practitioners—that they will be over-inclusive in the use of the category label, "resistance." Indeed, too often in our experience the label is virtually non-falsifiable for the simple reason that it is founded upon a tautology: client-families are perceived to be resistant because they have not responded to the therapist's interventions by exhibiting pattern change in the desired direction; the reason they have not changed in that direction is because they are resisting the therapist's therapeutic injunctions.

This tautology may have several negative consequences. For one thing, it may tend to insulate the therapist from his or her own incompetence. If every intervention failure is attributed to some form of client resistance, then there is no reason for the therapist to critically examine his or her own techniques, preferences, skills, and so forth. There is also the further tendency for the therapist to slide into accepting the false dichotomy of the "good" and "bad" client. These are defined as one would expect: "good" clients are those who consistently yield intervention successes while "bad" clients are those who yield intervention failures. This dichotomy, insofar as it precludes any distinction between "good" and "bad" therapists, necessarily smacks of "blaming the victim" (44) for the therapist's own shortcomings. Still another consequence is the tendency for therapists to engage in a process known as "creaming" (42), in which only clients with problem types that have previously yielded intervention successes are selected for treatment. Allegedly rationalized by some vague notion of treatability ("I have never had any success with these types of cases; they're untreatable."), this selection strategy has tragic consequences: client-families with severe problems and, therefore, most in need of treatment are denied potentially beneficial service. As often as not, they may be consigned to institutional care (21), either overtly or by indirect means—the application of diagnostic labels, the use of large doses of medication, the revolving door of multiple (unsuccessful) treatments by a variety of practitioners, the transfer to other services (dumping)—all of which gives the client-family the impression that it has somehow failed.

2. To a significant degree, resistance and error tend to shade into each other. A fundamental tenet of our recursive model (6) is that the therapist is responsible for the course and outcome of therapy. One facet of this responsibility is the selection, construction, and delivery of intervention tasks. This, in turn, should necessarily take into account the expected level of

family resistance; that is, intervention tasks should be designed to overcome such resistance. It follows that, with certain qualifications noted immediately below, intervention failure provides at least prima facie evidence of therapist error.

This is not to suggest that our clinical knowledge is so complete that therapist error is the only explanation for intervention failure; the "tough stability" (2) of schizophrenic families, for example, is well-known. Nor is it to disregard the fact that the "fit" between therapist and client—in style, language, culture, class, and so on—is seldom perfect. Indeed, intervention failure may be the only way to gather certain data that will subsequently be invaluable in guiding the course and ensuring the success of future intervention. Rather, our formulation is intended to draw attention to several salient features of the family therapy literature in general and the therapeutic process in particular:

1. The therapeutic encounter is at its root an interactional process involving two or more active participants, each of whom *necessarily* affects the other in at least some respects (12, 52). All too often, the therapist's narrow focus on the interactional processes which characterize the client-family causes him or her to lose sight of the fact that the system in therapy includes *both* family and therapist. This, in turn, distorts the fact that a significant proportion of client-family behaviours will occur, not solely as a function of intrafamilial interaction, but also in response to the therapist's behaviour.

2. Family therapists, like all professionals, may vary widely in their level of expertise, experience, acumen, creativity, flexibility, and so forth. This occurs not only among therapists, but even with individual therapists as factors such as the demand characteristics of the situation (39), fatigue, marital and financial difficulties, physical problems or ill health, age, and so forth come into play from day to day.

3. While practitioners, both "beginners" and "old-hands," routinely acknowledge *to each other* that they make mistakes, the notion of therapist error is formally contained neither in existing models of practice (13) nor in that portion of the family therapy literature concerned with training (23, 4, 51, 5, 50, 7). This is not to suggest that the notion of therapist error is not explicitly noted in the literature (31, 21), but that it is not systematically employed as part of any available model of therapy practice.

4. An unknown but probably significant proportion of intervention failures—both at the task and case levels—can be traced to therapist error. Logically, three levels of error may be distinguished: (1) "Beneficial" errors, in which the therapist employs intervention failure for the purpose of either data collection, hypothesis testing, or formulation verification. (2) "Neutral" errors resulting from Number 2 above, in which intervention success is expected but does not materialize; such errors are benign in the sense that they neither help nor hinder (except in terms of wasted time)

either the course of therapy or the client-family; indeed, to the extent that failure to respond to a specific intervention is "new" information, such errors in some cases may be beneficial, helping to insure the success of future interventions, albeit only accidentally; alternatively, repeated intervention failures may be both destructive—in the sense that they produce client frustration and increase the likelihood of client drop-out—and beneficial—in the sense that they at least indicate to the therapist that he or she is "stuck" and should either refer the case elsewhere, seek supervisory aid, or try a radically new approach to intervention. (3) Finally, "destructive" errors resulting, again, from Number 2 above, which does harm to the client-family by causing it unnecessary emotional distress, further stabilizing existing problem-maintaining interactional processes, exacerbating symptomatic behaviour, or causing the perceived level of functioning of the client-family to deteriorate.

These considerations would suggest, first, that client resistance is a relatively weak explanation of therapist intervention failure in all but the initial stage of the therapeutic encounter; second, that in most cases therapist error is a more fruitful explanation of intervention failure and, together with client and therapist characteristics, provides the basis for a more complete understanding of all forms of family therapy outcome; and, third, that a typology of therapist error, tied to some model of family therapy practice, would be of both practical and theoretical importance.

Therapist Error: A Typology

In what follows below, we present a typology of therapist error. This is grounded upon a series of salient assumptions:

1. The therapeutic process contains a finite number of "choice points" or "decision nodes."

2. At each choice point, the therapist is confronted with the need to select among two or more alternative courses of action.

3. In any given instance, some choices will be "better" or more efficient than others with respect to achieving certain desirable ends; conversely the therapeutic process is sufficiently variable and the technology sufficiently "soft" that there are seldom situations in which one and only one response is best.

4. Specifically with respect to intervention, to the extent that it is possible to put into operation and specify the "target" interaction process at which interventions are "aimed," it is also possible, at least in principle, to put into operation and differentiate between interventions that are, in context, correct or erroneous with respect to intended outcome. In other words, "correct" interventions are those in which the target pattern, observed to occur regularly prior to intervention, cannot be observed following intervention and are replaced by some alternative, more functional pattern; "erroneous" intervention yields no such "positive" change

and, indeed, may have "negative" consequences.* Similar logic applies to all other decision nodes (e.g., assessment).

With these assumptions in mind, the therapist will be said to have made an error if the outcome is judged either "neutral" or "destructive" as in Number 4 above; "beneficial" interventions that are not intended to produce change but, in fact, yield valuable data will be said to involve an "error strategy" and, as such, are not "errors" in the proper sense.

Inspection of our recursive model of family therapy (6), reveals that the family therapy process involves five major decision nodes. Consequently, these correspond to the five major categories into which our typology is divided. Furthermore, on the assumption that there is an inverse relationship between practice experience and the number and scope of therapist error, each category (where appropriate) is subdivided into errors that typify the "beginner" as opposed to those which typify the "old hand." For present purposes, the "beginner" therapist has been in practice less than five years whereas the "old hand" therapist has been in practice five or more years. Although somewhat arbitrary, these cut-off points were selected as a reflection of our own experience. Moreover, the following typology is necessarily tentative insofar as it is based on anecdotal evidence, specifically the experience of the second author as a private practitioner, therapist supervisor, case consultant, and (with the first author) an appreciative observer of some of the most prominent family therapists in North America. Finally, for each major error category, one or more case examples will be provided for illustrative purposes.

Category One: Assessment Error

Assessment involves the collection and interpretation of information concerning the problem or problems which client-families present. Assessment errors, therefore, essentially involve errors in information.

-----

*While methodological considerations are beyond the scope of the present paper, two test procedures come readily to mind. The first involves use of a panel of experienced family therapists, all of whom operate from within the same practice and theory model, who are asked to independently rate the "correctness" of interventions based on the videotaped record of a case. A pre-tested level of inter-rated reliability of 0.80 or better is presumed. The second approach similarly involves the use of a panel of raters but involves use of a rehearsed family scenario using professional actors rather than real families. The scenario in question would be constructed so as to severely limit the range of "correct" intervention responses of the therapist. Neither the therapist nor the judges would be told in advance of the scenario nor of the use of professional actors. The scenario would have been pre-tested to ensure inter-rater reliability of 0.80 or better amongst a different panel of judges with respect to the range of "correct" intervention responses.

The Beginner

Four different types of error are common to the new therapist:

1. First, and perhaps most common, beginners often run into difficulties with the techniques of data collection. Thus, information may be incomplete because the wrong combination of assessment techniques has been employed, such techniques have been employed incorrectly, or all proper information "targets" have not been "hit" (6).

2. A related problem involves the tendency for new therapists to commit themselves too readily to inaccurate data. This is especially likely to occur if the therapist naïvely accepts the family's portrayal of itself at face value. For example, the therapist may overlook the family's tacit refusal to discuss "sensitive" or "secret" information (27) or may fail to recognize family accounts as "myths" (26, 45, 9). Consequently, in their eagerness to get on with the case, beginners may commit themselves to data which are seriously distorted, vague, or misleading. This may also occur because they are distracted by content—a juicy bit of sexual behaviour, an allusion to experience in the near or far past, the subject of longstanding dispute between marital partners—and so fail to attend to process.

3. A closely related difficulty of new therapists is their extreme hesitance to commit themselves to accurate data. In effect, the therapist gets "stuck" at the assessment phase of therapy. Consequently, even though there may be ample data upon which to move to the formulation phase, the therapist fails to do so and instead continues to collect more information.

4. Finally, new therapists often have great difficulty in "reading" or interpreting accurate data. Reading the data means assembling them in such a way that patterns emerge. These, in turn, provide the basis for the construction of a case formulation. For new therapists, the data simply never coalesce to reveal patterns; rather, they remain randomly distributed and therefore quite meaningless. What appears to happen here is that the beginner is overwhelmed by the quantity and variety (behavioural, verbal, affective, informational, cognitive, motivational, etc.) of information to be processed in a relatively short space of time. Unable to cope with all of it, the therapist becomes "paralyzed" and refuses to deal with any of it.

Several of the foregoing types of error are apparent in the following case vignette:

> The A family came to the therapist complaining that son Todd, age three, was uncontrollable. This conclusion was primarily that of Mrs. A. who reported that Todd "threw a book," "stepped in hot tar," and "left his zipper open." Assessment revealed that this was a reconstituted family. Todd had only been with them for three weeks, prior to which he had lived with his biological mother who was known to have physically abused him on several occasions. From the therapist's perspective Mrs. A. appeared as the "wicked stepmother," behaving in a harsh and distant manner towards Todd, who appeared unable to do anything right in her eyes. Despite this, the therapist remained uncertain as to exactly what was

going on in this family and as a result did not know what to make of the available data. Evaluation of the therapist's performance by her supervisor revealed that she had been distracted by content, had been too ready to accept distorted and inaccurate data, and in the end had failed to commit herself to any specific interpretation. In fact, from his perspective, mother was over-involved, over-responsive, and overly responsible for this child, who, moreover, was at an age with which she had little recent experience. Rather than being harsh and punitive towards Todd, she was terribly concerned about him and equally disturbed over his abusive experience. Further assessment by the therapist around this interpretation subsequently confirmed its validity.

The Old Hand

With experience comes confidence and patience. Consequently, experienced therapists seldom commit the foregoing types of error. However, experience is a double-edged sword; just as it brings advantages, so it also includes certain hazards, which may translate into error.

Two common errors to which old hands are vulnerable are the following:

1. The first, and by far the most common, has already been alluded to, namely, "tunnel vision." This refers to the tendency to experientially associate certain family-presenting problems with certain interpretations, which gradually become virtually non-falsifiable. For example, having found marital conflict at the root of a child acting out in many cases, assessment of all subsequent cases automatically focusses on marital conflict to the exclusion of all other data. Even assuming that such an interpretation may be correct in the majority of cases, clinical experience clearly suggests that families are far too complex for any given interpretation to apply in all cases. Consequently, this "cognitive set," however well-intentioned, must inevitably be incorrect in some cases, with negative results for the families in question.

2. A second source of error for experienced therapists might be described as "assessment habituation," that is, the tendency to collect data in a rigidly predetermined manner. This may include seeing all families in a fixed setting, asking questions in a standard manner, regularly stressing or excluding certain family members, and so forth. While the development of such habits over years of experience may be easy to understand, they must inevitably become inappropriate, given the immense variability of the client-family population. Accordingly, in at least some cases, they will generate assessment data which are incomplete, inaccurate, distorted, or vague, as a standard procedure is applied to a non-standard case.

The problem of tunnel vision is well-illustrated by the following case vignette:

> The B family came into therapy complaining of rebellious behaviour on the part of their adolescent son Brian, age fourteen. Assessment revealed

that this was a reconstituted family. Brian's mother had remarried, while Brian continued to live with his father and his stepmother. The therapist saw the case as a standard example of a transitional problem in a reconstituted family. Brian's behaviour was interpreted as a means of deflecting attention from underlying marital conflict. The solution to the family's problems would be to shift power from the father to the stepmother, thus integrating her into the family and clarifying the boundaries about the parental subsystem. In contrast, Mr. B. argued that the problem, as he saw it, was that his first wife's new husband was systematically undermining his son's respect for him and his new wife. Based on his wide experience with reconstituted families, the therapist dismissed the father's claim as a rationalization intended to conceal the real problem, that is, the problematic relationship with his new wife. Therapy proceeded on this basis for the next ten sessions, but with little result; Brian continued to misbehave. The therapist was baffled and frustrated. In accord with his interpretation of the case, he had tried everything to shift power to the stepmother and appeared to have succeeded, but with no change in the presenting problem. At this point, the therapist learned that Brian's (biological) mother's new husband had approached Brian to come and live with them and, indeed, had been in regular contact with Brian for several months. This confirmed that Mr. B.'s simple interpretation had been correct all along and gave the lie to the therapist's more sophisticated but erroneous interpretation.

Category Two: Formulation Error

The development of the case formulation involves the interpretation and organization of available data into a coherent whole that permits the derivation of falsifiable hypotheses. This necessarily involves a high level of professional judgment, with few hard and fast guidelines available. As such, it is probably the hardest aspect of the therapeutic process to master and is thus correspondingly vulnerable to error. Interestingly, however, as we indicate immediately below, the nature of these formulation errors will vary significantly as a function of therapeutic experience.

The Beginner

The difficulties inherent in learning how to develop case formulations is evidenced by three types of error quite common to new therapists.

1. The first and almost universal problem faced by new therapists is learning to develop an hypothesis-testing cognitive style. Basically, this involves learning to accept ambiguity and uncertainty as inherent in the therapeutic process. Often, case formulations are generated precisely in order to demonstrate that they are incorrect, thus increasing one's confidence in the validity of an alternative formulation and the hypotheses which flow from it. Furthermore, even formulations which appear to account well for available data must continually be viewed with a skeptical eye, as they may still need to be abandoned or substantially modified as new

data become available. Such uncertainty is extremely difficult for beginners to accept, as they tend to perceive failed formulations, not as a necessary part of the therapeutic process, but rather as failure of their skills and expertise. Consequently they may doggedly pursue a specific formulation long after it has outlived its usefulness.

2. A second and closely related difficulty involves the generation of formulations and the derivation hypothesis which are true to data. From the perspective of the theoretical base of family therapy (general systems theory), this involves a focus on process and pattern rather than on personality or motivation. The mastery of this is often difficult for new therapists who have only succeeded in covering their traditional conceptual core with a surface patina of family systems theory. Consequently, they often tend to explain dynamic processes in static terms—terms derived from personality theory, psychoanalytic theory, Rogerian theory, and so on—from which only simplistic hypotheses can be derived. Such hypotheses invariably fail, leaving both therapist and client-family bewildered, frustrated, and angry.

3. Finally, even if a beginner masters the appropriate cognitive style, succeeds in developing a viable formulation, and derives fruitful hypotheses, he or she is still faced with the problem of finding a way to put the hypotheses to the test. Thus, sophisticated conceptual skills may founder over the issue of putting into operation the therapist's clinical hypotheses. This includes difficulty in developing a plan to test the hypotheses, enacting the plan in an awkward or bumbling manner, or being unable to "read" or decipher the feedback that the plan generates. Any or all of these difficulties may result in weak data highly vulnerable to either false positives or false negatives, which, in turn, provide an uncertain base from which to proceed to the next phase of therapy.

Brief examples of these types of error include case formulations such as the following: "Father does not play enough with his son" or "Father is stubborn and passive." In neither case does the formulation give evidence of process, that is, both fail to indicate what the attribute (e.g., stubborn) means in relation to any other member of the family, nor do they specify the interactional circumstances in which they come into play.

The Old Hand

Unlike beginners, experienced therapists have usually mastered the appropriate cognitive style and have little difficulty in generating formulations and deriving hypotheses. The nature of their formulations, however, continues to be problematic. Specifically, two types of formulation error typify this group of therapists.

1. The first involves use of formulations which prove to be inaccurate in the light of subsequent data. However, the therapist's confidence and conceptual sophistication work against him or her. So sure is the therapist that the formulation is correct that he or she disregards feedback from the

client-family. Consequently, the therapist persists in using a specific formulation even when the outcome of the intervention based upon it clearly indicates that it is inaccurate and should either be abandoned or modified.

2. A related problem, quite distinctive of the experienced therapist, involves the development of an overly elaborate and complex formulation in respect to a relatively simple problem. Here the sensitivity of the therapist to the complexity of family life leads him or her to see problems where they do not exist, and so may seriously distort the treatment plan which evolves from the formulation. This type of error is difficult to root out for two reasons: (1) elaborate formulations appeal to the therapist's justifiable pride in his or her conceptual sophistication; and (2) the more elaborate the formulation, the more likely it is to be non-falsifiable, as the therapist will almost certainly find some evidence of what he or she is seeking.

An apt instance of the latter error can be seen in the following case vignette:

> Mrs. C., a divorced single mother, brought her son George, age seven, to treatment because he refused to go to school. Based on his experience, the therapist disregarded Mrs. C.'s plea that she really wanted George to go back to school, and reasoned that this was camouflage for the real problem: mother's over-involvement with George and her failure to successfully make the transition from married to single status. Subsequent efforts to focus on marital conflict had little effect; George remained adamant that he would not attend school. At this point the therapist suspected that the problem was much simpler than he had initially believed. Perhaps George simply needed more structure than his mother was giving him. Accordingly, he had mother assert her executive authority and positively insist that George return to school. He did, and the case was terminated.

Category Three: Support Error

Supportive operations are needed throughout the therapeutic process in order to permit the therapist to establish a working relationship with the client-family. Failing this, it is unlikely that the client-family will respond positively to any intervention efforts the therapist may make, however sincere or brilliant. Support errors, then, occur when the therapist is unable to establish this working relationship. The reasons that such a relationship does not evolve between therapist and client-family show much overlap between beginners and old hands.

The Beginner and the Old Hand

As noted in Bross and Benjamin (6), the therapist seeks to establish a working relationship with client-families by means of a series of supportive manoeuvres. Proper use of these techniques involves a certain level of skill that may or may not be present in the new therapist. Consequently, a common support error simply involves a technical failure, that is, a therapist who is insufficiently attentive, fails to be sympathetic or respect differences, does not reinforce strengths, and so on.

A related difficulty concerns the new therapist's tendency to attach clinical significance to behaviour that the client-family intends as mere convention. Thus, it is not uncommon for beginners to misinterpret simple social courtesy as an effort at joining. This misreading of client feedback may act to set in motion a "comedy of errors" in which the therapist responds in accord with this misinterpretation, the family misinterprets this as a request for intensified politeness, and so forth. In the process, of course, a valuable opportunity to collect data may be replaced by a mutual experience of frustration, annoyance, and puzzlement.

A further problem of new therapists is that they focus on or emphasize client weaknesses, rather than see this as an opportunity to reframe these weaknesses as "strengths." Such an interpretation serves as a joining manoeuvre and simultaneously functions to pre-empt anticipated client resistance. Thus, the workaholic father may be viewed as either a man who neglects his family or as a dedicated provider. While the former interpretation may represent a family problem, the latter is more useful in reducing the distance between the therapist and the client.

A fourth problem area affecting both beginners and old hands concerns the timing of interventions. Supportive manoeuvres, while essential, become counter-productive if cut short abruptly or carried on too long, with no effort to undertake some specific intervention. This is because both processes contravene the generalized expectations of client-families; on the one hand, they expect the therapist to be warm and supportive, but, on the other hand, expect him or her to do something to alleviate the problem that brought them to therapy. Consequently, they respond with alarm and anger to a therapist who gives only lip service to support, while responding with frustration to a therapist who is overly effusive in his or her support. In our experience, both responses are associated with a dramatic increase in the probability of client drop-out.

Finally, the experienced old hand is more likely than the beginner to misinterpret client-family resistance. Due to the clinical significance attached to resistance, the experienced therapist will have spent much time learning to overcome it, in particular by learning to "go with it," as in the use of paradox. While this may be appropriate in some contexts and with some families, it has been our experience that such a response renders the therapist insensitive to instances in which resistance may be effectively reduced by seeing it as a time for joining. In this sense, "resistance" may indicate, not resistance to therapeutic destabilization, but rather resistance to forming a therapeutic relationship with a particular therapist. Consequently, joining is the most effective response. Conversely, the use of paradox in this context may, quite predictably, unnecessarily increase distance between therapist and client, thus reducing the former's effectiveness in the long run.

Three brief examples of supportive errors are as follows:

— In an effort to be supportive, the therapist frequently makes positive statements about the client-family and regularly reflects back their own statements, asking them rather than telling them what they think they ought to do. In response, client-families, who expect the therapist to be more directive, emerge from therapy frustrated and bitter, grumbling that "All we ever did was talk."

— In an effort to get to the clinical heart of the matter as quickly as possible, the therapist may simply dispense with supportive manoeuvres and, five minutes into the first session, ask the marital partners a series of intimate questions about their sex life. The clients hesitantly respond but feel overwhelmed and deeply threatened. They fail to show up for any further sessions with this therapist.

— Again, in an effort to induce change as quickly as possible, the therapist may disregard the need for support and instead get caught up in a power struggle with client-families. Such efforts to force them to change in accord with the therapist's wishes leaves the client-families feeling bruised and misunderstood. Accordingly, they perceive therapy as a waste of time and drop out.

Category Four: Tactical Error

Tactical or strategic manoeuvres are those interventions the therapist uses, either singly or in combination, with the intention of producing change in dysfunctional interactional processes. This includes the selection, construction, and delivery of therapeutic tasks. Such complex technical tasks necessarily afford the therapist, especially the beginner, with a series of opportunities for error.

The Beginner

Each of these components of the intervention task represent different classes of error. With respect to task selection, three related types of error tend to plague new therapists. The first stems from lack of confidence: new therapists often exhibit great reluctance to commit themselves unequivocally to one or another category of intervention task (6). This is primarily because they do not trust their own judgment. As a result, they often tend to oscillate rapidly between digital and analogic tasks.

Even when they come to a decision and select a task category, this is no guarantee that they will know how to put into operation the task in question. It is one thing to know intellectually what an analogic task is, but quite another to construct one yourself. In this regard, the examples of the dominant figures in the field are of little help. The analogic tasks of Milton

Erickson (8), for example, are so elegantly simple yet so profoundly sophisticated—a tour de force in some cases—that the new therapist can only despair of ever being able to live up to this high standard.

A common result is that the beginner simply "screws" his or her courage to the sticking point and forges ahead as well as possible. Without careful preparation and thoughtful analysis, however, such efforts are often awkward, bumbling, and not especially well-received by the client-family.

These difficulties rarely affect the old hand. Instead, if difficulties are encountered, they tend to derive not from the selection procedure per se, but rather from the therapist's tendency to develop a strong preference for certain types of intervention. Such preferences may result in a therapeutic style that is inflexible, a potentially catastrophic attribute given the immense variability of client-families. Thus, an experienced therapist may show a strong preference for analogic tasks and may use them to superb effect with highly verbal and articulate families only to have less articulate families react to them with blank incomprehension.

Turning next to task construction, new therapists frequently exhibit at least two major types of error:

1. The first is that the beginner often has difficulty constructing a task so as to make it acceptable, desirable, and believable for client-families. There are two variants of this error. (a) The first concerns the construction of appropriate pretexts or methods of reframing so that the task is prescribed for reasons which appear to the client-family to be sensible and, indeed, logical. The ability to do this well develops with experience that the beginner does not have. Consequently, the new therapist's efforts to develop a pretext may impede rather than facilitate client participation. Parents with an enuretic child who are told to make the child wet the bed at night and then sleep in it (19), are not likely to comply if this apparently bizarre procedure is explained by saying that "it is good for him." (b) A complementary difficulty is that new therapists construct tasks which are simply not acceptable to the client-family. Whereas aversive tasks, for example, may be acceptable to a client-family with a child exhibiting life-threatening behaviour (e.g., anorexia nervosa, 37), this is unlikely to be so when simple disobedience is the reported problem ("Doctor, I tell him to be home not later than 11 on a school night, but he never listens to me."). Similarly, it may be practical for a husband to "take your wife out to a nice restaurant once a week" if he is gainfully employed but not if he is receiving social assistance (i.e., welfare).

2. The second major type of error involves the beginner's attempts to use complex tasks. Again, two variants may be noted. (a) First, ideas for complex tasks typically do not spring unbidden into the therapist's mind. Rather, they require thoughtful and meticulous planning, often up to and including the precise choice of words, the length of sentences, the use of

examples, and so forth. Ideally, such interventions should, as much as possible, use the language of the client and must necessarily cloak the true intentions of the therapist. All of this planning takes time, time that the beginner (and more rarely the old hand) may not provide. Consequently, such interventions may be hastily conceptualized and sloppily constructed, with entirely predictable results: intervention failure.

Alternatively, sloppy construction may simply reflect the new therapist's lack of expertise. The elegant constructions of therapists such as Selvini-Palazzoli (52), Papp (40), and Minuchin and Fishman (38) involve a level of sophistication that reflects years of experience, for which there is simply no shortcut. This relates to the unique aspects of each case; even if the general principles of task construction are mastered (38), these must still be adapted to the individual case. Without the requisite field experience, this may simply be an insuperable problem for the new therapist. While they cope as best they can, their pride refuses to allow them to refer such cases to more experienced practitioners. The result, in our experience, is a high proportion of intervention failures.

Finally we come to the last component of intervention, namely, task delivery. Even provided sophisticated task selection and construction, the intervention may still falter or fail if task delivery is not done properly. The primary problem of beginners in this regard is that their delivery lacks polish and is clumsy. This may take a variety of forms: the therapist may be too brash or too timid, too polite or too aggressive; the therapist's facial expression or body posture may contradict or disqualify his or her words; or the task may be delivered in language which is either too erudite or too simple-minded for the client-family. Whatever the form such clumsiness takes, the result tends to be the same: intervention failure.

Several of the foregoing errors will be illustrated in two brief case vignettes. The first pertains to the beginner while the second applies to the old hand.

> The D family came to therapy complaining of marital difficulties centring primarily around the issue of parenting. The therapist constructed and delivered an intervention that would involve both marital partners: Father would help Mother with parenting and household chores, while Mother would stop making unreasonable demands upon Father. At the next session, the therapist learned that the intervention had failed. Upon investigation, the therapist discovered that Father, his attention riveted upon the therapist, had heard and understood the task, while Mother, her attention distracted by the children, had no recollection of the task whatsoever. The therapist had neglected to ensure that she had the undivided attention of both Father and Mother when the task was delivered.

> A low-income Italian family, the E's, came to therapy complaining of marital problems. In this case, the therapist, an experienced practitioner,

used the disengaged style that was her preference. This involved the collection of much data by verbal means alone, within a highly structured setting. Intervention tasks were constructed and delivered at the end of each session, with the expectation that change would occur between sessions. With the E family, this approach yielded repeated intervention failures, leaving the therapist feeling frustrated and the E's feeling misunderstood. Evaluation of the case by a consultant suggested that the therapist's preferred intervention style was inappropriate for this client-family. Whereas the therapist attempted to collect all data by verbal means, much of the most important data were being transacted before the therapist's eyes, a fact that suggested the need for an engaged intervention style. The therapist's habitual style, developed over years of experience, blinded her to this conclusion.

Category Five: Evaluation Error
Once a therapeutic intervention has been made, the therapist's evaluation of the feedback from this effort will organize his or her subsequent course of action. This "reading" of the feedback is crucial to the success of the treatment process, necessarily includes some degree of experientially guided judgment, and thus is vulnerable to error. While the degree of vulnerability to error may vary from beginner to old hand, the type of error does not.

The Beginner and the Old Hand
The primary evaluation error to which all therapists are vulnerable is that of inaccurately "reading" the feedback that results from some intervention. This may take a variety of specific forms—the therapist may re-apply the same intervention when an alternative would have been more appropriate; an entirely different intervention may be used when a small refinement of the same intervention would have sufficed; and so on—but these may all be accounted for by two basic variants.

1. The first may be described as a "false positive," that is, the case in which the therapist perceives a given intervention to have been successful when in fact it is not. Thus the therapist may conclude that termination is appropriate when in fact all treatment objectives have not been achieved. In such cases, the family is ahead of or moves too quickly for the therapist, such that they inadvertently fool the therapist into thinking that all is well. Conversely, this usually means that the therapist has employed criteria of success that are too narrow for the case in question, and, consequently, has inadvertently excluded from consideration additional valuable information.

2. The second variant may be described as a "false negative," that is, the case in which a successful intervention is mistakenly perceived to have failed. Thus the therapist may doggedly pursue a specific therapeutic goal long after it has already been reached. Since the therapist has been taught to trust his or her own judgment in such matters and to be sceptical of those of the family, the client-family is unable to convincingly inform the therapist

of the error. In such cases, the therapist is usually ahead of or has moved too quickly for the client-family, and has applied criteria of success that are so broad that some residual indication(s) of a "problem" may always be identified.

These common variations of evaluation error are briefly illustrated by the following two case vignettes:

> The F family came to therapy with Mrs. F. complaining of deprivation because of what she considered the inordinate number of hours her husband spent at work. In accord with this presenting complaint, intervention was designed to increase the involvement of Mr. F. in the marital relationship. In subsequent sessions, the F's reported a significant change in their relationship; Mr. F. was spending more time with his wife and, consequently, Mrs. F. reported feeling better. The therapist, however, felt that Mr. F. could provide still further involvement and so continued to pursue this goal. In contrast, Mr. and Mrs. F. felt that their level of marital involvement was sufficient to eliminate the problem for which they had sought treatment. The conflict thus created between therapist and client subsequently generated repeated arguments between them. In short, the therapist's "false negative" evaluation overlooked the disappearance of the presenting problem and replaced it with a new problem, the recurring conflict between therapist and client.

> The G family came to therapy in regard to their daughter Alice, age 14, who was afraid to confront her parents with her complaints about the way they treated her. Instead, she made repeated suicidal gestures. In order to alleviate Alice's mythical fear, the therapist intervened in such a way as to force Alice to initiate some action in regard to her complaints about her parents. At the next session, Alice was asked if she had initiated any action about her complaints. She replied that she had initiated such action on one occasion and was now satisfied that the problem was solved. Her parents were equally content. Having concluded that the problem was resolved, the therapist terminated the case. This action was premature; three weeks later Alice made a serious (although unsuccessful) attempt to take her own life. The therapist had applied an excessively narrow criterion of success, had excluded much valuable data from his evaluation, and so had misread the family's feedback. While the consequences of his "false positive" evaluation error in this case were not fatal, they might well have been.

The foregoing typology identifies 23 types of typical therapist error distributed over five generic categories. For analytic purposes, each of these errors has been described and discussed in isolation. In practice, they are more likely to occur in some combination, with an error in one phase of therapy significantly increasing the probability of error in subsequent phases. Taken together with our comments regarding "beneficial" errors, the present section suggests that (1) error is a common, indeed inevitable, feature of the family therapy process; (2) such errors may be invaluable as an aid to selecting among competing case formulations and as a guide to subsequent clinical practice; (3) alternatively, therapist error may have negative consequences for the client-family, ranging from client (and therapist) frustration and anger, to client drop-out, to the exacerbation of presenting symptoms; (4) the notion of therapist error appears to be crucial to the explanation, as opposed to the mere description, of treatment outcome, either at the level of the single intervention or of the entire case; and (5) knowledge of the range of therapist errors, while unlikely to eliminate their occurrence, may (a) sensitize the practitioner to them; (b) shift the therapist's attribution of responsibility for intervention failure from the client-family to him or herself; and (c) possibly reduce the frequency of "destructive" errors.

Discussion

The notion of therapist error is not new. Several of the most prominent practice models in this area of family therapy implicitly place heavy emphasis on the clinical use of deviation or "error"-reducing feedback, with respect to practitioners as well as students (36, 20). Indeed, several well-known authors in the area have explicitly used the term in their recent works (21, 31). Yet nowhere in the literature is the idea used in a systematic way, as an integral part of a model of clinical practice.

Why is this so? In closing, we should like to speculate that there are four primary reasons for this:

1. The first reason concerns the traditional image of the relationship between therapist and client. In this view, the therapist is seen as one who is impartial, objective, detached, and selfless (30). The task is to help the client-family recognize the dysfunctional interactional patterns in which they are "stuck" and to express their feelings regarding their presenting problem(s). In this sense, it is the client who is the focus of the therapeutic process; while the therapist's role is an important one, it is the client who is ultimately responsible for the outcome of therapy, whether positive or negative. The therapist thus fades imperceptibly into the background, hence the preoccupation in the literature with client resistance and how to overcome it. It is true, of course, that more attention has come to be focussed on the therapist with the evolution of "directive" modes of therapy, which do not seek to engender client insight (32). However, this seems to us to be more than offset by the tendency for family therapists to enter the field from disciplines which are still heavily involved in a traditional model of clinical practice (e.g., psychiatry; see 50).

2. A related reason concerns the historical focus of disciplines, such as social work, on the process as opposed to the outcome of therapy (30). This is manifested in a preoccupation with the methods of family therapy (13, 38), which, in turn, encourages practitioners to disregard outcome, or more precisely, to disregard the relationship between process and outcome (10).

From this perspective, the issue of therapist error simply never arises. While it is widely assumed that all therapists make "mistakes," this is dismissed as something to be overcome, as an impediment to be eliminated through supervision and/or consultation.

3. A third reason is the practitioner's image of the essential nature of the therapeutic process. This involves the twin notions that (a) the therapeutic process is an art form that is, in principle, not subject to quantification, and that (b) the idiosyncratic nature of each family is so complete as to preclude the identification of regularities or the derivation of generalizations regarding the therapy process (34). While we have no data concerning the proportion of practitioners who subscribe to these beliefs, our impression is that their acceptance is fairly widespread. Adherence to such beliefs once again focusses attention on the process whereby clinical skills are acquired, and thus considers the notion of therapist error as a flaw whose importance lies solely in its elimination.

4. A final reason is the ideological position which tends to arise when practitioners routinely employ a "soft technology" such as family therapy. As Perrow (41) notes, whenever work involves a heavy reliance on human judgment, is guided by inexact theories significantly influenced by beliefs, and is difficult to assess in terms of outcome (47), the organization of that work is likely to be unstable and problematic. One solution to the uncertainty that such instability creates is the development of a belief system or ideology that indicates how relevant experience is to be perceived, understood, and interpreted. One such belief is that of the dichotomy between "good" (i.e., treatable) and "bad" (i.e. untreatable) clients. Another is the notion that clinical mastery pertains primarily to the development of technical skills in the "art" of therapy and is thus independent of outcome. A third refers to the therapist's non-falsifiable faith in the family therapy modality as equal to or better than all other treatment modalities. And a fourth concerns the practitioner's anecdotal and individualized experience of treatment success as both objectively valid and generalizable to the population of family therapists and client-families. This ideological position—the existence of which is based on our own anecdotal impressions—allows the practitioner to feel secure in the belief that he or she is doing the best that he or she can and that that best is quite good enough. This precludes the need to be continually self-reflexive, eliminates the distasteful and unpleasant task of regularly being confronted with one's own fallibility, and implies that therapist error is the exception that proves the rule.

References

1. Ackerman, N.W., and Sobel, R. "Family diagnosis: An approach to the preschool child." *American Journal of Orthopsychiatry.* 20 (1950): 744-753.
2. Bateson, G. "The group dynamics of schizophrenia." In L. Appleby, J.M.

Scher, and J. Cumming, eds. *Chronic Schizophrenia: Explorations in Theory and Treatment.* Glencoe, Ill.: The Free Press, 1960.

3. Bateson, G., Jackson, D.D., Haley, J., and Weakland, J. "Toward a theory of schizophrenia." *Behavioral Science.* 1 (1956): 251-264.

4. Beal, E.W. "Current trends in the training of family therapists." *American Journal of Psychiatry.* 133 (1976): 137-141.

5. Bloch, D.A., and Weiss, H.M. "Training facilities in marital and family therapy." *Family Process.* 20 (1981): 131-146.

6. Bross, A., and Benjamin, M. "Family therapy: A recursive model of strategic practice." In A. Bross, ed. *Family Therapy: A Recursive Model of Strategic Practice.* Toronto: Methuen, 1982.

7. Cooper, A., Rampage, C., and Soucy, G. "Family therapy training in clinical psychology programs." *Family Process.* 20 (1981): 155-166.

8. Erickson, M.H., and Rossi, E.L. *Hypnotherapy: An Exploratory Casebook.* N.Y.: Irvington, 1979.

9. Ferreira, A.J. "Family myth and homeostasis." *Archives of General Psychiatry.* 9 (1963): 457-463.

10. Fisher, J. *Effective Casework: An Eclectic Approach.* N.Y.: McGraw-Hill, 1978.

11. Foley, V.D. *An Introduction to Family Therapy.* N.Y.: Grune and Stratton, 1974.

12. Framo, J.L. "Personal reflections of a family therapist." In J.G. Howells, ed. *Advances in Family Psychiatry.* Vol. 1. N.Y.: International University Press, 1979.

13. Goldenberg, I., and Goldenberg, H. *Family Therapy: An Overview.* Monterey, Cal.: Brooks/Cole, 1980.

14. Guerin, P.J. "Family therapy: The first twenty-five years." In P.J. Guerin, ed. *Family Therapy and Practice.* N.Y.: Gardner, 1976.

15. Gurman, A.S., and Kniskern, D.P., eds. *Handbook of Family Therapy.* N.Y.: Brunner/Mazel, 1981.

16. Gurman, A.S., and Kniskern, D.P. "Family therapy outcome research: Knowns and unknowns." In A.S. Gurman and D.P. Kniskern, eds. *Handbook of Family Therapy.* N.Y.: Brunner/Mazel, 1981.

17. Haley, J. "The family of the schizophrenic: A model system." *Journal of Nervous and Mental Disease.* 129 (1959): 357-374.

18. Haley, J. *Strategies of Psychotherapy.* N.Y.: Grune and Stratton, 1963.

19. Haley, J. *Uncommon Therapy: The Psychiatric Techniques of Milton H. Erickson.* N.Y.: Ballantine, 1973.

20. Haley, J. *Problem-Solving Therapy.* San Francisco: Jossey-Bass, 1976.

21. Haley, J. *Leaving Home: The Therapy of Disturbed Young People.* N.Y.: McGraw-Hill, 1980.

22. Harbin, H.T., and Maziar, H.M. "The families of drug abusers: A literature review." *Family Process.* 14 (1975): 411-432.

23. Harvey, M.A. "On becoming a family therapist: The first three years." *International Journal of Family Therapy.* 2 (1980): 263-274.

24. Jackson, D.D. "The question of family homeostasis." *Psychiatric Quarterly,* 31 (1957, Suppl.): 79-90.

25. Jackson, D.D., and Satir, V. "A review of psychiatric developments in family diagnosis." In N.W. Ackerman, F.L. Beatman, and S.N. Sherman, eds. *Explor-*

ing the Base of Family Therapy. N.Y.: Family Service Assoc. of America, 1961.

26. Kaplan, S.J. "Utilizing myth/game systems with couples in conflict." In A.S. Gurman, ed. *Questions and Answers in the Practice of Family Therapy.* N.Y.: Brunner/Mazel, 1981.

27. Karpel, M.A. "Family secrets." *Family Process.* 19 (1980): 295-306.

28. Kaslow, F.W. "History of family therapy in the United States: A kaleidoscopic overview." *Marriage and Family Review.* 3 (1980): 77-111.

29. Lebow, J. "Issues in the assessment of outcome in family therapy." *Family Process.* 20 (1981): 167-188.

30. MacFadden, R.J. *Stress, Support and the Frontline Social Worker.* Toronto: University of Toronto, Faculty of Social Work, 1980.

31. Madanes, C. *Strategic Family Therapy.* San Francisco: Jossey-Bass, 1981.

32. Madanes, C., and Haley, J. "Dimensions of family therapy." *Journal of Nervous Mental Disease.* 165 (1977): 85-98.

33. Masten, A.S. "Family therapy as a treatment for children: A critical review of outcome research." *Family Process.* 18 (1979): 323-336.

34. Mayer, M.F. "Program evaluation as a part of clinical practice: An administrator's position." *Child Welfare.* 54 (1975): 379-394.

35. Meissner, W.W. "Family process and psychosomatic disease." In J.G. Howells, ed. *Advances in Family Psychiatry.* Vol. 1. N.Y.: International University Press, 1979.

36. Minuchin, S. *Families and Family Therapy.* Cambridge, Mass.: Harvard University Press, 1974.

37. Minuchin, S., Rosman, B.L., and Baker, L. *Psychosomatic Families: Anorexia Nervosa in Context.* Cambridge, Mass.: Harvard University Press, 1978.

38. Minuchin, S., and Fishman, C. *Techniques of Family Therapy.* Cambridge, Mass.: Harvard University Press, 1981.

39. Orne, M.T. "On the social psychology of the psychological experiment: With particular reference to demand characteristics and their implications." *American Psychologist.* 17 (1962): 776-783.

40. Papp, P. *Family Therapy.* New York: Gardner, 1977.

41. Perrow, C. "Hospital: Technology structure and goals." In J. March, ed. *Handbook of Organization.* Chicago: Rand-McNally, 1965.

42. Prottas, J.M. *People-Processing: The Street-Level Bureaucrat in Public Service Bureaucracies.* Lexington, Mass.: Lexington, 1979.

43. Ruesch, J., and Bateson, G. *Communication and the Social Matrix of Psychiatry.* N.Y.: Norton, 1951.

44. Ryan, W. *Blaming the Victim.* N.Y.: Vintage, 1971.

45. Sederer, L.I., and Sederer, N. "A family myth: Sex therapy gone awry." *Family Process.* 18 (1979): 315-321.

46. Selvini-Palazzoli, M.S., Cecchin, G., Prata, G., and Boscolo, L. *Paradox and Counterparadox: A New Model in the Therapy of the Family in Schizophrenic Transactions.* N.Y.: Jason Aronson, 1978.

47. Slipp, S., and Kressel, K. "Difficulties in family therapy evaluation." *Family Process.* 17 (1978): 409-422.

48. Stanton, M.D. "Family treatment approaches to drug abuse problems: A review." *Family Process.* 18 (1979): 251-280.

49. Stein, J.W. *The Family as a Unit of Study and Treatment.* Seattle, Wash.:

Regional Rehabilitation Research Institute, University of Washington, School of Social Work, 1969.

50. Sugarman, S. "Family therapy training in selected general psychiatric residency programs." *Family Process.* 20 (1981): 147-154.
51. Tomm, K.M., and Wright, L.M. "Training in family therapy: Perceptual, conceptual, and executive skills." *Family Process.* 18 (1979): 227-250.
52. Walsh, F. "Preventing burnout in therapeutic work with severely dysfunctional families." In A.S. Gurman, ed. *Questions and Answers in the Practice of Family Therapy.* N.Y.: Brunner/Mazel, 1981.
53. Wells, R.A., and Dezen, A.E. "The results of family therapy revisited: The nonbehavioral methods." *Family Process.* 17 (1978): 251-274.
54. Woodward, C.A., Santa-Barbara, J., Streiner, D.L., Goodwin, J.T., Levin, S., and Epstein, N.B. "Client, treatment, and therapist variables related to outcome in brief systems-oriented family therapy." *Family Process.* 20 (1981): 189-197.

4

The Formation of the Reconstituted Family System: Processes, Problems, and Treatment Goals

Adele Wolpert-Zur and Allon Bross

This paper explores the processes and problems associated with the reconstituted family and suggests some of the strategies available to the family therapist in helping resolve such difficulties. The paper highlights three transitional stages in the formation of the reconstituted family and the goals of family intervention as it relates to problem formulation. Clinical implications for the family practitioner are discussed.

Introduction

Reconstituted or blended families are those in which one or both parents have previously been married and bring with them children from the first marriage. Such families are becoming more numerous. For example, it has been estimated that in 1975 in the United States, 15 million children, 18 years of age or under, lived in step-families and that a minimum of 25 million husbands and wives were stepfathers or stepmothers (27). While comparable Canadian statistics are not currently available, it has been shown that in 1975, nearly one out of five Canadian marriages included at least one person who had previously been divorced (33). In view of the fact that the divorce rate appears to be steadily rising, and, considering that the majority of the divorced subsequently remarry (i.e., 75%, 20), it is probable that the reconstituted family may become the predominant family form of the future. If correct, this reasoning would suggest that it is increasingly important for family therapists to understand the impact that remarriage has on the family system and the processes to which its members must adapt.

Accordingly, this paper will begin by examining the formation of the reconstituted family in terms of a series of three transitional processes or stages. It will be argued that specific tasks need to be accomplished during each of these stages. Concomitantly, families that fail to accomplish these tasks successfully may evolve dysfunctional family processes. Building on this relationship between stage-specific tasks and family problems, the goals of family intervention with respect to each problem type will then be highlighted.

Stages in the Formation
of the Reconstituted Family

For families to function in a healthy manner, boundaries between sub-systems need to be clear and well understood. Such boundaries may be defined as rules that determine the parameters of the family and that serve to "protect the differentiation of the system." (21) Members of a family who experience divorce and then remarry must undergo a series of relationship changes as well as the process of rebuilding boundaries. As Messinger et al. (20) observe, "This process requires a redefinition of individual identity and involves major changes in family structure and functions."

The consolidation of these new relationships and boundaries occurs within the context of a transitional process essentially involving three stages, extending from marriage to a period of single parenting, including recovery from the loss of the previous marital relationship (Stage 1), to the establishment of a new relationship and remarriage (Stage 2), to the reconstruction of the new family system (Stage 3), (20, 26, 32). At each stage, the development of symptomatic behaviour in one or more family members is an indication that the family has not been able to adapt successfully to the changes and tasks associated with the stage in question.

Stage 1: *Mourning the loss.* There appears to be general agreement in the literature that adequately mourning the loss of the previously intact family is the first task to be accomplished by those individuals who will later form the reconstituted family. In fact, the degree to which conflicts and feelings associated with the first marriage have been successfully resolved appears to be the single major determinant of a satisfactory remarriage (19, 16, 13, 35, 26, 32).

In adjusting to the loss, both parents and children will experience feelings of guilt, sadness, and anxiety. For the child, this process involves the gradual acceptance of the fact that his parents will not be getting back together and the equally difficult task of establishing a different kind of relationship with the non-custodial parent (16). For the parents, this process involves the task of terminating their previous marital relationship, while redefining their relationship as parents. To accomplish this, it is important that boundaries between and within subsystems be clarified (1). Establishing such clear boundaries allows ex-spouses to deal with conflict directly, without going through a child who too often becomes triangulated in the parents' problems (21). Furthermore, defining clear rules about how each parent will continue to relate to the child will facilitate "the child's understanding and stabilization of his or her relationship with each parent." (1) In turn, this enables the child to have an independent relationship with each of them.

One of the consequences of not establishing these clear boundaries is the tendency of the custodial parent to tighten the boundaries around the parent-child system in an effort to deal with the loss and compensate for family disruption (20). The result is that parent and child may develop an overly close relationship in which the child may overtly or covertly be expected to behave like a substitute for the absent spouse. This not only interferes with the child's relationship with the non-custodial parent, but makes it extremely difficult for a new member to enter the system (33, 15).

In sum, then, the tasks of this stage include the disengagement of the spouses from their former marital relationship and the redefinition of the boundaries around their co-parental relationship. This will confine conflict to the parental subsystem and permit the children to maintain a separate relationship with both parents. Failure to accomplish these tasks may push the custodial parent and the child into a destructive relationship in which the child is expected to behave like an adult.

Stage 2: *Planning to remarry.* The next transitional stage involves planning to remarry. An important task of this stage concerns the efforts of the prospective marriage partners to strengthen and unify their relationship. This is essential as it has been widely noted that a primary characteristic of a healthy family is cohesion of the marital subsystem (32).

In their uncertainty about their relationship, however, and in their urgency to bring the family together into one "happy unit," the new couple may neglect this important task (35). In contrast to first marriages in which the couple has time to develop a clear subsystem boundary, protected from the demands of other subsystems, a reconstituted couple is confronted with the challenge of simultaneously working out their marital and parental subsystem boundaries, and the concomitant relationships associated with them. As Ransom et al. (26) observe, "The presence of children at the earliest stage (of remarriage) prevents the establishment of an exclusive spouse-to-spouse relationship which predates the undertaking of parenthood."

Consequently, while the development of solidarity in the marital relationship is crucial, closing the boundaries around the spouse subsystem may undermine parent-child interaction, a process equally important to the formation of the reconstituted family. The result may be to precipitate acting out behaviour on the part of the child, who is now put in the position of having to strive desperately to get parental attention.

Other difficulties are also associated with the formation of this new marital relationship. For example, each member of the new couple may enter the relationship with fresh memories of hurtful experiences from a previous marriage. Fearful that this relationship may also fail, they may feel especially vulnerable and sensitive to conflict. Consequently, they may tend to deny existing difficulties so that a "pseudo-mutual" (37) style of interaction may evolve, subsequently impeding the negotiation and resolution of conflict (10). Indeed, if pseudo-mutuality is present prior to marriage, it is likely to persist, if not intensify, in the formation of the reconstituted family. In turn, this sets the stage for an interactional process in which conflict episodes will be dealt with by triangulating a child; the resulting "symptoms" of the child will thus permit the new couple to avoid conflict while maintaining family solidarity (26). These processes thus imply that in addition to stabilizing the marital relationship, a further task for the couple is to develop an interactional style characterized by communication which encourages them to negotiate differences and deal directly with conflict, without resorting to involving the children.

In sum, the tasks of this stage involve, first, the development of solidarity and cohesion in the marital relationship; second, the evolution of an interactional style that permits negotiation of differences and flexibility in undertaking simultaneous parental and marital relationships; and, third, the creation of boundaries around the marital subsystem that are neither too tight nor too close. Failure to accomplish these tasks may result in either the triangulation of a child or its exclusion as the marital relationship becomes enmeshed (21).

Stage 3: *Family reconstruction*. The final stage, family reconstruction, fundamentally involves the tasks of restructuring the family around new relationships and boundaries. This is a difficult process as remarriage may precipitate a crisis; members do not have prescriptions for handling multiple new relationships, nor can they utilize definitions of subsystem boundaries from the previous nuclear family (15). This creates a sense of disequilibrium affecting all family members.

In this context, dysfunctional patterns of behaviour may represent the system's attempts to restore balance. Children may respond by attempting to exclude the new member, the step-parent, who is perceived as a threat to the stability of present relationships. As Kent (15) explains, "they are attempting to close the boundaries of the old family in an effort to resist potential floods of energy for the new member that may threaten the existence of the family system they have known."

Furthermore, while it is important that the system maintain some continuity in family structures and functions, they must also be able to adapt sufficiently to integrate a new member into the system (15). This process involves accommodation and assimilation.

Both processes, however, may be problematic. Remarriage calls for the blending of two systems, each with different histories, memories, rules, and values. In addition, there is a non-custodial parent outside the system. Consequently, the process of assimilation is made difficult, requiring that both the step-parent and the children adapt to the new family system by "chang(ing) their expectations and behaviour in order to accommodate themselves to be able to use the new energies from new relationships." (15)

Similarly, given the absence of clearly defined relationships within the reconstituted family and the negative myths often associated with the step-parent-step-child dyad (i.e., the notion of the wicked, cruel step-parent), the process of accommodation may be particularly problematic. Specifically, difficulties may arise in the areas of discipline and nurturing, in which the position of the step-parent implies contradictory functions (6).

On the one hand, both the step-parent and the step-child have the same expectations of "instant love" (29) and "instant adjustment" (11) that are typically associated with the relationship between parent and biological child (33).

On the other hand, the step-parent is not accorded equal parental rights around the issues of discipline and control. This is because financial obligations, child socialization, and decision-making must be shared with the non-custodial parent.

This situation is further exacerbated by the ambivalence of the spouse about the issue of sharing parenting responsibilities. The natural parent wants help with child discipline—indeed, they may even remarry partly for that reason—but is resentful of any interference with his or her relationship with the child. In a sense, the parent wants to maintain exclusive control and power, only allowing the step-parent to "borrow power" under specific and rather narrow circumstances (4). What frequently results is an interactional sequence in which the step-parent withdraws from all disciplinary activity with the children, thus precipitating an over-involved parent-child relationship together with a disengaged step-parent. Alternatively, the step-parent may prematurely impose his or her views of discipline on the children, thus leading to their emotional withdrawal (15). Again, this encourages a parent-child coalition and reinforces the disengaged step-parent position. Under both circumstances, the boundaries between the parent and child subsystems will not be clearly defined, resulting in confusion of the family hierarchy.

A related dysfunctional process may evolve with respect to parental nurturing. The step-parent attempts to counteract the derogatory image of the "mean step-parent" by making intense efforts to be affectionate and loving toward the child. These efforts may backfire, however, as "stepmothers in general make the error of simply trying too hard to be the perfect step-parent." (31) In the process, a dysfunctional interactional sequence may unfold in which the traditional myth of the wicked step-parent is confirmed: the stepmother makes constant attempts to reach out to the stepchild by showing affection and interest; the child is unresponsive and cold; the stepmother persists but is continually rebuffed; eventually, she withdraws and distances herself from the child; the child's original assumption that the stepmother is cruel is confirmed; the child now feels justified in creating conflict between the marital pair; the stepmother retaliates by demanding of father that the step-child be around less, heightening the hostility between step-parent and step-child, and maintaining negative step-parent-step-child interaction (27).

A similar process may also spring from slightly different roots. Like the step-parent, the child too is expected to automatically feel affection towards the step-parent when in fact these feelings and loyalties are invested in the non-custodial parent. In this sense, any alliance with the step-parent may be perceived by the child as a betrayal of the mother or father. The child's efforts to grapple with this problem may be manifested in a range of symptomatic behaviours, including acting-out behaviour, either at home or at school, or in withdrawal from family and friends, thus further complicating the process of family reorganization (18).

Still further difficulties in the area of nurturing may arise insofar as efforts at being affectionate may be misconstrued in a family composed of non-biological relationships. Specifically, in these types of families, the usual prohibitions surrounding the incest taboo may become confused (6, 29, 10, 31, 32, 16, 15). The resultant blurring of the boundaries about the parent and child subsystems may be associated with intense fear and uncertainty on the part of the natural parent. Such feelings may be especially pronounced when the children reach adolescence and are curious about sexual issues, and may be stimulated by their awareness of an affectionate, sexual relationship between the natural and the step-parent.

In this context, Schulman (29) reports that mothers are often fearful that their husbands will find their daughters more attractive than they are. As a result, an interactional sequence may be established in which every act of affection between stepfather and stepdaughter may be misinterpreted as potential incest. The stepfather may thus find himself caught in a double bind: his wife wants him to show affection to her daughter, yet misconstrues his attempts to do so as sexual. Consequently, marital conflict may develop, which, paradoxically, may lead to an even closer tie between stepfather and stepdaughter, thus apparently confirming the mother's initial suspicions. Moreover, this tense situation may be exacerbated as the relationship between step-siblings comes under suspicion. These difficulties clearly suggest the importance of making subsystem boundaries and the sanctions associated with inappropriate behaviour sharp and clear; failure to do so may result in increased interpersonal conflict as family members attempt to mask their sexual feelings; it may even result in a child leaving home prematurely (15).

The importance of having clear subsystem boundaries notwithstanding, it is important to recognize that reconstituted families need more permeable boundaries than intact nuclear families. The existence of a non-custodial parent outside the household, one who shares in parental authority and decision-making, means that reconstituted families need flexibility, that is, the capacity to expand and contract their boundaries as they allow their own and visiting children to come and go freely (18).

This is not to deny that reconstituted families must develop their own stable life style, history, culture, rituals, and rules around which all families are organized. Nevertheless, Walker and Messinger (33) have suggested that the reconstituted family may be fruitfully seen as a system whose constituents have "dual membership" in two family systems. This perspective attempts to take into consideration the affiliation and affection that often exists between the non-custodial parent and the child, but simultaneously recognizes that child's membership in the new household. In short, it is important that neither system demand total loyalty from its members, but rather that the child in particular be permitted to have an independent relationship with both systems.

Further, not only do the boundaries between the two family systems need to be negotiated, but boundaries between the reconstituted family and the network of extended kin need to be re-established (15). In addition to the pre-existing ties to kin through the custodial and non-custodial parents, the new step-parent also brings a network of relatives who need to become established parts of the family system. Indeed, nurturing by grandparents may especially need to undergo change. The process of reconstituting the family, then, requires redefinition of relationships and boundaries with extended kin, in order that they continue to serve as sources of support during a stressful period, rather than as sources of potential conflict (15).

In sum, it is apparent that the primary tasks of this final stage involve the clarification and redefinition of boundaries and the integration of new and sometimes difficult relationships. These processes have as their ultimate goal the establishment of a cohesive family system with boundaries that are sufficiently permeable as to allow the free movement of at least some members from one household to another. Clearly, these processes are fraught with difficulty and must be allowed to develop gradually; they cannot be ascribed as in the nuclear family (33). Failure, either to accomplish the required tasks or to allow sufficient time for these processes to unfold, may result in a disengaged step-parent and disturbed marital and/or parent-child interaction.

More generally, the present section has sought to discuss the various tasks associated with the formation of the reconstituted family and to highlight the various family problems that may arise (see Figure 4.1) if these tasks are not accomplished successfully.

Clinical Implications

The foregoing discussion provides a series of insights into the nature and dynamics of the transitional processes involved in the formation of the reconstituted family. Such insights contain within them a range of implications, both general and problem-specific, of value to the family therapist confronted with the challenge of offering treatment to such clients.

1. *General Implications.* The foregoing discussion makes clear that reconstituted families may involve a more complex network of persons and relationships than would typically apply to the nuclear family. Accordingly, it is important for the family therapist working with reconstituted families to carefully evaluate the past and present relationships with

ex-spouses and grandparents. This will serve to determine the extent to which they should be part of the treatment process. In general, the clearer these relationships and the more open the communication between family members, the more functional the new family structure is likely to be (18).

In a similar vein, Schulman (29) notes that when reconstituted families come into treatment, mythical (i.e., the wicked step-parent) as well as real expectations, hopes, and fears are interwoven in the system. The fact that some of them are, moreover, culturally reinforced makes them highly resistant to change. It is important, therefore, for the family therapist to intervene in the system by explicitly challenging these myths, thus diminishing or nullifying their impact. Expectations that each member has, both of themselves and of each other, also need to be clarified. In the process, it is often helpful to allow members to share their past histories together. This not only gives them "permission" to express their feelings of loss, but may serve also as a "bonding ritual" or "ritual of reintroduction" for members of this new family, who may still be struggling to create a new history and set of rules together (9).

Furthermore, while the presenting problems of the reconstituted family may frequently centre around the same issues as those of the nuclear family, it is important for the therapist to be aware of, and appreciate the structural differences and greater complexities of this family type (18). Dysfunctional structural formation may be seen in the development of rigid relationships, boundaries, and patterns of negotiation. Difficulties in such families frequently arise because of attempts to draw "firm boundaries around new household membership; to push for primary loyalty and cohesiveness similar to first-marriage families; to exclude or combat the influence of natural parents and grandparents on their children; to deny differences and difficulties, or to try to act 'as if' this family is just an ordinary household of parents and kids like the one next door." (18)

In this context, approaching the reconstituted family as though it were a continuously intact nuclear family impedes its capacity to grow and change. Peck (24), for example, comments that "highlighting and defusing their differences paradoxically 'seduces' the individual into a familylike endeavour." This can make it easier for the family to move from pseudo-wholeness to genuine unity whereby they come to value their uniqueness (29).

Finally, a general goal of working with the reconstituted family concerns helping them achieve family reorganization, with a good marital relationship, while permitting freedom of movement for children between two households. Duberman (5) argues that a key to the successful comple-tion of these processes is a viable parental coalition accompanied by mutual support, open negotiation, and interactional flexibility. This, in turn, influences the success of the relationship between the parents and the children. Thus affective coping in such families requires that members "make conscious efforts to establish themselves as an entity, yet avoid the illusion of approximating the normative patterns of the nuclear family." (5)

2. *Problem-specific Implications.* As shown in Figure 4.1, transitional processes may be associated with a range of family problems. These tend to fall into three broad categories: (a) the "adult" child, (b) acting out behaviour, and (c) heightened interpersonal conflict. It would be a serious error, however, for the therapist to assume that all forms of acting out, for example, warrant a similar therapeutic response; rather, the goals of treatment will vary systematically as a function of the transitional stage at which such problems occur and the interactional processes which underlie them.

(a) *The "adult" child,* for example, appears to be uniquely associated with Stage 1 and is manifested either by "role reversal" in which the child attempts to nurture the parent, or by "pseudo-precocity" in which the parent treats the child like an adult confidant. In either case, such a relationship is clearly inimical to the development of both participants; it robs the child of the opportunity to develop its own unique identity while preventing the parent from seeking close ties with other adults, including the search for another spouse. Consequently, the twin goals of therapy are (1) to create distance between parent and child, thus strengthening the boundary around the sibling subsystem, and (2) to confront the parent with the abdication of executive functions, thus strengthening the boundary around the parental subsystem and, in turn, freeing the parent to go outside the family system for adult companionship.

(b) In contrast to the "adult" child problem, *acting out behaviour* may be found in Stages 2 and 3, and may include school difficulties, emotional problems, temper tantrums, aggressive behaviour, extreme dependence, and so on. In this instance, the choice of specific therapeutic intervention will vary primarily as a function of the interactional process underlying the problem. More specifically, the therapist is confronted with three relatively distinct interactional alternatives.

1. The therapist may be faced with a pseudo-mutual couple presenting with no difficulties other than (1) a child with behavioural or school difficulties, or (2) constant fighting between two sets of children. In the former case, it is likely that the child is being triangulated as a means of deflecting marital conflict, thus maintaining the "illusory harmony" (21) of the marital relationship. The goal of therapy here is to strengthen the marital subsystem boundary in order to allow differences between the spouses to be negotiated directly and brought to a resolution. This, in turn, will free the children from the marital relationship, eliminate the interactional basis of the child's behaviour, and thus allow the child to give up his or her symptom.

In the latter case, "the children are usually fighting out the conflicts denied by the remarried couple either in their own marriage or in the

The Reconstituted Family System / 123

Figure 4.1

Manifest Problems Associated with Formation of Reconstituted Family, with Stage-specific Latent Problems From Which They Arise and Interactional Processes Through Which They Are Made Manifest

Transitional Stage	Latent Problem	Interactional Process	Manifest Problem
1 Mourning the loss	Incomplete mourning of the loss of the former relationship	Increased frequency and intensity of parent-child interaction	"Adult" child
2 2 Planning to re-marry	Conflict avoidance (pseudo-mutuality) Enmeshed marital relationship	Triangulation Decreased interaction between parent and child; child has no access to parent	Child acting out behaviour Child acting out behaviour
3 Family reconstruction	Disengaged step-parent Spouse's fear of step-parent intrusion into parent-child relationship Spouse's fear of incest; insecurity in marital relationship Child's fear of loss of parental love and affection	Over-involved parent-child relationship; step-parent no authority Increased interaction between step-parent and child Refusal of step-parent affection; over-involved parent-child relationship	Child acting out or dependent behaviour Increased marital conflict Increased conflict: marital and/or step-parent-child

relationship with either or both ex-spouses." (18) Accordingly, family assessment should pay particular attention to the involvement of ex-spouses, for they will then need to be included in treatment. If so, the goal of intervention will be to establish clear boundaries between ex-spouse and parental subsystems. This will enable the ex-spouses to deal with their differences directly instead of through the children, while allowing the children an independent relationship with each natural parent. If not, the goal of treatment will be to strengthen the boundaries around the parental and sibling subsystems, again constraining the marital partners to deal with their own difficulties by themselves.

2. The family may present itself as a conflicted marital relationship focussed on the acting-out behaviour of a child. This configuration is typically associated with an over-involved, parent-child coalition together with a disengaged step-parent shorn of disciplinary authority. The goal of therapy is to shift the balance of power from the over-involved parent to the disengaged step-parent (4). In so doing, the therapist must seek to clarify two issues: first, acknowledge that the step-parent is not the child's mother or father; and, second, establish whether or not the natural parent wants help with parenting. Given an affirmative response to the latter issue, the therapist will ask the natural parent to "lend" the step-parent the power (4). This will draw the peripheral parent into the family and strengthen the boundaries around the parental and sibling subsystems. Once the step-parent has established that he or she can exert authority, the couple can then negotiate a mutually acceptable balance in its parental functioning.

3. The family may present itself as an intensely close marital pair distressed over the acting out of a child. In this instance, it is likely that the marital relationship has become enmeshed, and thus rigidly and impermeably bounded, such that the child is denied access to parenting. The goal of therapy is to loosen the boundary around the marital relationship, thus decreasing the distance between parents and child, and giving the child access to the parenting that it needs. This will often involve encouraging the parents to spend time with the child in age-appropriate activity.

(c) The third category of behaviour, *heightened interpersonal conflict*, tends to be associated primarily with Stage 3 and may include either intense marital or parent-child conflict. Again, the intervention of choice will depend on the interactional processes underlying the difficulty. Specifically, two alternative processes are most common.

In the first instance, the family may present itself around the issue of intense conflict between the step-parent and the child. This typically suggests that the child's fear of losing the natural parent, together with that parent's ambivalence towards remarriage, has resulted in an over-involved parent-child dyad leaving the step-parent in the disengaged position. In this case, the goals of treatment are, first, to normalize the situation by pointing out that "instant" love between step-parent and child is not to be expected; second, to strengthen the boundary around the marital sub-system, thus bringing the step-parent into the family; and, third, to open a channel of communication between the parents and the child, thus permitting them to explicitly negotiate the form they want their relationship to take, while, simultaneously, giving the child the time it needs to work through its natural fear.

In the second instance, the family may present itself as an intensely conflicted marital relationship centring around the intensity of the stepfather-stepdaughter relationship. In this case, the mother's fear of incest between her husband and daughter typically conceals a number of as yet unresolved—perhaps even unperceived—differences between the marital partners, particularly around the issue of an appropriate level of marital intimacy. The stepfather-stepdaughter relationship represents the family's way of avoiding this highly charged and very threatening emotional issue. The goals of therapy then, are, first, to strengthen and clarify the boundary around the marital subsystem, thus distancing the stepdaughter; and, second, to confront the marital partners with their differences, thus affording them an opportunity to directly negotiate not only the intimate nature of their relationship, but also the relationship between a stepfather and stepdaughter.

Conclusion

The purpose of this paper has been to explore the processes and problems associated with the reconstituted family and to suggest some of the strategies available to the family therapist in helping resolve such difficulties. Of necessity, our treatment of this complex area remains incomplete; constraints of space and our exclusion of problems associated with the extended family were partly responsible. A far more important reason is simply that the reconstituted family has yet to receive the research attention it deserves. This is especially ironic if, as we suggested in the introduction, this is likely to be the predominant family form of the future. Accordingly, if the present paper has not only indicated what we do know, but in addition hinted at the amount that we do not know, then our purpose will have been served.

References

1. Ahrons, C. "Redefining the Divorced Family: A Conceptual Framework." *Social Work.* 25 (6, 1980): 437-440.
2. Ahrons, C. "Divorce: A Crisis of Family Transition and Change." *Family Relations.* 29 (1980): 533-540.
3. Bernard, J. *Remarriage: A Study of Marriage.* N.Y.: The Dryden Press, 1956.

4. Bross, A. *Treatment of Families—A Manual.* Unpublished work, Toronto, 1980.
5. Duberman, L. *The Reconstituted Family: A Study of Remarried Couples and Their Children.* Chicago: Nelson Hall Publishers, 1975.
6. Fast, I., and Cain, A. "The Step-parent Role: Potential in Disturbances in Family Functioning." *American Journal of Orthopsychiatry.* 36 (1966): 485-491.
7. Goldman, J., and Coane, J. "Family Therapy After the Divorce: Developing a Strategy." *Family Process,* 16 (1977): 357-362.
8. Goldmeier, J. "Intervention in the Continuum from Divorce to Family Reconstitution." *Social Casework,* 1980, 39-47.
9. Goldner, V. "Blended Families." Workshop held at Interfaith Pastoral Counselling, Kitchener, 1980.
10. Goldstein, H. "Reconstituted Families: The Second Marriage and Its Children." *Psychiatric Quarterly.* 48 (1974): 433-440.
11. Jacobson, D. "Stepfamilies: Myths and Realities." *Social Work.* 24 (1979): 202-207.
12. Johnson, H. "Working with Stepfamilies: Principles of Practice." *Social Work,* 23 (1980): 304-308.
13. Jones, S.M. "Divorce and Remarriage: A New Beginning, a New Set of Problems." *Journal of Divorce.* 2 (2, 1978): 217-221.
14. Kaplan, S. "Structural Family Therapy for Children of Divorce: Case Reports." *Family Process.* 16 (1977): 75-83.
15. Kent, M. "Remarriage: A Family Systems Perspective." *Social Casework,* 1980, 146-153.
16. Kleinman, J., Rosenberg, E., and Whiteside, M. "Common Development Tasks in Forming Reconstituted Families." *Journal of Marital and Family Therapy.* 1979, 78-86.
17. Maddox, B. *The Half-Parent.* New York: M. Evans and Company, Inc., 1975.
18. McGoldrick, M., and Carter, E. "Forming a Remarried Family." In E. Carter and M. McGoldrick, eds. *The Family Life Cycle: A Framework for Family Therapy.* New York: Gardner, 1980.
19. Messinger, L. "Remarriage Between Divorced People with Children from Previous Marriages: A Proposal for Preparation for Remarriage." *Journal of Marriage and Family Counselling.* 1976, 193-199.
20. Messinger, L., Walker, K., and Freeman, S. "Preparation for Remarriage Following Divorce: The Use of Group Techniques." *American Journal of Orthopsychiatry.* 48 (2, 1978): 263-272.
21. Minuchin, S. *Families and Family Therapy.* Cambridge, Mass.: Harvard University Press, 1974.
22. Nichols, W. "Divorce and Remarriage Education." *Journal of Divorce.* 1 (2, 1977): 153-161.
23. Osman, S. "My Stepfather is a She." *Family Process.* 11 (1972): 209-218.
24. Peck, B. *A Family Therapy Notebook: Experiential Techniques of Family and Couples Psychotherapy.* New York: Libra Publishers, 1974.
25. Perkins, T., and Kahon, J. "An Empirical Comparison of Natural-Father and Stepfather Family Systems." *Family Process.* 18 (1979): 175-183.
26. Ransom, J., Schlesinger, S., and Derdeyn, A. "A Stepfamily in Formation." *American Journal of Orthopsychiatry.* 49 (1, 1979): 36-43.

27. Roosevelt, R., and Lofas, J. *Living in Step.* N.Y.: McGraw-Hill, 1976.
28. Schlesinger, B. "Remarriage—An Inventory of Findings." *The Family Coordinator,* 1968, 248-249.
29. Schulman, G. "Myths That Intrude on the Adaptation of the Stepfamily." *Social Casework.* 1972, 131-139.
30. Simon, A. *Stepchild in the Family: A View of Children in Remarriage.* New York: The Odyssey Press, 1964.
31. Visher, E., and Visher, J. "Common Problems of Stepparents and Their Spouses." *American Journal of Orthopsychiatry.* 48 (2, 1978): 252-262.
32. Visher, E., and Visher, J. *Stepfamilies: A Guide to Working with Stepparents and Stepchildren.* New York: Brunner/Mazel, 1979.
33. Walker, K., and Messinger, L. "Remarriage After Divorce: Dissolution and Reconstruction of Family Boundaries." *Family Process,* 18 (1979): 185-192.
34. Walker, K., Rogers, J., and Messinger, L. "Remarriage After Divorce: A Review." *Social Casework.* 58 (1977): 276-285.
35. Whiteside, M., and Auerbach, L. "Can the Daughter of My Father's New Wife Be My Sister?" *Journal of Divorce.* 1 (3), 1978.
36. Wilson, K., Zurcher, L., McAdams, D., and Cunitis, R. "Stepfathers and Stepchildren: An Exploratory Analysis From Two National Surveys." *Journal of Marriage and the Family.* 1975, 526-536.
37. Wynne, L.C., Irving, M.R., Day, J., and Hirsch, S.I. "Pseudomutuality in the Family Relations of Schizophrenics." *Psychiatry.* 21 (1958): 205-220.

5
Contracts and Contracting*

Michael A. Rothery

The concept of the contract has been invoked with increasing frequency in the therapy practice literature in recent years.

Since the process of negotiation that is present in all relationships takes many different forms, the idea of contracts is complex, and can be confusing. This paper outlines the different meanings associated with the term and suggests that a complete understanding needs to be seen as an ongoing transaction as well as a series of static agreements.

We promise according to our hopes, and perform according to our fears.—Duc de la Rochefoucauld

Introduction

Twenty years ago, the notion of a contract between therapists and their clients was rarely discussed. Today, this concept enjoys enough popular appeal that most current texts on practice give it at least a passing reference, and some explore its application and essential features at length.

Certain developments in the theory and assumptions on which practice is based have created a climate conducive to ideas such as the contract. Ego psychology has encouraged an increased respect for people's cognitive tools and creative problem-solving abilities. There has also been a renewed recognition that action is not secondary to insight and emotional integration as a valid resolution of problems and preferred outcome of intervention (7). Behaviouristic models (in the broadest sense of the word) have also emphasized action, along with demands for clarity about goals and the procedures for realizing them. As for basic assumptions, increased interest in contracts reflects the influence of a number of beliefs about practice, including: (1) that people can and should make informed choices about the nature and goals of the services they receive; (2) that this carries with it a concomitant share in the responsibility for their treatment and its consequences; (3) that this responsibility includes full participation in the process of making decisions and choices and acting on them; and (4) that there is value in maximizing a client's cognitive involvement in his or her own problem-solving from the outset of the helping process.

An examination of the ways contracts and contracting are described in our literature reveals areas of consensus as well as substantial areas of

---

*Reprinted with the permission of the journal *Clinical Social Work*.

confusion. The latter require attention, particularly since the concept is being invoked with increasing frequency. Other writers (8) have recognized the need that motivated the preparation of this paper—to clarify and elaborate a potentially useful concept that is still incomplete in its development. My goal is to examine the current state of our thinking about contracts and to suggest theoretically and practically useful extensions of this.

Definitions and Review

Seabury (15) notes that "In social work, the contract has generally been defined as an agreement between client and worker that sets forth the purpose of their interaction and the processes through which that purpose is to be achieved." Maluccio and Marlow (8) also emphasize the aspect of agreement about goals and procedures, adding that this needs to be stated explicitly. Other definitions are consistent with these.

An apparent agreement as to the meaning of the term breaks down with an examination of the ways in which it is actually applied. Maluccio and Marlow (8), for example, having emphasized explicitness as a defining characteristic, go on to recognize "corrupt contracts" that are normally unstated or tacit agreements. Some writers use "contract" to designate specific (preferably written) commitments to particular behavioural goals (3, 17), while others apply it to the norms that naturally evolve as part of the development of the client/worker system (4).

There are also differences regarding the point of time in the development of the relationship at which a contract should be negotiated. Schertz (14) indicates that the formation of a contract is preceded by the development of a therapeutic alliance, but Brammer (1) sees contracting occurring after agreed-upon goals have been established. Hollis (6) sees the contract as "the end result of . . . the initial phase of work," and Reid and Epstein (10) prescribe contract completion by the end of the first or second interview. Other writers (2, 8, 15) emphasize that the contract should not be considered a single event that occurs at the end of the initial phase of intervention, but as an integral and central part of the entire helping process.

Fischer, Siporin, Seabury, and Goldstein (16), among others, recognize the need to distinguish among different types of contracts. Although different labels may be used, there is widespread accord that there are preliminary contracts, or whatever agreements are made, to meet and discuss matters which sustain the relationship at its inception as it acquires focus and purpose. There is similar consistency in the view that these preliminary contracts are supplanted by a primary working contract, which is the first formal agreement about goals, procedures, and responsibilities. A number of writers are careful to note that this contract remains open to change or renegotiation if the assessment of the situation requiring service or the situation itself should change. Finally, it is widely accepted that additional secondary contracts may be developed as interventions aimed at particular tasks which represent steps in the fulfillment of the general goals agreed upon in the primary working contract. Behavioural contracts are a specialized type of secondary contract.

With respect to the content, purposes, and functions of contracting, there are differences in emphasis, but no apparent inconsistencies. Contracts are said to spell out the goals, limits, expected roles, responsibilities, time constraints, organizational requirements, target problems (often prioritized), and procedures that service from a particular therapist or agency entails. Only when these have been negotiated and agreed upon, according to some writers, can the "applicant" or "target system" properly be considered a client. The contract is seen as a primary requirement and defining characteristic of the therapist-client relationship.

Several authors have noted that, by spelling out the goals of intervention, the contract also provides a framework for assessing accountability. Siporin (16) makes the useful related point that therapists should not be accountable for the failure to achieve changes for which a client will not contract or in cases where agreed-upon secondary contracts are not followed through.

Other frequently mentioned advantages of contracting include the opportunity to dispel unrealistic expectations, including inappropriate dependent fantasies (9). Contracting is said to involve clients more fully in the problem-solving process and to minimize the chances of their being subject to procedures that they are expected to trust on faith. It also protects the client in situations where he could be treated "behind his back" (10). Fischer (3) points to general efficacious side effects in terms of an enhanced relationship based on greater openness and shared commitment. Less widely discussed but hardly less important is the suggestion that contracting renders the helping process more efficient and increases the possibility of positive outcomes.

Extending the Concept

There are two major points that are touched on in the literature but insufficiently developed so that their full potential for providing a clearer, more complete understanding of contracting remains to be explored. First, the process is a developmental one. Second, contracting can be seen as a transactional, communicative process in action as well as a relatively static agreement or series of such agreements.

The Developmental Perspective

Rhodes (11) obtained the information from 91% of the social workers in her sample that, after three interviews, an ulterior expectation or set of expectations was being entertained by the therapist with respect to the client. Her implied disapproval of this situation seems to be based on an unrealistically simple model of contracting and practice. While she, as well as others, call for a recognition of contracting as a continuous process, problems arise from an insufficient appreciation of its developmental aspect.

Good practice often requires a redefinition of the problem. The goals embodied in the primary working contract may differ markedly from those contained in the initial request for help. Such a development is not unusual. Indeed, a competent therapist initially should be somewhat ahead of the client, considering options and ways of understanding problems that the client has not entertained. Nor is it unusual that some groundwork or preliminary exploration is required before such ulterior goals responsibly can be introduced. One works toward an understanding of the problem and shared goals, ends that may be reached very quickly with some clients but never completely reached with others.

The first phase of the contract is often simply an agreement to consider the possibilities of the worker's and the agency's services. Realistically, all that is achieved is a tenuous and limited commitment which, according to some empirical findings (13), usually either dies or is confirmed near the time of the third interview. This phase of the process includes aspects of "role induction" (3), exploration of problems and needs, possible reframing of problems in terms of goals, and agreements about the type of service to be provided, including salient organizational details.

Another phase begins with a commitment to work toward certain ends. It can include a redefinition of problems and goals, a choice of priorities, and more specific agreement about appropriate procedures for achieving these. While roles are increasingly stable and less of an issue, negotiations about the distribution of responsibility may be an ongoing requirement.

A third phase contains all the possible secondary contracts designed to deal with specific steps toward established goals. Clarity of contract or a continuous recognition of the purposes of the relationship is an ongoing task. The general aim is successful action, realistic choices, and the generalization of the learning of more adaptive coping patterns. Ideally, the therapist's contributions become less important to the success of problem-solving throughout this phase, and the responsibility for maintaining goal-directedness and focus is more evenly distributed.

A final phase of contracting involves negotiating an end to the relationship (15). Referral, plans for ways to solidify and maintain gains, and arrangements for follow-up contracts are examples of the possible content of negotiation at this time.

This overview, admittedly general, already invites discussion of exceptions. Being a dynamic and developmental process, contracting will vary with the context in which it is practised, and the contexts are never exactly the same. However, such a framework is clearly necessary for an adequate conceptualization of practice, and it reflects realities that need to be recognized by research into the contracting process. Within it, research can contribute substantially, both by refining the general outlines of the phases and providing details of variations on the main developmental theme.

The Transactional Perspective

While considerations of contracting that do not take developmental aspects into account are limited, similar limitations are imposed by a view that takes insufficient cognizance of the fact that contracting is also an ongoing transactional process and a reality to be contended with from the moment a relationship begins.

From a transactional point of view, for example, there is no debate about when contracting takes place because there is no choice but to negotiate the terms of our relationships if we are to relate at all. There are choices about how explicit to be about the contracting process and at what point to formalize it, but non-negotiation itself is not an option. To paraphrase a popular communications' axiom: one cannot not contract (18).

Often, discussion of formal and behavioural contracts is based on a limited paradigm: the problem-solving process as an orderly, linear series of events, progressing logically from exploration through decision-making and planning, culminating in action that resolves the problem. As useful as this paradigm is, reality is usually considerably less tidy, and a complete view of contracting needs to accommodate the disorderly as well as the orderly forces at work as help proceeds.

A number of difficulties can be associated with a rigid reliance on formal contracting that does not incorporate a respect for the interpersonal dynamics that occur during contract negotiation. The limited view does not provide the conceptual tools necessary to do effective contracting with clients who are experiencing conflicting needs and motives, where there are ulterior or hidden agendas operating, and where inconvenient irrational beliefs and feelings may mount a strong opposition to the client's attempts to conform to the logical program that is offered. A related problem is the possibility of procedural dogmatism: clients will not be served well by workers or agencies with a preconceived formula for change, whether this requires that they talk about their transference reactions or adapt to an expectation that their problems can be neatly broken down into prioritized "target behaviours."

Seabury (15) directs attention to similar pitfalls that may appear if the concept of contracting is misused and also raises the issue of "involuntary clients" who may be ambivalent about formulating a contract, especially initially. This concern is shared by Reid and Epstein:

> Forming contracts becomes far more difficult when the client is reluctant to accept the services of a social worker . . . (although) we would argue that they are even more important with this group. A vast amount of time in clinical social work is unproductively spent in unclarified, ambiguous,

and covertly conflicted relationships with recalcitrant clients . . . do clients mean what they say when they contract to work on problems in agencies such as juvenile court, which hold considerable power over their lives? More generally, verbal agreements may not reflect felt commitments (10, p. 9-10).

As Samuel Goldwyn is supposed to have said: "A verbal contract isn't worth the paper it's written on." The option of making agreements more binding by writing them down may not be desirable as a general rule, but the issue raised is a central concern whenever contracting is under way. The "New Year's Resolution Principle" recognizes that good intentions seldom translate easily into change, and commitments made in one context or frame of mind are subject to undermining or distortion with changes in time, place, and mood.

It is by now a commonplace that communication occurs at many levels simultaneously, often reflecting different cognitive processes, emotional responses, and needs. When two or more such levels contain messages that are incongruent, we can observe the transactional expression of an interpersonal conflict. Another common observation is that aspects of messages can be sent or received outside of the conscious awareness of one or more of the communicants. Incongruent and unrecognized beliefs, needs, or feelings often are, of course, the problem when a contract made at one time and place is not followed through at another.

To avoid the self-defeating practice of making "corrupt" contracts, therapists need to be attuned to certain signals, which are the various communicational clues to incongruence and conflict:

> The goal of the therapeutic contract, of course, is what the patient offers to do for himself, to change; the goal of the psychological contract may be the secret resolve . . . not to change anything. The latter is usually stated in what I call the first "con," when I first hear the (patient's hidden) statement that he has no intention of changing.
> There are hundreds of clues to the first con: "would like to," "perhaps," "just," "maybe," "you know," "can't" (which usually means "won't"), "I should quit drinking" means, "I don't intend to, but my husband wants me to." (5, pp. 206-207)

The scope of this discussion does not permit an attempt to detail techniques for circumventing the effects of "psychological" or ulterior contracts, a list which would ultimately include the full range of helping skills. The general principle involved, clearly, is that the possible operation of such contracts has to be a central concern, and that formally agreed-upon goals cannot be effectively pursued unless ulterior contracts are simultaneously dealt with. Another principle affirms the desirability of explicitness. It is hard to think of exceptions to a general rule that an ongoing responsibility of the worker is to make as much of the contract, including its transactional aspects, as explicit as is possible, given due consideration for the many other factors that may need to be taken into account.

An important implication of the transactional viewpoint is that research on formal contracts alone can go only so far since the communication process by which they are developed and implemented is a critical variable. Fortunately, sound research methodology for measuring such variables and their relationship to outcome is being developed (11, 12), so the opportunity is available to anchor this aspect of practice in a solid empirical base.

One final point remains. As an ubiquitous transactional event, the contract should not be considered of interest to direct practice alone. The clinical focus of this paper is not intended to imply a limited application of the concept. The fact that an aspect of agreement operates in any interpersonal situation means that contracts are a tool that can be put to use wherever people need to collaborate. It also means that inattention to formal and ulterior agreements is a potential problem far beyond the boundaries of the helping relationship.

Summary

Contracts have been viewed through three different lenses in this discussion. The first differentiates various kinds of contracts, identifying and organizing a number of usages of the word in the literature. Most uses can be accommodated if the concept is understood to be complex rather than simple, representing events that take various forms. The second lens brings the developmental aspect of contracting into focus, highlighting the linkage between the changing tasks called contracting and the fluid context of the helping relationship within which they are performed. The third lens isolates the aspect of contracting which gives the concept unity. Whatever forms it may take, the thread that runs throughout is the transactional process of negotiating agreement about the limits, goals, and structure of any relationship.

Each focus brings special problems and features into the foreground, and there are several examples of unfortunate consequences that can arise if a limited understanding prevails. It is hoped that each way of viewing the contract has been demonstrated to contribute substantially to practice, education, research, and the simple management of daily affairs.

References

1. Brammer, L. *The Helping Relationship: Process and Skills*. Englewood Cliffs, New Jersey: Prentice-Hall, 1973.
2. Estes, R., and Henry, S. "The Therapeutic Contract in Work with Groups: A Formal Analysis." *Social Service Review*. 50 (4, 1976): 611-22.
3. Fischer, J. *Effective Casework Practice: An Eclectic Approach*. New York: McGraw-Hill, 1978.
4. Goldstein, H. *Social Work Practice: A Unitary Approach*. Columbia, South Carolina: University of South Carolina Press, 1973.
5. Goulding, R., and Goulding, M. *The Power is in the Patient: A TA/Gestalt Approach to Psychotherapy*. San Francisco: TA Press, 1978.
6. Hollis, F. "The Psychosocial Approach to Casework," In R. Roberts and R. Nee, eds. *Theories of Social Casework*. Chicago: University of Chicago Press, 1970.
7. Maluccio, A. "Action as a Tool in Casework Practice." *Social Casework*. 55 (1, 1974): 30-35.
8. Maluccio, A., and Marlow, W. "The Case for the Contract." In B. Compton and B. Galaway, eds. *Social Work Processes*. Homewood, Illinois: The Dorsey Press, 1975.
9. Rapoport, L. "Crisis Intervention as a Mode of Treatment." In R. Roberts and R. Nee, eds. *Theories of Social Casework*. Chicago: University of Chicago Press, 1970.
10. Reid, W., and Epstein, L. *Task Centered Practice*. New York: Columbia University Press, 1977.
11. Rhodes, S. "Contract Negotiation in the Initial Stage of Casework Service." *Social Service Review*. 51 (1, 1977): 125-140.
12. Rhodes, S. "Communication and Interaction in the Worker-Client Dyad." *Social Service Review*. 52 (1, 1978): 122-31.
13. Saltzman, C., Leutgert, M., Roth, C., Creaser, J., and Howard, L. "Formation of a Therapeutic Relationship: Experiences During the Initial Phase of Psychotherapy as Predictors of Treatment Duration and Outcome." *Journal of Consulting and Clinical Psychology*. 44 (4, 1976): 546-555.
14. Schertz, F. "Theory and Practice of Family Therapy." In R. Roberts and R. Nee, eds. *Theories of Social Casework*. Chicago: University of Chicago Press, 1970.
15. Seabury, B. "The Contract: Uses, Abuses and Limitations." *Social Work*. 21 (1, 1976): 16-21.
16. Siporin, M. *Introduction to Social Work Practice*. New York: Macmillan, 1975.
17. Thomas, E. "Behavioral Modification and Casework." In R. Roberts and R. Nee, eds. *Theories of Social Casework*. Chicago: University of Chicago Press, 1970.
18. Watzlawick, P., Beavin, J., and Jackson, D. *Pragmatics of Human Communication: A Study of Interactional Patterns, Pathologies, and Paradoxes*. New York: Norton, 1967.

6

Paradox: A Common Element in Individual and Family Psychotherapy

Allon Bross and Peter Gove

This paper advances the thesis that "paradox" represents a common element underlying both individual and family psychotherapies. In support of this position, a selected array of individual and family psychotherapies is examined. In each case, paradox is shown to be an important element of the therapeutic model in question. On the basis of this data, it is concluded that (1) the client must accept the therapist's interventive pretext for change to occur, (2) the design and delivery of the directive is crucial, (3) the use of paradox is especially helpful with clients who engage in repetitive interactional sequences, and (4) all therapies contain paradoxical elements.

Introduction

In generic terms, psychotherapy is an approach to treatment. Relying primarily on verbal means, its practitioners seek to reduce or eliminate dysfunctional behaviour in a client (whether an individual or a family) and to induce more adaptive means of coping with life's exigencies. The means by which these ends are to be achieved, however, are legion. Not only is a wide range of models of psychotherapy available, but wider variation exists within and among existing models—Goldenberg (11), for example, lists no less than nine models of family therapy (to which we would be inclined to add several more).

In view of this, how is one to choose among these models on grounds other than personal preference or taste?

1. One method is to compare and contrast models on the basis of their empirical performance. Not only are such tests notoriously complex and difficult (18), but those models that claim to achieve theoretical closure (e.g., psychoanalysis) resist quantitative analysis in principle.

2. A second approach is to compare and contrast models on purely logical grounds (5). While interesting and certainly intellectually stimulating, this approach cannot hope to offer definitive results and will certainly fail to sway those already committed.

3. A third approach eschews the effort to select any competing model, and instead seeks to integrate two or more of them into a new more general hybrid model (18). While often creative and extremely interesting, such

efforts face the very real difficulty of accommodating assumptions which may be diametrically opposed. Furthermore, they are often quite rightly used with scepticism, as they may seek to incorporate elements of existing models which have themselves yet to receive empirical validation, thus compounding one aspect of ignorance with another.

4. A final approach endeavours to transcend existing models altogether, not by degradation, but rather by abstraction, that is, by seeking to determine what elements are common to all approaches to psychotherapy (8). On the one hand, this approach is clearly highly risky; it is the most general, the most abstract, the most difficult to test, and the most likely to be rejected. On the other hand it may be the most fruitful of the various approaches listed above; it is the most enlightening, the most potentially practical, and has the most explanatory power. In these senses, the search for common elements of psychotherapy is not only potentially fruitful, but it has only received relative and scanty attention in recent years.

In this context, increasing recent attention to the use of "paradox" in psychotherapy (19) is of signal importance. For purposes of the present paper, therapeutic paradox may be defined as any intervention in which a practitioner prescribes an ongoing course of dysfunctional behaviour with the intent of mobilizing client resistance such that the behaviour in question either diminishes or ceases.

Unfortunately, it has been our experience that this technique is either poorly understood and/or is badly misused. Often, average therapists learning about this technique either "sanctified" it as a magical, complex notion that only a few gifted therapists dare tamper with, or they have oversimplified it to the point where it has become the solution for every clinical problem, simply at the cost of a clear understanding of the dynamics of the case. Furthermore, the technique is often exclusively associated with family therapists' approach to treatment. In contrast to this view, it will be the thesis of the present paper that "paradox" represents a common element of virtually all psychotherapies, whether oriented towards the individual or the family. Accordingly the objectives of this paper are threefold: (1) to explore the use of paradox in a range of conventional, individually oriented psychotherapies; (2) to examine the use of paradox among family therapies; and (3) to indicate the several ways in which "paradox" represents one aspect of all the psychotherapies discussed.

Conventional Approaches to Individual Psychotherapy: The Use of Paradox

At the level of theory, individual psychotherapies have several features in common: first, as the name implies, they focus on the individual client seen alone, and thus assume that it is both possible and appropriate to see the individual in isolation from his or her social surround; second, they accept a linear view of causality, that is, dysfunctional behaviour may be understood in terms of a cause-and-effect chain stretching from the present into the past; finally, they assume that causality is uni-directional, that is, effects in the present are always the product of events or causes in the past.

At the level of practice, however, individual psychotherapies vary widely, from the insight of psychoanalysis to the environmental shaping of behaviour modification. Despite these variations, however, paradox plays at least some role in all of them. Indeed, two very well-known individual psychotherapists, Victor Frankl and Alfred Adler, can properly be described as pioneers in the development of the technique of paradox.

Of the two, Adler was probably the first to write about paradox as a therapeutic strategy. Essentially, he viewed paradox as dialectic wherein the patient wants to maintain but simultaneously relinquish his symptom (15). Change, he felt, occurred as a result of an increase in self-esteem by the client when, in a power move, the client rejects the therapist's suggestion that he or she maintain the symptom.

A closely related formulation is advanced by Frankl (9), as part of his theory of existential psychiatry known as logotherapy. This is especially evident with respect to his techniques of "paradoxical intention" and "de-reflection." With respect to the former, Frankl (10) suggests paradoxical intention is an appropriate technique for use with obsessive-compulsive or phobic individuals. The occurrence of a given symptom, for example, evokes from the patient the fearful expectation (anticipatory anxiety) that it will recur. However, the fear itself tends to bring about that which is feared, so a problem-maintaining, vicious cycle is established. In this context, the therapist encourages the person to do what he or she fears the most in order that the person stops fleeing his or her fears, thus breaking the feedback loop and solving the problem. Frankl suggests that this intervention forces the individual to step back from his problems, viewing them with detachment, something he calls "self-transcendence" (10).

With respect to the latter, Frankl (10) describes the use of "de-reflection" in situations in which there is sexual dysfunction between members of a couple. He suggests that when an individual is concerned about a problem of sexual satisfaction the individual tends to withdraw from his or her partner and concentrates on what is happening within himself or herself. This decreases the amount of sexual excitation available from the partner escalating the degree to which the person withdraws into self. The result of this process is again a vicious cycle. In this situation, Frankl's intervention is to prescribe that the couple not have sex at all for a certain amount of time, the rationale being that this will tend to relieve the anticipatory anxiety which initiates the vicious cycle. The technique is paradoxical in that the client is directed to do what is feared the most—abstain from sex.

Another variation on the use of paradox is to be found in that form of psychoanalysis known as "direct analysis" (20). Developed as a method for working with schizophrenic patients, the therapist takes the metaphoric statements of the schizophrenic patient completely seriously and insists that the patient do the same. Theoretically, this creates deliberate confusion between the symbol and the thing symbolized, thus emphasizing the difference between the metaphoric and the literal, and forcing the patient to distinguish between the two. The approach is paradoxical insofar as the schizophrenic's difficulty is the inability to distinguish between the different levels of a message; by deliberately confusing them, the therapist is simply asking the patient to keep having the same problem (3).

In a related fashion, the change process within Gestalt therapy contains important paradoxical elements. As Beisser (4) explains, "Change occurs when one becomes what he is, not when he tries to become what he is not. Change does not occur through a cohesive attempt by the individual or by another person to change him, but it does take place if one takes the time and effort to be what he is—to be fully invested in his current positions. By rejecting the role of change agent, we make meaningful and ordinary change possible." The reason for this, Naranjo (16) suggests, is that "Experiencing the compulsive quality of brooding (past) or planning (future) may be inseparable from an appreciation of an alternative to them, and of a true understanding of the distinction between these states of mind and present centredness."

Finally, perhaps, the explicit description of the use of the therapeutic paradox is found among the behavioural therapies. An early example is the work of Dunlap (7), who developed a technique that he refers to as "negative practice." At the time, he was concerned with a particular problem: whether repeating a particular behaviour made the behaviour more or less likely to occur under any given circumstances. Dunlap hypothesized that sheer repetition of a behaviour was not enough to increase the rate of occurrence of that behaviour; rather, the behaviour had to be paired with certain positive factors in a simple operant-conditioning paradigm. Conversely, he suggested that pairing the same behaviour with negative factors would lead to its extinction. More specifically, Dunlap proposed that two major factors would need to be paired with the behaviour at any time, these being affective factors (i.e., feeling) and ideational factors (i.e., emitting the behaviour because one has been told to do so as opposed to having the behaviour occur involuntarily). If the behaviour could be made to occur when these factors differed from involuntary occurrence, the behaviour should cease. Accordingly, Dunlap's approach to treatment was to simply have the patient "practise" the unwanted behaviour.

This approach to treatment is strikingly similar to the early behavioural technique of "massed practice" (19). In accord with this approach, the patient is encouraged to emit as many of the unwanted behaviours as possible within the permitted time frame. Raskin and Klien (19) suggest that the resultant fatigue or boredom creates a change in the stimulus properties making it unlikely that the behaviour will be spontaneously emitted again in the same setting.

A similar process would appear to underlie a number of more recent behavioural techniques. Flooding and desensitization, for example, involve confronting the patient with the stimuli which cause the distress. These two techniques may be considered to be opposite ends of a continuum of intensity, with "flooding" involving rapid confrontation of the patient with distressing stimuli resulting in the evocation of intense emotion, while "desensitization" involves a more gradual build-up to the problem stimuli with the intent of maintaining emotional response at a lower level (2). These and related techniques may utilize mental imagery or actual confrontation with the stimulus, and may or may not be paired with relaxation techniques. Suggested mechanisms for the success of such approaches include habituation of the subject to the anxiety-invoking stimuli, suggestion, and expectancy; and, where the anxiety-producing stimuli are paired with relaxation, the incompatibility of the learned response (anxiety) with the relaxation response (28). In any case, however, all of those techniques have at their root the use of paradox, that is, the injunction that the patient engage in behaviour, whether metaphorically or in fantasy, that is intensely distressing as a means of extinguishing that behaviour.

In sum, then, in the present section we have briefly examined a selected array of well-known and commonly used individual psychotherapies. While the treatment methods across therapies vary widely, all involve, as a central component, the use of a therapeutic paradox.

Family Therapies: The Use of Paradox

Like individual therapies, family therapies share a number of common features. These features, however, contrast sharply with those of the individual therapies. More specifically, family therapies (1) focus on the relationship between and among family members, thus assuming that individual behaviour is meaningless or, more precisely, uninterpretable, when seen in isolation from the social context of which it is a part; (2) adopt a non-linear or circular view of causality in which dysfunctional behaviour is seen as the reflection of a particular pattern of reciprocal, interpersonal interaction, and is thus interpreted as a relational phenomena; and (3) accepts the notion that such patterns of interaction are created and maintained by interpersonal forces in the present and thus have no necessary relationship to past states or processes.

Given this assumptive base, however, family therapies vary widely in actual practice, although many of the most well-known are explicit in their use of paradox. Before briefly reviewing the similarities and differences among those therapies, however, it is instructive to consider their common roots in the work of Gregory Bateson.

Bateson (3) begins with the notion that all mammals are capable of changing to adapt to their circumstances, but that the changes are a product of trial-and-error feedback loops which are psychically and biologically expensive. To deal with this expense, mammals are capable of forming habits (interactional patterns) which can be applied to classes of problems. One such problem class concerns the relationship between mammals. When an individual animal is put in the "wrong" regarding its rules or habits concerning a relationship with another animal, the individual is placed in what Bateson calls a "double bind," what is, in effect, a paradox. He suggests that such a situation can promote severe pain and maladjustment. However, if this pathology can be warded off or resisted, the experience can promote "deutro-learning," that is the development of habits, rules, or patterns which creatively transcend the contradictions (i.e., the paradox) of the previous relational context.

This theoretical foundation is the essential basis upon which a number of clinical theoreticians apply paradoxical interventions to systems of interpersonal relationships (12, 13, 14, 17, 22, 26). Despite their common roots, however, it is all too apparent that these diverge sharply in the ways in which they conceptualize and apply paradox.

Jay Haley (12, 13), for example, discusses the paradox inherent in both the general context of the psychotherapeutic process and the function of a symptomatic family member within a network of relationships.

With respect to the former, the context of psychotherapy dictates that while the client participates in a voluntary relationship for the purpose of change he or she does so within a framework of the involuntary necessity for change. Haley suggests that it is the successful resolution of this paradoxical situation that produces a successful outcome. In other words, it is the successful resolution of paradox that is the basic mechanism of change rather than increased self-awareness and understanding.

With respect to the latter, the symptom-bearer has an advantage in gaining control and defining the relationship with other family members. Distortions in hierarchy may occur when a member of a lower hierarchical level gains control over the emotional state of members of a higher hierarchical level. For example, by developing a symptom a child may control the emotional state of its parents. Paradoxically, then, the harder the parents try to deal with the child's difficulty, the more powerful the symptom (and the child) becomes.

The application of paradox occurs when the therapist encourages the client or family to maintain the undesirable behaviour, but within the context of the necessity for change. Consequently, the paradox always involves the communication of two messages, "change" but "don't change" (13). The client moves towards the treatment goal by proving the therapist wrong. In turn, giving up the symptom produces a change in the relationships which previously maintained it, thus re-establishing an appropriate parent-child hierarchy. This interpretation derives from

Haley's claim that the symptom has a function for all members of the family.

In complementary fashion, Madanes (14), an associate of Haley, has suggested a number of paradoxical approaches to the re-establishment of an appropriate family hierarchy. She suggests that having parents demand that the child exhibit the symptom destroys its effectiveness by bringing a formerly uncontrollable behaviour under the control of the parents. Madanes also describes a number of techniques wherein family members are asked to play act overtly what is actually happening covertly. For example, the therapist may ask a parent to request that the child "pretend" to help them. By "pretending" in this way the distorted hierarchy becomes overt, thus inducing the child and the parents to resist the inappropriateness of this form of family organization.

Watzlawick et al. (25, 26) provide a somewhat different interpretation of paradox. From their perspective, symptomatic behaviour evolves and is maintained as a result of repetitive circular sequences which become embedded in the interactional patterns of the system. The individual members of the system are not able to meta-communicate on the sequences which are maintaining the problem because any such communication would be part of the sequence. In accord with the theory of logical types, a communication that is part of a set (the sequence) cannot be a generalization about the set because the result would be self-reflexive and paradoxical, and therefore impossible to respond to. In other words, the player cannot comment on the game because all comments are part of the game.

A good example of this situation is the mother who insists that her son do his homework because he enjoys it, not only because he has been told to do it. The command to do homework is made on a primary logical level and can be responded to quite effectively by the son. The command to enjoy it, however, is made on a secondary logical level; it is a comment on how the homework is to be done. Consequently, the son is left in the "bind" of doing his homework for the wrong reasons, or not doing his homework for the right reasons. Either the son does not do his homework, or does it for the wrong reasons, so the mother re-applies her paradoxical injunction, and the cycle perpetuates itself, creating what Watzlawick et al. have called "the game without end."

In order to disrupt these "vicious" cycles, Watzlawick et al. have designed a number of therapeutic interventions aimed not at what the family defines as the problem, but rather at the family's attempted solutions. Their interventions are based on the concept of "second-order change," which involves placing the situation, including both the problems and the attempted solutions, in a different "frame" which "lifts the situation out of the conflict-engendering trap created by the self-reflexiveness of the attempted solution. . . ." (26) The paradoxical intervention, prescribing the continuation of the problem, "defuses" the paradoxical nature of the attempted solution applied by system members and results in the disappearance of the problem.

Still another variation on the theme of paradox is advanced by Selvini-Palazzoli et al. (21, 22) who view family interaction as consisting of a series of symptom-maintaining paradoxes. The behaviour of family members is not viewed as benevolent attempts to deal with the symptoms; rather, family members are seen as engaged in a struggle for control in which paradoxical and dysfunctional communication are both tactics in the struggle, and indeed attempts to disguise it.

There are two main components to their approach:

1. Positive connotation is applied to everything that the family offers in therapy. The authors suggest that the dysfunctional family is an extremely rigid system and that all requests for change are perceived as threatening. Consequently, connoting all that the family does as positive is beneficial because the therapist is received by the system as a co-conspirator interested in maintaining the homeostasis.

2. Symptomatic behaviour is connoted in a particular way for interventive purposes. This is done in such a manner as to leave family members in an untenable position, thus throwing the system into confusion and reshuffling the relational forces of the family. The therapist is thus aligned with the homeostatic tendency of the system, but, in so doing, has paradoxically reframed the behaviour in such a way that change becomes necessary.

In a recent article, Deff (6) has suggested that this approach be called "double paradoxical" because there are actually two paradoxes contained in the directive. The initial positive connotation applied to all of the family's behaviours can be seen as equivalent to "prescribing the symptom," which is a paradoxical manoeuvre in itself. The second part of the intervention involves presenting the family with benevolent reasons for their behaviour (e.g., "You behave in the way you do out of loving, self-sacrificing motivation."), but, paradoxically, these reasons radically contradict family members' premises about the family.

Recently, Selvini-Palazzoli (23) has suggested that the approach of the Milan group is not necessarily paradoxical in accord with any dictionary definition of the term. Rather, she states that people are most influenced when they expect a certain message and receive instead a message at a totally different level. The most effective therapeutic interventions, therefore, are those which are the most unexpected. The intervention is not necessarily designed to be logically paradoxical. Rather, it is designed to be completely unexpected in the context of the premise or meaning system of the family, the expectation being that in so doing the internal coherence of the system will be disrupted, forcing reorganization into a different configuration.

A further variation on the use of paradoxical intervention is seen in the work of Peggy Papp (17). The distinguishing characteristic of the Papp approach is the utilization of a consultation group, composed of colleagues observing the therapy, that acts as a Greek chorus. This group is utilized at the discretion of the therapist to "support, confront, confuse, challenge, or provoke the family" (17). This approach to paradox is based on three concepts: "the concept of the family as a self-regulatory system, the concept of the symptom as a mechanism for self-regulation, and the concept of systemic resistance to change."

Moreover, Papp describes three different types of paradox. The first involves "redefining" the symptom in such a benign way as to make it an essential part of the family system. The second involves "prescribing" that the symptom maintain patterns of behaviour positively, in order that it lose its power of problem maintenance. The third involves "restraining" the family from changing so that in fact they can continue to change.

Once again, we have seen, in sum, that while wide variation exists among family therapies, in terms of the interpretation and implementation of therapeutic paradox, it nonetheless remains a central component of each of these therapeutic approaches. Furthermore, unlike their individual counterparts, these approaches to psychotherapy make the use of paradox explicit and continue to work at developing increasingly effective, paradoxical intervention techniques.

Paradox as a Common Element of Psychotherapy

The present paper has examined the use of paradox in a series of individual and family therapies. This examination suggests that in several respects paradox may represent a common element underlying all of them.

First, the underlying assumptions of the psychodynamic, behavioural, and interpersonal approaches to treatment result in a variety of therapeutic pretexts designed to encourage more of the client's undesirable or symptomatic behaviour with a view to eliminating it. This suggests that a common feature of effective psychotherapy is that the client accept the therapist's interventive pretext, which, in turn, must match the client's reality. This is crucial, for acceptance, paradoxically, means rejection of the problem-maintaining behaviour and this is independent of the therapeutic model employed. Consequently, it appears that the design and delivery of the paradoxical directive per se may supersede the particular theoretical framework from which the directive is derived. By implication this calls attention to the need for further work on the characteristics of effective paradoxical directives.

Second, it appears that paradoxical interventions may be useful with clients who engage in repetitive interactive sequences, especially in their solution to family problems, whether in relation to another person, idea, or behaviour. The repeated theme of employing paradox to intervene in the "vicious" circle transcends both linear and circular models.

Finally, it would appear that a critical element of all therapeutic modalities examined is that undesirable behaviour be prescribed. This is consistent with Haley's (12) position that all therapies contain paradoxical elements and that it is those elements, rather than the type of therapy itself, which produce effective therapeutic change. Much of what has been discussed in the present article is supportive of that position.

References

1. Adler, A. *Understanding Human Nature*. Greenwich, Conn.: Fawcett Company, 1954.
2. Agras, W. *Behavior Modification: Principles and Clinical Applications*. London: Little, Brown and Company, 1972.
3. Bateson, G. "Double Bind." In G. Bateson, *Steps to an Ecology of Mind*. New York: Ballantine Books: 1972.
4. Beisser, A. "The Paradoxical Theory of Change." In J. Fagan and I. Sheppard, eds. *What is Gestalt Therapy?* New York: Science and Behavior Books Inc., 1970.
5. Benjamin, M. "A Comparative Analysis of Three Explanatory Models of Mental Disorder and a Preferred Focus of Explanation." Unpublished M.A. thesis. Concordia University, Montreal, 1977.
6. Deff, P.F. "Some Irreverent Thoughts on Paradox." *Family Process*. 20 (1, 1981): 37-41.
7. Dunlap, K. *Habits, Their Making and Unmaking*. New York: Liverright, 1932.
8. Frank, J.D. *Persuasion and Healing: A Comparative Study of Psychotherapy*. Rev. ed. Baltimore: Johns Hopkins University Press, 1973.
9. Frankl, V. *Man's Search for Meaning: An Introduction to Logotherapy*. Boston: Beacon Press, 1959.
10. Frankl, V. *The Unheard Cry for Meaning*. New York: Simon and Schuster, 1975.
11. Goldenberg, I., and Goldenberg, H. *Family Therapy: An Overview*. Monterey, California: Brooks-Cole, 1980.
12. Haley, J. *Strategies of Psychotherapy*. New York: Grune and Stratton, 1963.
13. Haley, J. *Problem Solving Therapy*. New York: Harper and Row, 1976.
14. Madanes, C. "Protection, Paradox, and Pretending." *Family Process*. 19, 1980.
15. Mozdierz, G., Maccitelli, F., and Lisiecki, J. "The Paradox in Psychotherapy: An Adlerian Perspective." *Journal of Individual Psychology*. 32 (1976): 169-184.
16. Naranjo, C. "Present Centeredness: Technique, Prescription and Ideal." In J. Fagan and I. Sheppard, eds. *What is Gestalt Therapy?* New York: Science and Behavior Books, 1970.
17. Papp, P. "The Greek Chorus and Other Techniques of Paradoxical Therapy." *Family Process*, 19, 1980.
18. Peterfreund, E. *Information, Systems and Psychoanalysis*. New York: International Universities Press, 1971.
19. Raskin, D., and Klien, Z. "Losing a Symptom Through Keeping It: A Review of Paradoxical Treatment Techniques and Rationale." *Archives of General Psychiatry*. 33 (1976): 548-55.
20. Rosen, J.N. *Direct Analysis*. New York: Grune and Stratton, 1933.
21. Selvini-Palazzoli, M., et al. "The Treatment of Children Through Brief Psychotherapy of the Parents." *Family Process*. 13 (1974): 429-442.

146 / Related Topics

22. Selvini-Palazzoli, M., et al. *Paradox and Counter Paradox*. New York: Jacob Aronson, 1978.
23. Selvini-Palazzoli, M. "Comment," *Family Process*. 1981. A response to the article by P.F. Deff, "Some Irreverent Thoughts on Paradox." *Family Process*. 20 (1, 1981): 37-41.
24. Slipp, S., and Kressel, K. "Difficulties in Family Therapy Evaluation." *Family Process*. 17 (1978): 409-422.
25. Watzlawick, P., Jackson, D., and Weakland, J. *The Pragmatics of Human Communication*. New York: Norton, 1967.
26. Watzlawick, P., Weakland, J., and Fisch, R. *Change*. Toronto: George J. McLeod Ltd., 1974.
27. Weeks, G.R., and L'Abate, L. "A Compilation of Paradoxical Methods." *American Journal of Family Therapy*. 7 (4, 1979): 61-75.
28. Wolpe, J., and Lazarus, A. *Behavior Therapy Techniques*. New York: Pergamon, 1966.

PART 3
CASE STUDIES

7
The Systemic Treatment of
Hysterical Paralysis: A Case Report

Pam Grosman, Allon Bross, and Michael Benjamin

*This report describes the use of strategic family therapy with an adolescent girl diagnosed as hysterical paralysis-conversion type. Treatment involved a total of eight sessions spread over an eleven-week period, with complete symptom removal at termination. The report focusses on (1) the importance of family system processes in the creation and maintenance of symptomatology, and (2) some of the problems of doing this type of therapy within the context of a psychiatric in-patient ward. Several implications of the findings are discussed.**

Introduction

Current psychiatric nosology recognizes two forms of hysterical neurosis, dissociation and conversion reaction (2). The latter is a functional disorder characterized by a variety of physiological symptoms, including blindness, deafness, the loss of smell (anosmia), general or circumscribed loss of feeling or sensation (anesthesia, paresthesia), failure of muscle co-ordination (ataxia), restricted or irregular movement (akinesia, dyskinesia), and, finally, paralysis. The disorder (conversion reaction) is usually associated with adolescent females (18) and is comparatively rare (19). Nevertheless, it has received an inordinate amount of attention in the research literature, dating back to the classic works of Charcot and Freud (see 19).

Most of this work has focussed on the question of etiology, with treatment per se receiving relatively scanty attention (22, 18). In general, two etiological perspectives prevail in the literature. The first is behaviouristic in orientation and views conversion reaction as an adaptive response to a frustrating life situation (3). Physiological symptoms are thus thought to represent the product of an instrumental learning process shaped by a specific set of environmental reinforcement contingencies (23).

The second and rather more influential view is psychoanalytic in orientation. This holds that conversion reaction results from the displace-

*To ensure confidentiality, the names, ages, and family particulars of this case have been altered.

The authors wish to thank Dr. A. Froese for his co-operation and support on this case.

ment or "conversion" of psychic energy from the psychic to the somatic realm (21). Precipitated by a stressful or threatening situation in the present, the process is thought to originate in childhood, wherein unacceptable incestuous or aggressive ideas and impulses are frustrated through repression. Unavailable to the ego, the resulting intrapsychic conflict seeks unconscious expression through somatic means (7, 8).

Both behavioural and psychoanalytic approaches, then, place primary emphasis on the individual as the symptom bearer and, concomitantly, view the individual patient as the unit of treatment.

While this view of conversion reaction is widely accepted, a number of authors in recent years have begun to call attention to the role of parents in symptom formation. Rock (22), for example, notes a parental configuration involving an over-protective mother coupled with a peripheral father in each of the ten cases he examined. This, he suggests, indicates that parents contribute to symptom formation by encouraging the child's symptom(s) as a way of deflecting anxiety away from their own problems. Erhlich and Fisher (9) present a similar formulation with respect to orthopedic conversion reaction, noting in addition the "symbiotic" nature of the parent-child relationship. Finally, Yates (29) supports this view, concluding that attention to family dynamics is a prerequisite for successful treatment outcome.

While suggesting the need for a revision of the traditional conception of conversion reaction, these authors remain firmly attached to a psychodynamic perspective. While parents may contribute to symptom formation, the disorder clearly remains "within" the patient and it is the individual who remains the central focus of treatment. Further, even if symptoms are associated with environmental events or figures, they remain fundamentally epiphenomenal and, as such, are to be understood merely as indicators of an underlying intrapsychic process. Consequently, it is the amelioration of that process that is the primary aim of treatment and the only sure and certain route to a permanent cure (19).

This approach to conversion reaction rests on the fundamental assumption that it is possible to view and treat the individual in isolation from the social surroundings. There is a growing body of work, however, that suggests that this assumption is untenable (12, 26, 5, 4, 6, 14, 28). Operating from a systems perspective, proponents of this view argue that a family unit, for example, represents an indivisible whole in which the term "family member" refers to a relational, rather than an individual status. In this sense, the family system involves much more than "merely" the sum of the personalities which make it up; rather, it involves a complex network of emergent, patterned interactional processes, many of them not apparent to the participants. In the present context, this suggests that conversion reaction may be conceptualized, not as an indicator of individual psychopathology, but rather as symptomatic of a dysfunctional family system.

Accordingly, it is the family system per se, rather than just the symptom bearer, that requires treatment. The aim of such intervention is not to "cure illness," but rather to restructure and reorganize dysfunctional family relationships (16, 11).

Efforts at family intervention, however, are complicated by a related systemic issue, namely, that the context of intervention itself has systemic properties. This is especially evident with respect to a common context within which patients suffering conversion reaction are offered treatment: the psychiatric in-patient ward. When seen through the "lens" of systems theory, the array of professionals comprising ward staff themselves constitute a system within which the patient family is embedded and with which it interacts. It follows that effective system intervention must include the participation of all relevant system elements, that is, the patient and family together with those members of the staff with whom they regularly interact (13).

Unfortunately, neither family intervention with respect to conversion reaction nor the systemic properties of the treatment context has thus far received focussed attention in the research literature. The present paper is a contribution aimed at remedying this situation.

Specifically, this paper describes the treatment of a case of hysterical paralysis (conversion type) using strategic family therapy (10, 27). This is a mode of therapy that is directive, present-focussed, goal-oriented, and is primarily concerned with symptom alleviation and family restructuring, rather than the induction of insight. In addition, we describe some of the difficulties associated with employing this technique in the context of a psychiatric in-patient ward.

The Presenting Problem

The identified patient, Sheila H., age 14, was referred to the Adolescent Medicine Clinic in January, 1980. This is an out-patient medical facility, part of a major children's hospital in Metropolitan Toronto, Canada. At that time, her presenting problems included weight loss, social isolation, stomach aches, and progressive weakness that had developed over the preceding month to the point where Sheila was paralyzed, unable to walk, or even hold up her head. Medical testing had immediately ruled out all possible organic causes; she was diagnosed "hysterical paralysis-conversion type." Treatment primarily consisted of individual psychotherapy together with physiotherapy exercises aimed at retaining muscle strength; the attending psychiatrist also saw the parents alone on several occasions. No medication was given.

After twelve weeks of treatment (January to March), the patient showed minimal improvement. It was concluded by the attending psychiatrist that the patient required more intensive treatment than could be provided on an out-patient basis. Accordingly, Sheila was transferred to the

Adolescent and Family Unit, an in-patient psychiatric facility in the same hospital.

Initial Assessment

The Adolescent and Family Unit is a 12-bed facility. Treatment is eclectic in orientation, with the average patient remaining on the ward for three to six weeks, followed by continued out-patient treatment.

Initial contact with Sheila and her mother was made by nursing staff. This revealed that (1) father was an alcoholic; (2) mother and daughter attended Al-Anon together; (3) mother and daughter had an extremely close relationship; (4) the marital relationship was a source of bitter and continuing conflict; and (5) mother was seriously thinking of leaving father but was restrained from doing so by the seriousness of her daughter's illness.

A routine family assessment was then done by a psychiatric resident. Together with observations made by ward staff, this uncovered the following information: physically, Sheila was unable to walk, sit in an unsupported position (except with the use of a wheelchair), or make her bed independently; while she had normal strength and movement in her arms and could feed herself, she required assistance with hygiene, full dressing, and getting into and out of bed; further, she was underweight by approximately ten pounds (4.5 kg), was vomitting on admission to the ward, complained that she had previously had headaches and dizziness, and showed wide muscle-tone fluctuation; significantly, however, it was noted that she showed occasional, slight, voluntary leg movements when she believed herself to be unobserved; emotionally, Sheila was sad and forlorn, refused to join her peers in ward activity, and preferred to sit alone; she believed that ward staff was unsympathetic to her dilemma and was herself resistant in consequence; she showed no insight, being unable to relate her medical problem to a psychological cause; finally, she had little motivation to work on a pre-planned exercise regime and, generally, seemed unwilling to change.

This assessment also provided the following brief family vignette. Including Sheila, the H family consisted of four members. Mr. H., age 54, was an alcoholic and had not worked for the past eight years, since having had a "nervous breakdown." The family existed on his D.V.A.* pension. Mrs. H., age 47, was a housewife; while Sally, age 16, was a high school student. The mother's earlier report of chronic, severe marital conflict and the father's excess drinking were confirmed. Significantly, it was also learned that the family was athletically inclined—both parents loved to go for long walks—although Sheila was the "real" athlete in the family.

This case presented ward staff with a dilemma. A similar case had not

---

*Department of Veterans' Affairs.

been seen on the ward since its inception, in 1977. Consequently, none of the staff had any professional experience to serve as a guide in treatment. Moreover, the patient's resistance and her apparent lack of insight made her an unlikely candidate for individual psychotherapy. It was in the search for some alternative that the therapist suggested strategic family therapy. It was reluctantly and rather sceptically agreed that this could be attempted.

Family Assessment and the Treatment Plan

In order to formulate a treatment plan, another family assessment was conducted by the first author; the second author, acting as consultant, was stationed behind the one-way mirror. This working arrangement was, with only a few exceptions, maintained throughout the course of treatment.

On the basis of this interview, it seemed to us that Mr. H. was the centre of power in the family. He treated his wife like a child, refusing to allow her to go out to work or even to have any significant social contacts. By word and deed, he repeatedly indicated that he believed his wife to be incompetent and therefore constantly in need of his protection. For her part, Mrs. H. acted in a childlike manner in response to her husband, refusing to confront him, instead turning to her daughters, especially Sheila, for advice and support. This emotional distance between husband and wife helped explain Mrs. H.'s unhappiness and her repeated threats to leave him. It also illuminated the intensely close relationship that had gradually evolved between Mrs. H. and her daughters.

In this context, Sheila's response to the nature of her parents' relationship was to align with mother while attacking father. The result was a highly regular and cyclic pattern: father would attack mother; mother would give evidence of anxiety and distress; Sheila would deflect this conflict by attacking father; father and Sheila would argue; then the entire cycle would repeat. Throughout this process, Sally tended to remain aloof, having little contact with her family, especially Sheila. However, because mother and Sheila were aligned against father, he tended, unsuccessfully, to seek support from Sally.

These data suggest a family pattern all too familiar in the family therapy literature (17), namely, one of triangulation involving the violation of hierarchy (16). In other words, Sheila had gradually been sucked into the marital relationship where she was expected, on the one hand, to serve as the medium through which her parents could communicate, thus allowing them to get close without getting too close; on the other hand, she served as the glue that kept her parents together and prevented them from getting so far apart as to threaten the continued stability of the family system. In short, Sheila served to regulate distance and preserve family homeostasis (14).

This particular relational configuration was dysfunctional for the family in a number of ways:

1. The intense closeness of the relationship between Sheila and her

mother interfered with Sheila's ability to grow up and separate from her mother (15).

2. This relationship interfered with the relationship between mother and father, preventing them from confronting and perhaps resolving their differences; it also engendered resentment in father at being excluded from his wife's relationship with Sheila.

3. Father inappropriately turned to Sally, rather than his wife, for support, thus impeding her efforts at separation.

4. The involvement of both daughters in their parents' marital relationship simultaneously prevented them from developing a mutually supportive relationship of their own.

5. Sheila's tendency to attack her father on behalf of her mother meant that Mrs. H. had no opportunity to learn to fight her own battles.

6. Finally, Mr. H.'s "bottle" acted to precipitate conflict between him and his wife, while preventing them from resolving the differences thus created.

This formulation helps explain the maintenance of Sheila's paralysis and suggests the kernel of our treatment plan. Despite the fact that Sheila was able to function autonomously in some areas, as her condition worsened, her mother perpetuated the problem by responding to her daughter's every need. While father was somewhat less accepting of Sheila's state, his concern about her and his desire to help her kept him involved. Moreover, it was apparent that this arrangement had gradually stabilized to the point that it had acquired homeostatic properties.

From this perspective, the objectives of family intervention were clear, namely, (1) to block the parents' efforts to "help" Sheila, and (2) to create distance between Sheila and her parents, thereby extracting her from the marital subsystem and returning her to the sibling subsystem where she belonged. Intense family resistance, however, made it unlikely that the family would respond in a co-operative manner to requests for change in the form of simple tasks. Consequently, we elected to employ a series of "non-co-operative" strategies which primarily involved the use of paradoxical manoeuvres (11, 25). Essentially, such manoeuvres involve two interlocking components: (1) the therapist "prescribes" the symptom in an effort to encourage change by mobilizing the family's tendency to reject (i.e., resist) the therapist's thoughts and ideas; (2) the therapist then offers the family an "illusion of alternatives" whereby it is disadvantageous for them to maintain the symptom as a means of organizing their ongoing relationships.

While this approach to family intervention has proven remarkably effective in a wide range of cases (26, 27), its use in the present instance was complicated by the need to involve ward staff as an integral part of the overall treatment. This was problematic in two respects.

1. First, it was logistically complex. We felt it essential that Sheila and

her family interact consistently with only a limited number of staff members. Moreover, it was important that these staff members be willing, at least temporarily, to accept our treatment plan and carry it out faithfully. Consequently, this required not only careful recruitment of staff, but also the juggling of ward schedules. The co-operation of the chief-of-staff and the head nurse made this task immeasurably easier.

2. Second, and perhaps more important in the long run, we anticipated the possibility of staff resistance. The use of a strategic approach was clearly inconsistent with the psychoanalytic training and perspective of most staff members. Furthermore, the plan placed the therapist, a social worker, in charge of intervention planning and forced the psychiatric resident assigned to the case to withdraw from any active participation and to remain as an observer. This represented a violation of the ward's traditional authority structure. In an effort to pre-empt such resistance, the therapist made extensive and intensive efforts at joining with, and providing support for relevant ward staff. Nevertheless, we suspected such efforts might not be enough. As will readily become apparent, such fears turned out to be well founded.

The Treatment Process

Session 1
The extensive data already available concerning the H family were subsequently confirmed in our first family interview. The family in general and Sheila in particular were each given a paradoxical intervention. To the family as a whole, we said:

> "Mother has been thinking of leaving her husband for a long time, and she has come to the point where she is making that decision again.
>
> Sheila has decided to act like a baby so that mother will not have to make a decision about leaving. Sheila has understood the impending doom, and has decided to stop walking, sensing her mother's strength and conviction about leaving, in order to keep her mother and her father together.
>
> Because she stopped walking, father all along has known that there was no physical problem. It worked precisely the way Sheila planned since father has gotten more involved in getting Sheila to walk.
>
> If Sheila begins to walk, the risks are that mother might leave with the girls, father might increase his drinking, and the family will split up.
>
> This way the family stays together; father is more involved, mother has a reason not to leave, and Sheila has only to sacrifice her legs."

To Sheila alone, we stated:

> "Our team has decided that although your case is most unusual, we thought that part of your problem lay with your subconscious and that we believe that you 'have forgotten how to walk.' We want to trigger this memory in your subconscious, with your approval. You will relearn how

to walk, just as an infant does, progressing from dragging yourself along the floor, to balancing on all fours, to crawling, then to standing, and then finally to walking. Although we aren't certain it will work, it may be worth the effort to try. These training sessions are to be held three times a day in half-hour periods. As much as we hate to do it, you will have to be withdrawn from certain programmes on the ward in order that you can devote your full attention and efforts towards your training programme which includes physiotherapy."

The family intervention had a threefold purpose. First, it redefined or "reframed" Sheila's symptom as useful for each member of the family as it was then organized. Second, it described and explained the meaning of Sheila's symptom for each member of the family. Finally, by describing the functional aspects of Sheila's paralysis in this manner, it became difficult for each family member to continue to relate to each other in the usual manner in order to maintain it.

The intervention directed at Sheila was equally complex in its intent. First, it defined Sheila's symptom in such a manner as to remove any interpersonal advantages it might offer her in relation to ward staff. Second, by making reference to "your subconscious," we were using symbolic language that was acceptable to both Sheila and the relevant ward staff. Third, it created a situation whereby the ward staff could benevolently accept Sheila's paralysis as real, be supportive of her dilemma, and yet make it difficult for her to maintain her symptom. Fourth, it delivered a metaphoric message to Sheila directly and, through her, to the rest of her family: if Sheila was going to behave like a helpless "baby," then she must act like a baby. Fifth, by referring to Sheila's "approval," it sought to pre-empt refusal, while simultaneously giving her the illusion of choice. Finally, physiotherapy was included in the treatment plan, since muscular inactivity results in muscle atrophy. Muscle building would be required for a successful outcome.

Neither of these interventions was spontaneous. Rather, like all of our subsequent interventions, it was carefully planned ahead of time. Moreover, this approach to the problem was not undertaken lightly. Not only might Sheila have refused to co-operate, but there was also the possibility that the staff might balk as well, in the face of an aversive procedure that was quite outside their clinical experience. Despite these very real risks, an incisive intervention seemed essential because we regarded Sheila's paralysis as extremely serious and likely to become chronic if not interrupted quickly.

The results of these interventions were dramatic: within five days, Sheila showed visible improvement; she was able to extend her head and had increased her trunk strength; she was determined to reject the "truth" of our message and vigorously attempted to prove that her paralysis was not needed in order to keep the family together; at the same time, ward staff members were amazed at the results and were very enthusiastic.

Session 2

By Session 2, not only had Sheila begun to improve, but Mr. and Mrs. H. reported that they totally rejected the need for Sheila to remain paralyzed in order to keep them together. Furthermore, as part of an alliance both against our therapeutic message and Mr. H.'s alcoholism, Mr. and Mrs. H. jointly attended an A.A. meeting, the first time this had occurred. The combination of Sheila's physical improvement plus the change in the marital relationship had the family in an optimistic mood. In order to maintain this momentum and further mobilize the family's resistance, we reiterated our central message:

> "If Sheila is to begin to walk, mother will be depressed without someone to look after, and father might turn to the bottle. Sally might feel alone. We still feel that the family needs Sheila's symptom."

At the same time, we wanted to increase the physical and emotional distance between Sheila and her mother. Since Sheila was to go home that weekend, we delivered the following "homework" task:

> "Father, it will be your job to keep mother from helping Sheila at home. Sally, if your sister needs anything, you are to help her. The exercises that Sheila does on the ward are to be done at home, and Sally, not mother, is to help her with them."

Finally, as a further hedge against a cessation of therapeutic change, the consultant (behind the one-way mirror) was used to caution everyone in the family against "improving too quickly" since this would, in his view, only have negative effects.

Following this session, Sheila continued to improve on the ward. By dragging her body, she was doing many lengths of her room, and had progressed to the point where she was practising leg and neck raises in each "training session." In physiotherapy, she had begun to stand with support at the parallel bars. Ward staff continued to play its role faithfully and remained impressed by Sheila's improvement.

Session 3

Father and Sally did not attend the third session. Available data on the case showed a number of positive changes. Our intention in this session was to continue the process of separating mother and Sheila by indirectly encouraging mother to deal with her marital problems by herself. We also wished to introduce the idea that Sheila might soon be returning home.

Accordingly, we presented mother and Sheila with the following observation:

> "Considering our observations of Sheila's progress on the ward, her tremendously hard work, terrific potential for athletics, and her present muscle strength, the team is puzzled as to her lack of progress. We

wondered whether there was some reason she would not like to go home, and hence, preferred to stay in the hospital."

We also pointed out that Sheila may prefer to avoid the fighting at home:

"We know Mom and Dad fight and that you protect mother by fighting with father. We don't blame you for not wanting to return to that situation."

We had Sheila and her mother discuss these observations. In the process, we commented on Sheila's admirable loyalty to mother, even to the extent that Sheila would willingly give up boys, dating, and girlfriends. In the discussion that ensued, Sheila rejected our interpretation, insisting that she was making progress and that the family was beginning to change.

We closed the session by telling Sheila that "she can't *stand* up to her mother and father so that she might never be able to leave them." While directed at Sheila, this metaphorical message was intended for both mother and daughter: with respect to Sheila, it implicitly equated standing with independence; with respect to mother, it suggested that Sheila would walk when mother was able to "stand up" to her husband by herself.

Finally, we suggested to Sheila that "she could go home as soon as she wished." The message offered her an "illusion of alternatives." *We* gave her permission to take control of her progress, thus making it appear as if she was in charge; moreover, it suggested that her choice consisted of walking "now" or walking "later." In either case, the outcome would achieve our treatment goal.

Session 3 appeared to us to be the turning point in the case. While Sheila had previously been making progress, the pace of change had slowed considerably. From this point on, however, she showed sustained progress. She began to make a sincere effort to crawl, could lift her head partially, and could stand up at the parallel bars. Most important, she began to talk about walking.

Things were also going well at home. Father continued to attend A.A. meetings, and mother and father reported an improvement in their marital relationship.

For the first time, we decided to join in the family's excitement about these changes. To this end, the following comment was made to Sheila by the therapist: "This is a miracle. You will begin to walk." Sheila's response was ecstatic. However, to ensure continued progress, the following message was delivered by the therapist: "The consultant predicts that Sheila's progress will be short-lived. Father will start to drink again, which will rekindle mother's frustration, requiring assistance from her two daughters."

Interestingly, it was at this juncture that staff interest in the treatment plan began to flag noticeably. Rather than commenting on these changes, as they had done previously, they appeared to lose interest entirely. While this may, in part, have been a function of habituation, we tended to view it more as a form of passive resistance. Such changes in Sheila were inconsistent with a psychoanalytic perspective and thus threatened a variety of long-held views regarding what "proper" psychotherapy should be about. Further, these changes appeared to justify a radical (if temporary) change in ward structure and organization. This too was threatening.

Sessions 4 and 5

Our efforts to reunite mother and father while creating distance between mother and daughter continued in Session 4. In all important particulars, this session was a repeat of Session 3.

Following this session, Sheila continued to make progress. She was angry with the ward staff who spoke about her "forgetting how to walk" and complained bitterly about being treated like a "silly little baby." Consequently, she became increasingly anxious to try to walk. In order to pre-empt failure and mobilize resistance, the ward staff encouraged her to become stable on all fours before trying to walk.

Session 5 then followed, at which Mr. H. did not appear. We interpreted this as his effort to sabotage therapy, but chose to pass over it lightly; to do otherwise risked deflecting the direction of the treatment plan. Instead, we used his absence to join with mother, intervening with her in such a way as to mobilize her resistance and thus encourage further marital change.

Accordingly, the session began with a comment by the therapist on the advice of the consultant; this stated that mother did not have the strength to stand up to her husband alone. In response, Mrs. H. reported that she felt insecure in her relations with friends and in her efforts to find a job, sentiments that were echoed by Sally. Furthermore, both Mrs. H. and Sally admitted that they were afraid to confront Mr. H. It appeared that only Sheila could "stand up" to her father while, ironically, unable to "stand up" for herself. The session ended with the family feeling frustrated; no explicit task was delivered.

Despite this conclusion, Sheila's progress continued. She was able to hold her head up with no support, could stand, and actually began to walk, either with the support of staff or with a "walker."

In addition, serendipity intervened to give her progress a further boost. Terry Fox, a one-legged cancer victim, was running his "marathon of hope" in aid of the Canadian Cancer Society. This was celebrated at Toronto City Hall, with Sheila and her family among the crowd in attendance. Sheila was visibly shaken after this dramatic affair. She returned to the ward comparing herself to this brave and tragic young man, declaring to staff that she would be walking within two weeks. It is unlikely that we could have planned a better intervention.

At the same time, staff resistance appeared to be mounting. Despite Sheila's "progress" to date, suggestions were made regarding the importance of alternative treatment modalities, specifically hypnotherapy and individual psychotherapy. In light of Sheila's improvement this resistance was dismissed as counter-productive.

Session 6

As the sixth session began, father was again absent. This seemed to us scarcely fortuitous; as real change in the marital relationship began, the couple's resistance to it stiffened perceptibly. Mrs. H., for example, reported openly challenging her husband about his drinking and in relation to her desire to get a job. Mr. H.'s response was to threaten to have a nervous breakdown, thus reawakening all of the negative feelings and fears associated with his previous breakdown. This resulted in Mrs. H. becoming timid and fearful. It was impossible, she insisted to us, to stand up to her husband and make a life of her own.

In response, we joined with Mrs. H.'s resistance, paradoxically suggesting that she remain dedicated and loyal to her husband, as he needed her now that he was falling apart, and that she must relinquish any hope of making a life for herself or getting a job. Similarly, the girls were instructed to remain dedicated to helping their parents' marriage and, for that reason, should stay close to home.

At the same time, the following letter was sent to Mr. H. in the mail:

Dear Mr. H.,

I understand the reason that you could not attend this session. You understood that Sheila was making progress in her effort to begin to walk again. Your attendance and the continued problems that you're having at home with drinking and getting along with your wife, indicated to you that it was best not to attend. You felt that if marital issues came up again, it would discourage your daughter from walking. Thank you for understanding and allowing your daughter to continue to make this progress.

Sincerely,

Pam Grosman

This was intended to accomplish three things: first, it redefined father's absence as useful, thus nullifying its disruptive effects; second, it attempted to mobilize father's resistance in order to have him return to therapy; finally, whether or not he returned, it defined him as necessarily a part of the therapeutic process, thus permitting us to give him and, through him, the family directives by means of the mail.

Despite father's resistance, Sheila's progress was unabated. By now she was walking with crutches and without the aid of a "walker." Indeed, the physiotherapist reported that, in her view, Sheila had the ability but not the confidence to walk. In an effort to enhance her confidence, both the therapist and the ward staff told Sheila that she would be discharged five days after she had begun to walk without any external support.

Session 7

With all family members in attendance, the seventh session focussed on a discussion of what was stopping Sheila from throwing away her crutches. Paradoxically, the therapist suggested that perhaps Sheila was "afraid to go home."

In order to overcome this impasse, both therapists, in a consultation during the session, decided to create a dramatic scenario in which Sheila would walk for the first time without external assistance. We reasoned that Sheila's apparent inability to walk unaided primarily reflected her own mental set rather than her physical state. Following Erickson and Rossi (10), we elected to employ a "confusion" technique in order to "depotentiate" her current frame of reference and provide her with an opportunity to reorganize her thinking along "therapeutic pathways."

Accordingly, the therapist asked the family to meet the consultant in the busy hospital corridor. They were informed that the consultant had noticed "something" in Sheila that would clarify why she remained unable to walk unaided. Stationing Sheila about 60 feet (20 m) away from him, the consultant instructed Sheila, still on crutches, to walk toward him (with the family and many hospital staff members as observers). As she approached him he quickly said, "Look at your feet. See how your crutches are interfering with your ability to walk." Confused, she was left standing, looking at her feet. The consultant then told her to turn around and, with a single movement, removed her crutches, telling her to walk toward her family; spontaneously, she did so. This sequence was repeated twice.

Following this episode, the therapist told Sheila that her crutches would now be taken away; if she needed support, she could use the walls of the hospital. Since all good hospital walls eventually come to an end, the nature of this task would force Sheila to continue to walk without support. Within two days, Sheila had given up all external support (including the walls) and began to walk and even jog in the hallways.

Session 8

The eighth and final therapy session was held just prior to Sheila's discharge from hospital (in August), 11 weeks after the initiation of family therapy and five days after she began walking without external support. We congratulated the family on its progress, but encouraged continuation of therapy on an out-patient basis. In view of their earlier resistance, we were not surprised when they refused, stating that now that Sheila was "cured," therapy was no longer necessary. Since it appeared to us that many of the problematic marital issues remained unresolved, we closed the session by predicting that some other family member would need to develop a problem in order to keep the family together.

Follow-up

Strategic intervention with the H family produced several positive changes that freed Sheila so that she no longer needed to use her paralysis in order to keep her family together: boundaries had been established around the marital and sibling subsystems; the parents' marital problems were resolved at least to the extent that mother no longer needed to turn to the girls as her main source of support; most important of all, Sheila felt free to be distant from her mother, began to pursue a life of her own, and no longer needed to monitor her parents' relationship.

This is not to say that all the problems in the H family had been resolved. The marital conflict between Mr. and Mrs. H. remained serious and we anticipated the possibility that Sally might now become the focus of her parents' attention. Unfortunately, this expectation proved to be well founded. In a letter sent to the authors over the summer, Sally stated that as a result of therapy, she was now aware of her inability to express her feelings, a state she referred to as "emotional constipation." Her father continued to be a major source of frustration for her, as she remained unable to deal with him effectively. Under some distress, she requested advice that would "help her get through the summer."

Unlike her sister, however, Sally's distress was not disabling. This became evident in our follow-up six months after Sheila's discharge. Sheila described herself as fully mobile and participating in all school sports. Sally, though upset, appeared to be doing reasonably well. Even Mrs. H. reported that she had just found a part-time job. Only Mr. H. showed minor change; he remained unemployed, had discontinued A.A., and maintained a highly conflictual relationship with his wife.

With respect to the ward staff, the aftermath of this "experiment" in strategic family therapy was both positive and negative. Initially, the fact that this approach violated the ward's hierarchical structure produced initial resistance. Eventually this approach came to be seen as one alternative therapeutic modality.

Implications

This case study permits the derivation of a number of clinical implications and raises a number of questions.

1. This case clearly suggests that it is fruitful to conceptualize conversion reaction in terms of intrafamilial interaction processes. Concomitantly, it implies that strategic family therapy may provide an extremely effective, short-term method of therapeutic intervention. Parenthetically, we would add that the outcome of this case was not a complete success; although symptom alleviation was achieved, serious marital dysfunction remained.

2. It graphically highlights the importance of the relationship between treatment context and therapeutic outcome. Traditionally, the

unit of treatment is determined a priori by the therapeutic model in use. Just as the psychoanalytic therapist is oriented toward the individual, so the family therapist is oriented toward the family system. But such a choice does not inhere in systems theory upon which family therapy is grounded. Rather, in theoretical terms, the system in question is operationally defined in terms of the purposes of the observer (6, 5). In light of the present report, this means that the unit of treatment must remain an empirical question; dogmatic adherence to one unit or another can only deflect the therapist from the primary goal, namely, the reorganization of dysfunctional social systems.

By the same token, this report makes clear that attempting to remain simultaneously aware of events and processes at both the family and the ward levels is a formidable task indeed. Families and wards are isomorphic; both constitute social systems and both are organized in terms of the maintenance of a homeostatic state. When one is embedded in the other, as in the present case, therapeutic destabilization of either system becomes that much more difficult. Indeed, if we knew then what we know now, we might have been considerably less willing to proceed with this case.

3. This case provides further empirical support for the utility of perceiving the patient's symptom(s) as primarily indicative of family, rather than individual, dysfunction. Furthermore, it suggests that symptom substitution, typically conceptualized in psychodynamic terms (19), may more fruitfully be seen as the efforts of a family system to realign in order to maintain and preserve a dysfunctional homeostatic state (14). Data from the present report, however, indicates that while symptom substitution may, in some cases, not be eliminated, it may at least be radically circumscribed. Therapeutic efforts with the H family appear to have redefined Sheila as no longer available as a marital intermediary. Indeed, we noted, after the fact, that such a message was embedded in our parting comments to the family in Session 8; while intended to mobilize resistance against dysfunctional interactional processes, our statement that "some *other* family member will need to develop a problem" clearly delineates Sheila as unavailable for that family position. Conversely, this implies that a similar process of definition was operative in the initial development of symptoms in Sheila as opposed to Sally. While the manner in which this process is generally initiated remains unclear, in the present case Sheila's ordinal status appeared crucial. The fact that she was the youngest resulted in an especially close relationship between her and her mother and hence her "selection" as the symptom-bearer.

4. Finally, this case calls in question the utility of standard psychiatric nosology for the family therapist. Based on a medical perspective, the notion that Sheila was suffering from a "conversion reaction" implies a particular model of etiology and calls attention to individual attributes while deflecting attention from interpersonal processes. Concomitantly, it acts to determine how therapists select, weigh, evaluate, and interpret

clinical data. In the present case, the knowledge that Sheila had been diagnosed "hysterical paralysis-conversion reaction" was of strikingly little clinical use. What was important was the function this symptom had in the family in question and how it fitted in with a cyclic process of "father attack—mother withdraw—Sheila attack."

On the one hand, this suggests the need for much greater research in the effort to develop a family nosology (e.g., 20). On the other hand, it calls attention to the important, but unresolved issues of symptom selection and development. The process of triangulation, for example, has been implicated in a variety of child problems, including school phobia (11), emotional disturbance (24), anorexia nervosa (17), and now conversion reaction. That some process or processes over and above triangulation are responsible for symptom choice and development seems clear. What these processes are remains to be determined. In the present instance the intersection of two processes appears significant. The first process involved the family's developmental stage. As an adolescent, Sheila was beginning to turn from her family to her peer group. This called for family readjustment, a process especially difficult for Mr. and Mrs. H., in view of their marital difficulties. Consequently, Sheila "chose" to become part of the marital system rather than risk the dissolution of her family (1).

In this context, we would speculate that symptom selection, the second process, in the H family was related to two factors. First, Sheila's paralysis was of symbolic importance in light of her reputation as the family athlete. Finally, Sheila was best suited to the position of symptom-bearer; she was both the most assertive and in the "best" physical condition.

References

1. Ackerman, N.J. "The Family with Adolescents." In E.A. Carter and M. McGoldrick, eds. *The Family Life Cycle: A Framework For Family Therapy.* N.Y.: Gardner, 1980.
2. American Psychiatric Association. *The Diagnostic and Statistical Manual of Mental Disorders.* Washington, D.C.: A.P.A., 1980.
3. Barr, R., and Abernathy, V. "Single Care Study: Conversion Reaction. Differential Diagnosis in the Light of Biofeedback Research." *Journal of Nervous and Mental Disease.* 164 (1977): 287-292.
4. Bateson, G. *Mind and Nature: A Necessary Unity.* N.Y.: Dutton, 1979.
5. Bateson, G. *Steps to An Ecology of Mind.* N.Y.: Ballantine, 1972.
6. Buckley, W. *Sociology and Modern Systems Theory.* Englewood Cliffs, N.J.: Prentice-Hall, 1967.
7. Engel, G.L. "Conversion Symptoms." In C.H. MacBryde and R.S. Blacklow, eds. *Signs and Symptoms: Applied Pathologic Physiology and Clinical Interpretation.* Fifth ed. Philadelphia: Lippincott, 1970.
8. Engel, G.L., and Schmale, A.H. "Psychoanalytic Theory of Somatic Disorders." *Journal of American Psychoanalytic Association.* 15 (1967): 344-365.
9. Erhlich, E.L., and Fisher, R.L. "Orthopaedic Conversion Reactions in Child-

hood and Adolescence." *Connecticut Medicine*. 41 (11, Nov. 1977): 681-3.

10. Erickson, M.H., and Rossi, E.L. *Hypnotherapy: An Explanatory Casebook*. N.Y.: Irvington, 1979.

11. Haley, J. *Problem-Solving Therapy: New Strategies for Effective Family Therapy*. San Francisco: Jossey-Bass, 1976.

12. Haley, J. *Strategies of Psychotherapy*. N.Y.: Grune and Stratton, 1963.

13. Haley, J. "Why A Mental Health Clinic Should Avoid Family Therapy." *Journal of Marriage and Family Counselling*. Jan. 1975, 3-13.

14. Jackson, D.D. "The Study of the Family." *Family Process*, 4 (1965): 1-20.

15. Lidz, T. *The Family and Human Adaptation*. N.Y.: International University Press, 1963.

16. Minuchin, S. *Families and Family Therapy*. Cambridge, Mass.: Harvard University Press, 1974.

17. Minuchin, S., Rosman, B.L., and Baker, L. *Psychosomatic Families: Anorexia Nervosa in Context*. Cambridge, Mass.: Harvard University Press, 1978.

18. Modrall-Jones, M. "Conversion Reaction: Anachronism in Revolutionary Form." *Psychological Bulletin*, American Psychological Association. 87 (3, 1980): 427-41.

19. Nemiah, J.C. "Conversion Reaction." In A.M. Freedman and H.I. Kaplan, eds. *Comprehensive Textbook of Psychiatry*. Baltimore: Williams and Wilkins, 1967.

20. Olson, D.H., Sprenkle, D.H., and Russer, C. "Circumplex Model of Marital and Family Systems. I. Cohesion and Adaptability Dimensions, Family Types, and Clinical Applications." *Family Process*. 18 (1979): 3-28.

21. Rangell, L. "Nature of Conversion." *Journal of the American Psychoanalytic Association*. 7 (1959): 632-662.

22. Rock, Nicholas L., M.D. "Conversion Reactions in Childhood: A Clinical Study On Childhood Neuroses." *Journal of the American Academy of Child Psychiatry*. 10 (1972): 65-93.

23. Ullmann, L.P., and Krasner, L. *A Psychological Approach to Abnormal Behavior*. Englewood Cliffs, N.J.: Prentice-Hall, 1969.

24. Vogel, E.F., and Bell, N.W. "The Emotionally Disturbed Child As The Family Scapegoat." In N.W. Bell and E.F. Vogel, eds. *A Modern Introduction to the Family*. Rev. ed. N.Y.: Free Press, 1968.

25. Watzlawick, P. *The Language of Change: Elements of Therapeutic Communication*. N.Y.: Basic, 1978.

26. Watzlawick, P., Beavin, J.H., and Jackson, D.D. *Pragmatics of Human Communication*. N.Y.: Norton, 1967.

27. Watzlawick, P., Weakland, J., and Fisch, R. *Change: Principles of Problem-Formation and Problem-Resolution*. N.Y.: Norton, 1974.

28. Wender, P.H. "Vicious and Virtuous Circles: The Role of Deviation-Amplifying Feedback in the Origin and Perpetuation of Behaviour." *Psychiatry*. 31 (1968): 309-324.

29. Yates, A., and Steward, M. "Conversion Hysteria in Childhood." *Clinical Paediatrics*. 15 (4, 1976): 379-82.

8

Strategic Intervention with an Individual: The Issue of Intimacy

Susan Cohen and Allon Bross

*This case speaks to the importance of understanding transitions in developmental life stages of family systems. The following case report of Barbara discusses (a) the treatment of a nineteen-year-old woman in transition from late adolescence to adulthood with a specific focus on the issues of sexuality and intimacy; (b) working individually utilizing a systemic framework; and (c) the use of consultation in the treatment process.**

Introduction

Traditional (i.e., psychodynamic) and family therapeutic views of psychiatric disorder diverge sharply. Three ideas characterize the traditional perspective.

1. The "monad" is the primary unit of analysis (7, 10). This holds that the individual may be seen in isolation from his or her social surround and conceptualizes symptomatic behaviour as a manifestation of underlying intrapsychic processes. Further, this necessarily assumes that the direction of effect is uni-directional, from parent to child and not vice versa (1). This is not to suggest that proponents of a traditional view are not sensitive to interactional processes, but rather, following Harry Stack Sullivan, such processes are viewed through the lens of individual introspection rather than *in vivo* behavioural interaction (14).

2. Causal processes are conceptualized in linear terms, with cause-and-effect sequences forming an unbroken chain from the past to the present. This perspective necessarily assumes that (a) the long term effects of early experience are, for all intents and purposes, irreversible; and (b) antecedent experience as opposed to proximal events has the status of causal primacy (4, 12). In other words, understanding current symptomatology requires a journey into the past where such behaviour is believed to have its roots. It is only by "working through" the scars of the distant past that the therapist can effect symptom removal.

3. Human change and growth is conceptualized in developmental terms. Whether this takes the form of Freud's "psychosexual stages" (2) or Erickson's "life stages" (5), development is seen to involve a cumulative

---

*To ensure confidentiality, the names and facts of this family have been altered.

linear progression, from the primitive and undifferentiated to the socialized and complex. It follows that the next stage can only be reached once the requirements of the preceding stage have been met. Consequently, the dominant image of the traditional developmental perspective is one of "blockage." Failure to master one stage "blocks" one's efforts to move into the next stage, with intrapsychic conflict and symptomatic behaviour the long-term, and perhaps the lifelong consequence.

In accord with the traditional view, the family therapeutic perspective also encompasses three components. Apart from this superficial similarity, their formulation could not be more different.

1. The unit of analysis is that of a social group, typically but not exclusively a family, containing two or more individuals (9, 10). In this context, symptomatic behaviour is conceptualized as indicative of the interactional patterns which characterize the larger family system within which such behaviour is embedded and from which it takes its meaning. This necessarily assumes that the direction of effect is bi-directional, with reciprocity of effect and mutual participation among members the rule (1).

2. Causal processes are conceptualized in circular terms such that the distinction between "cause" and "effect" ceases to be meaningful (10). This perspective is founded on twin assumptions: (a) that there need be no necessary relationship between antecedent events and proximal processes; and (b) proximal processes have the status of causal primacy (4). In other words, the explanation of symptomatic behaviour involves inquiry into those current interactional processes which are presumed both to produce and to maintain the behaviour in question. It is by altering the structure and organization of the dysfunctional family system that the therapist effects symptom removal (10).

3. Finally, like their traditional counterparts, family therapists conceive of human growth and change in developmental terms. Such development is seen to take the form of a "normal" trajectory of change, involving passage through a sequence of life stages (11, 13). These stages, however, are neither static nor need they progress in lockstep (3). Rather, each stage is thought to reflect a dynamic, interactional process which may, moreover, be significantly affected by situational factors. Furthermore, differentiation is not conceptualized in digital terms, as either present or absent, but rather as an analogical phenomenon, with increased differentiation on some levels (e.g., communication) and increased simplification (e.g., ritual) on other levels (e.g., meaning). Consequently, the transition from one stage to another, ordinarily fraught with difficulties, need not occur simultaneously at all levels nor for all family members. Thus, the dominant image of the family therapeutic developmental perspective is one of "being stuck." Interactional patterns around some issues or at some levels may be more resistant to change (i.e., stable) than others, such that the failure to complete the transition between life stages may give rise to symptomatic

behaviour in one or (more rarely) more members (6, 15). Such behaviour is thought to signal not merely the individual's difficulties with the transition in question, but more importantly the distress of the larger family system.

Unfortunately, with regard to the last component, the relationship between stage transition and symptom formation has received relatively little systematic attention in the literature. For the practitioner, there are relatively few studies and even fewer clinical examples that speak either to the issue in question or to the relationship between transition failure and treatment outcome. Indeed, it has only been in the 1970's that the first direct references to these topics have appeared in the family therapy literature (8, 13, 15).

In an effort to remedy this situation, the following case study underscores the importance of understanding the negotiation of transitional phases for assessment and treatment. More specifically, this paper will examine the treatment of a 19-year-old woman, Barbara S., in transition from late adolescence into adulthood. This will demonstrate the consequences of an unsuccessful transition in the form of symptomatic behaviour and will indicate that the primary goal of therapy was to help the client successfully complete the transition in question.

Late Adolescence-Adulthood: The Courtship Period

Haley (8), describing the work of Milton Erickson, identifies several important aspects of the "courtship phase" in late adolescence. These include:

(a) a specified period when courting practices are learned in adolescence;
(b) the possibility of conflict resulting from simultaneous involvement with one's family and peers as the adolescent moves toward autonomy;
(c) the failure to become independent of one's family of origin during the courtship phase, resulting in the individual acquiring a peripheral social status within the community;
(d) the inability to achieve autonomy possibly making it especially difficult for the individual to form age-appropriate intimate or work-related relationships.

With clinical experience, it has become clear that these elements of the courtship phase that exert pressure on the individual to move to the next phase of forming a lasting relationship, can become a central issue in the treatment process. In response to a client who has not successfully passed through this stage, the clinician must pay particular attention to the dual issues of (a) closeness and intimacy and (b) separateness and autonomy from one's family of origin.

With regard to the former, the ability to be comfortable with intimacy in a "new" relationship, including sharing information, mutual support, co-operation, and sexual intimacy, is often hard to acquire. Because we spend the first phases of our lives negotiating this within our family of origin, arriving at a solution to this issue in another relationship requires time, skill, and patience. Consequently, there are many occasions in the development of this new intimate relationship where problems can occur.

As for the latter, the ability to be separate or autonomous from one's family of origin and to move into new relationships often places the late adolescent in a "push and pull" position. In one sense, the person feels loyal to the family of origin, its beliefs and values. In another sense, there is a push to create a new relationship and to renegotiate with one's family of origin around the formation of a "new" family system.

It is getting "stuck" between the "push" and the "pull"—neither advancing completely into any new relationship nor holding completely to the old values and beliefs—that can lead to problem formulation, with the resultant request for therapy by a young adult or the family.

The Treatment Modality

In this context, treatment in the following case study is based on the following assumptions:

1. Dysfunctional behaviour is seen to be symptomatic of the interactional processes that typify the relationship among two or more individuals; this way of relating is responsible for the maintenance of the problem; furthermore, these processes are embedded within a developmental stage in the family life cycle wherein the family (with the adolescent) has "failed" to make the appropriate transition.

2. Diagnosis is based on information that accrues as a result of feedback following initial clinical intervention; this information is then used as the basis of a clinical formulation.

3. The client's history is regarded as of only incidental importance since dysfunctional behaviour is maintained by interactional process in the present.

4. In working with client-families, therapeutic change is a process that can occur relatively quickly.

5. The goal of therapy is to help people solve the problem that brought them to therapy; that therapeutic process is carefully planned and the responsibility for outcome success or failure rests with the therapist.

Taken together, these assumptions suggest that, as much as possible, therapeutic intervention is a planned and highly predictable process. Consequently, it is the therapist, rather than the client, who is ultimately responsible for the success or failure of the therapeutic process.

The Case Study

Barbara, age 19, was self-referred to an out-patient clinic. Her chief concerns included: an unsatisfying social life; difficulty in forming and maintaining relationships; dating experiences that had been frustrating in both contact and brevity; and contact with men that had been repetitively unsuccessful.

At first sight, these problems seemed anomalous. Barbara was a very attractive, bright young woman whose previous successes in life were based solely upon her academic achievements. At the time of referral, she had completed one year of university, living in an on-campus residence. Despite the fact that Barbara was living away from home, however, she remained extremely attached to her closely knit family. Further inquiry revealed that Barbara came from a strict Roman Catholic upbringing. Her parents had continued to reassure Barbara, telling her that through ongoing prayer she would be able to achieve a satisfying social life. To date, however, her efforts at prayer had yielded little success in resolving her reported difficulties.

The client was seen by the first author for three months on a regular weekly basis. The initial focus of treatment was around dating procedures, assertiveness training, and support. By the end of this period, however, there were no visible changes in the client's relationships and no improvement in her feelings about herself. Despite this, Barbara remained committed to working out her problems and also felt quite accepting and trusting in her relationship with the therapist. Since the problem persisted, the first author decided to seek case consultation.

In seeking this consultation, the following was presented to the client.

> "Barbara, you are obviously physically attractive, and have many positive qualities. Since we haven't made much progress, perhaps it would be important to obtain a male perspective that might shed some light on your difficulty in relating to men."

Although the client accepted this rationale, it was evident that she was experiencing some discomfort.

Prior to meeting with the client, an information-sharing session was held between the therapist and the consultant (the second author) in order to formulate a hypothesis based upon the therapist's previous knowledge. Our speculation was that this young woman was fearful of intimacy, although the basis of this fear was unclear. We conjectured that it was rooted in her religious upbringing; operating from a perspective in which sex and intimacy were to be saved for marriage and/or that sex is dirty, Barbara therefore considered anything to do with sex (i.e., intimacy) as wrong. It was jointly decided that this formulation would serve as a guide to treatment. Such treatment encompassed a total of four sessions, with the consultant taking an active role.

Session 1

After joining with the client around her frustrations, the consultant directly asked Barbara when she had last experienced "sexual intimacy."

While this question was not intended to imply anything specific, the client reacted with extreme embarrassment. Literally, Barbara tipped her chair back and threw her arms into the air as she made a valiant effort to retreat into the wall. Her face turned red and she appeared to be temporarily stunned. It was clear that simply using the word "sexual" had significantly raised Barbara's level of anxiety.

Following this, the consultant discussed Barbara's understanding of sexual functioning, her hopes around forming relationships, and how she felt that her own religious upbringing had influenced her present situation. It became quite clear that our hypothesis concerning fear of intimacy was accurate.

Upon further investigation, it also became clear that Barbara had developed a pattern of behaviour that perpetuated her feelings of inadequacy and unattractiveness. Specifically, she revealed that she responded to male advances by retreating and, because of her own level of discomfort, may not have been aware of second attempts for her attention. Further, she revealed a suspiciousness about men such that she was reluctant to pursue any involvements. Significantly, it became clear that Barbara was totally unaware of how her own discomfort possibly repelled men, thus maintaining her problem.

At this point, in view of Barbara's minimal knowledge or understanding of sexual functioning, we decided that part of the treatment plan was to introduce an educational component; this was intended to normalize the issue of sexuality with the hope of dissipating her stress. Accordingly, we directed Barbara to go to the university library where she was to obtain a copy of Masters and Johnson's *Human Sexual Functioning*, of which she was to read the first 100 pages. The following week, she was to return to discuss anything that was not clear to her.

In response to this task, Barbara expressed concern that someone (e.g., parents) might "catch her" reading this book, a comment that further confirmed our hypothesis that Barbara viewed sex and intimacy in a negative light. We replied that Barbara was only to read this book while in the residence and not when she was home on weekends. We further suggested that she could discuss some of the content with girlfriends in the residence. However, she flatly rejected this idea, deeming it outrageous. To ensure confidentiality, we encouraged Barbara to place a "book cover" over the text so that no one would catch her.

Session 2
Barbara reported that she did not feel comfortable reading the book in her parents' home and so confined this reading to the residence. However, a major incident occurred that we, in our best laid plans, could not have imagined. Barbara was approached, spontaneously, by a female friend (from her residence) who wanted to know what she was reading. Despite

her effort to conceal the book's identity by placing it in a book cover, her secret was revealed. Upon discovering the content matter, her friend asked where she had obtained this text. Too embarrassed to reveal the true source, Barbara's spontaneous response was that, "My mother gave it to me!" Barbara's friend responded by saying how lucky she was to have such a progressive and open-minded mother. The outcome was that Barbara discovered that her lack of knowledge was universal, that is, that she was not the only woman in the world with this type of problem. As a result of her reading, she became an expert in relation to her girlfriend, and was thus able to share accurate data with her while secretly receiving help for herself. During the course of the evening, a roomful of women from the residence filed into Barbara's room to join this discussion, further confirming Barbara's role as expert, and paradoxically dissipating both the magnitude and severity of her problem.

A discussion and clarification of those first 100 pages ensued, and another 100 pages were assigned.

Session 3

Since Barbara was clearly uncomfortable with intimacy, it was considered important that she be made to feel more at ease with her own body. Accordingly, we suggested that Barbara begin to explore her own body, coincident with the text, in order that she be able to identify her body parts in the vaginal area. She was to proceed in a very sterile manner, with the aid of a mirror. We also suggested that it would be "okay" if she masturbated, if she so desired. The consultant and therapist anticipated that, at worst, this would be a healthy, educational experience for Barbara and that, at best, she might experience sexual arousal. As an adjunct to this discussion, the consultant shared a metaphoric story adapted from the work of Milton Erickson:

> A sixty-five-year-old woman came to a mental health clinic with the presenting problem of severe depression. Upon enquiry the psychiatrist discovered that some five years earlier Mrs. X.'s husband had passed away. Further investigation discovered that although Mrs. X. could cope with the loss of her husband, she repeatedly emphasized that the most difficult aspect of her current situation was that she could no longer have any sexually intimate experience. As a result of her age, she could not replace the sexually active life that she had enjoyed with her husband. Mrs. X. felt that she could not "go out and pick up men," nor did she feel that men would be sexually attracted to her. The solution of her family doctor had been to prescribe a variety of medications for her depression since he could not think of any other solution.
>
> The psychiatrist decided that it would be best to help this woman overcome her "sexual problem" by having her experience sexual pleasure through masturbation. These sessions were spent helping the woman to be comfortable with the idea of masturbation, which Mrs. X.

had previously thought taboo. The results were astonishing. The woman gave up the use of medication and began to feel quite comfortable with the use of masturbation to fulfil her need. Her depression disappeared and she lived a normal life.

The purpose of this intervention was to normalize the client's ability to experience sexual stimulation through masturbation. While uncomfortable, Barbara did agree to attempt the task. She was then told that she now had all the knowledge and equipment to aid her in having satisfying relationships with men "as she so pleased."

Session 4

Returning several weeks later, Barbara reported that she had completed the assignment and could now identify her body parts. She also intimated that she had experienced sexual arousal. By this time, Barbara had moved home for the summer and had met a man who had asked her out a number of times. She reported dating regularly, and felt quite pleased about her ability to relate to this man. While Barbara was anxious to share her sexual experiences, the consultant and therapist told her that some things should be kept private. Although we expressed pleasure that she could experience a positive sexual relationship, we felt that these intimate experiences need not be shared. This response served to place a boundary between herself and the therapists that simultaneously allowed for appropriate discretion, while placing a similar boundary between herself and her parents.

Barbara thanked the therapists for their help and felt that her presenting problem, repeated negative relationships with males, was resolved. Accordingly, treatment was terminated, with no follow-up planned.

Clinical Implications

The case study of Barbara underscores the importance of understanding the developmental life cycle of the client within the system of which they are a part. This broader view of symptom formation takes the problem out of the realm of the individual and requires a more complete and more complex understanding of the client's situation. As a result, a number of important clinical judgments are required for the family therapist.

1. First and foremost, therapy entails making a decision, on empirical grounds, as to who to have in treatment. For most family therapists, the norm has been to invite all members of the system involved in maintaining the problem. By taking a broader view of symptom formation, the case of Barbara illustrates the need to leave this an empirical question. It was essential in this case that a "psychological" boundary be placed between Barbara and her parents. Her parents' beliefs and values were in fact affecting Barbara in her relationship with men at her current developmental phase. It would have been counter-productive to have invited Barbara's parents and family to the therapy because the area of sexuality is private. In

relation to her parents, the therapist would have encountered resistance (i.e., negative feedback) to confront this topic, thus further confirming and maintaining Barbara's mistaken beliefs in her relationships with men. Her parents would have reinforced this belief system, which, in turn, would have placed Barbara in a "no win" position. Her compliance would have maintained her problem whereas rebellion by a loyal and dedicated daughter was not an alternative in this case. In this context, working with the individual while utilizing a systemic understanding of the individual in context was deemed the most appropriate and efficient clinical route to problem resolution.

We must underscore, however, that seeing one member of the family in therapy does not prevent the therapist from placing the client's problem in a frame that encompasses the system of which he or she is a part. Rather, we would argue that it is entirely possible to work with individuals from a systems perspective; the choice of doing so will depend on the clinical situation.

2. A second consideration is the role and use of a consultant in therapy. It is important to obtain consultation in order to facilitate the therapeutic process in a situation wherein the therapy has continued but the client's problem has persisted. Clinical consultation may help the therapist get through this difficult situation. Moreover, a therapist will often use a pattern of problem assessment and response wherein a preconceived notion of what is required for problem resolution is in use. The result is therapeutic "tunnel vision." It is the therapist's responsibility to determine the reasons for problem maintenance, among them, as in this case, "tunnel vision." In other words, while problem maintenance may reflect client resistance, it may also or alternatively pertain to therapist error.

3. Third, this case points out the need for creativity in the construction of tasks and strategies. This case required a series of tasks, both direct and indirect, in order to achieve the treatment goal. In particular, the task of reading a textbook and its multiple ramifications could not have been created in any other treatment format. Although one does not always receive inspiration in terms of matching the right tasks to the client's needs, careful construction, delivery, and planning of tasks is essential.

4. Lastly, this case addresses the issue of human sexuality. It is our opinion that sexuality is too often a taboo area, making it difficult for mental health professionals to deal with this problem effectively. The existence of sexual myths, together with much inaccurate sexual information in the minds of both the general public and the practitioners, helps account for this sad state of affairs. The result, for family therapists, is often discomfort and/or ignorance resulting in ineffective practice. Barbara's behaviour and her family's response to it are one more reflection of the myths and values still prevalent in our society today.

In closing, the purpose of this case report has been to illustrate the importance of understanding problem formation as a function of transitional periods in the developmental life cycle of family systems. More specifically, it has discussed the issues of intimacy and sexuality in the transition from late adolescence into adulthood. Understanding this and other developmental phases requires a more complete and more complex perspective than has hitherto been the case. This paper has merely touched on a few selected, case-specific themes; the need to pursue this untapped area in future clinical and research investigations is apparent. Ultimately, our ability to more effectively achieve our therapeutic goal of problem resolution will depend on an ever-broadening knowledge base.

References

1. Bell, R.Q., and Harper, L.V. *Child Effects on Adults.* Hillsdale, N.J.: Lawrence Erlbaum, 1977.
2. Brenner, C. *An Elementary Textbook of Psychoanalysis.* Rev. ed. N.Y.: Anchor, 1974.
3. Carter, E.A., and McGoldrick, M. *The Family Life Cycle.* N.Y.: Gardner, 1980.
4. Clarke, A.M., and Clarke, A.D.B. *Early experience: Myth and evidence.* London: Open Books, 1976.
5. Erikson, E.H. *Childhood and Society.* 2nd ed. N.Y.: Norton, 1963.
6. Hadley, T., et al. "The relationship between family development crisis and the appearance of symptoms in a family member." *Family Process,* 13, 2, 1974.
7. Haley, J. *Strategies of Psychotherapy.* N.Y.: Grune and Stratton, 1973.
8. Haley, J. *Uncommon Therapy: The Psychiatric Techniques of Milton H. Erickson.* New York: Norton, 1973.
9. Madanes, C., and Haley, J. "Dimensions of family therapy." *Journal of Nervous and Mental Disease.* 165 (1977): 88-98.
10. Minuchin, S. *Families and Family Therapy.* Cambridge, Mass.: Harvard University Press, 1974.
11. Nock, S.L. "Family life-cycle transition: Longitudinal effects on family members." *Journal of Marriage and the Family.* 43 (1981): 703-714.
12. Peterfreund, E. *Informations, Systems and Psychoanalysis.* N.Y.: International University Press, 1971.
13. Solomon, M. "A developmental, conceptual premise for family therapy." *Family Process.* 12 (1973): 179-188.
14. Spiegel, J.P., and Bell, N.W. "The family of the psychiatric patient." In S. Arieti, ed. *American Handbook of Psychiatry.* Vol. 1. N.Y.: Basic, 1959.
15. Walsh, F. "Concurrent grandparent death and the birth of a schizophrenic offspring; an intriguing finding." *Family Process.* 17, 4, December, 1978.

9

Ritual, Reframing, and Written Prescriptions: The Techniques of Strategic Family Therapy

Nina Woulff

The following case study relates the experiences of a peer consultation group employing strategic family therapy in a mental health clinic. The case illustrates: implementation of the strategic model, the therapeutic techniques, ritual, reframing, and written prescriptions; the development and interpersonal dynamics of the peer consultation group; and a discussion of strategic therapy in the context of a mental health centre.

Introduction

This paper presents the experiences of a peer consultation group employing strategic family therapy in a mental health clinic. One half-day each week, three therapists* and I work with referred families.** Our goals are to improve our strategic tactics and to deliver efficient and effective therapy to families having difficult and seemingly intractable problems with their children.

The core theoretical constructs of this group follow the strategic therapy models of Haley (6, 7), Andolfi (1), Selvini-Palazzoli, et al. (17), Watzlawick, et al. (18), Watzlawick (19), and Madanes (10). The child's symptoms are understood as both the results of, and an attempted solution to a problem in the family. The symptoms seem to protect the family by focussing energy and attention away from other troubles, when, in fact, they sustain the problem. By not responding to the parents' efforts to solve the child's problems, the symptomatic child exerts power and influence over the family, creating an incongruous hierarchy in which the child appears to control the parents. In addition, the boundaries between subsystems in symptomatic families are either enmeshed or disengaged, and these structural anomalies contribute to the problem. The goal of therapy

---

*Wayne Hollett, M.S.W., Carolyn Humphreys, Ph.D., Valerie O'Brien, M.S.W.
**This consultation group was developed at the Atlantic Child Guidance Centre in Halifax several years ago and is modelled upon the brief therapy project at the Nathan Ackerman Family Institute in New York (Papp, 1977, 1980).
    To ensure confidentiality the names and facts of this family have been altered.

is to eliminate the problem of hierarchical incongruities—those interactions that recur around the problem—by creating perceptual crises, blocking dysfunctional habits, and choreographing new interactional sequences.

Such an approach requires considerable time for planning strategies, although there may be few actual sessions with the family (sessions being scheduled for approximately one hour every three weeks). For each session, the consultation group has three meetings: one of around 10 minutes beforehand, another of around 20 minutes in the middle of the session, and the last of 10 to 30 minutes afterward. In addition, the therapist working directly with the family spends time between sessions reviewing the tape and planning interventions. Each member of the consultation group works with his or her own case family, while the others observe through a one-way mirror, an arrangement that the family has agreed to. Except for the therapist, then, the consultation team ordinarily remains anonymous. There is telephone communication between therapy- and viewing-rooms so that group members can request additional information and make suggestions.

The case of Serena Salter (age 15) will demonstrate how we follow this model of therapy. Serena had been referred to us by a pediatrician whose extensive testing had identified no medical reason for multiple vague complaints of generalized fatigue, chest pains, headaches, loss of appetite, and insomnia. The girl had been suffering for nine months and had missed 30 days of school during the first half of the term. A virtual recluse, she spent most of her time in her room. The family included an older brother (Sam, age 17) and parents in their early forties. Because the father was in the armed forces, the family had moved to new surroundings every two years or so. The mother did not work outside the home.

Session I: Engaging and Reframing
The first session follows a fairly standard outline. It is a search for information to help us answer the following questions:

1. How does the family interact around the problem child?
2. What have been the family's attempted solutions to their problem(s)?
3. Who or what is being protected by the child's symptoms?
4. What are the family members' assumptions about the cause and nature of the problem?
5. What kinds of boundaries and hierarchies exist in the family?
6. What are the family's expectations of the treatment?

Direct questioning of the family and the group's educated observation of interactions and non-verbal behaviour provide our answers.

There are several goals for the first session: the therapist will construct a tentative hypothesis about how the symptom is maintained and the function that it serves; the therapist will usually reframe the problem and assign a task for homework; the therapist will want to give the family the hope that the consultation group will be able to help.

Before the first session, and before there have been any screening or assessment interviews, the therapist and the consultation group review whatever information has been compiled by the receptionist from the oral or written referral. Because this model of therapy assumes that the therapist will react to any piece of information, the therapist discusses the impressions and ideas, however tentative, based on the limited data. As therapists, we must acknowledge our assumptions and accept that they will influence our behaviour with the family. Because we are aware that our assumptions are *not* fact, we must be open to their revision in the face of information gleaned from our interactions with the family. Thus, by identifying our covert preconceptions in our consultation meetings, we hope to deprive them of undue influence.

Before my first meeting with the Salters, I explained to the group my expectation that the family would resist treatment, an impression I had gained from the pediatrician's referral letter. Serena's pediatrician had diagnosed her problems as psychological and had suggested that Serena was suffering from a "reactive depression," related to concern for an ill grandmother and dissatisfaction with the community where the family was living. My hypothesis was that, if the doctor had shared these impressions with the parents, they would view the problem as involving but one person—Serena. I was also expecting the family to show some of the common characteristics of psychosomatic families: the tendency to have enmeshed boundaries, to avoid expressions of conflict, to use the symptomatic child as a conflict detour, and to be pseudo-co-operative (12, 9, 20).

> During our first session, the Salters expressed great concern about Serena, who was experiencing such intense chest pains and fatigue that her parents had asked the school to excuse her from gym classes. After school, the girl would lie on her bed at home and talk to her mother about her problems. Occasionally, the father would sit with her instead. Both parents reported that Serena did not like school and that, when she was there, she constantly thought about being home. Such an attitude had apparently developed suddenly after the summer. Closer inquiry revealed that both Serena and her brother had been missing school fairly regularly for about a year. The parents could not make sense of Serena's problems and saw her as quite helpless. The father insisted that the difficulties were physical and that Serena should be given more medical tests.
>
> Serena remained very quiet during the session, answering questions only after glancing at her mother. She could not explain her illness, but suggested that it might have something to do with her hatred of school. When I asked her to specify what she hated, Serena was unable to isolate particulars. Sam behaved in much the same way as his sister. He would look at his mother before speaking in curt phrases. He admitted to having few friends and to engaging in solitary activities.

Mrs. Salter offered the thought that Serena might be worrying, as she did, about the health of her own mother, who lived about 200 miles (320 km) away. She recalled having spent two weeks with the mother, several months before; the family, Serena in particular, had missed her greatly. Mrs. Salter admitted to being torn between two responsibilities: one, to an ailing mother, and the other, to a sick daughter. She described herself as a "worrier," then suggested that she and Serena had very similar attitudes, an idea which did not seem to displease her: "I guess it's 'Like mother, like daughter'."

Although Mr. Salter was involved in a number of organizations, his wife would rarely leave the house and he would attend social functions without her. When I asked whether he minded his wife being such a "stick-in-the-mud" (my words), he became rather uncomfortable, acknowledging that he did wish she would go out more, but that he was really "used to it by now, and, anyway, that's just the way she is, I guess." As he admitted his lack of success, Mr. Salter seemed frustrated and demoralized by his general inability to motivate the women in his family.

During our group's mid-session meeting, I reviewed the new information in light of my original hypotheses. The family did appear to fit the psychosomatic profile, mother and daughter functioning as though they shared the same skin, and all family members avoiding expression of any annoyance, irritation, or disagreement. While the family was extremely cordial and would answer all my questions, their responses were brief and guarded. The parents stated that they wanted to do everything to help their daughter, yet they appeared annoyed about being at a mental health centre. On the other hand, I had incorrectly imagined the family understanding the problem as Serena's "depression." As it turned out, they remained convinced that some undiscovered organic ailment was the source of the problem, not some treatable emotional one.

The attention that Serena was receiving and the essential confirmation that her problems were beyond her control clearly supported and promoted her symptomology. The symptoms additionally seemed to resolve two potential crises in the family: Mrs. Salter leaving to devote herself to her mother, and increased tension between the parents. In other words, Serena's illnesses not only forced Mrs. Salter to care for the girl instead of her mother, but also maintained the distance between mother and father, who could avoid pressuring each other to change as long as there was a sick child to worry about.

Several challenges confronted our group: as well as defining both our goals and the goals which would be acceptable to the family and engage them in therapy, we needed to reach those goals without alienating our clients. Our own goals were to block the contingencies reinforcing Serena's symptoms, encourage the development of autonomy and independence in the two adolescents, strengthen the marital and parental coalition, create more differentiation between mother and daughter, and elicit the expression of conflict between family members and the development of independent problem-solving. Had I shared this list with the family, they most likely would have been overwhelmed and angered. The next step, therefore, was to translate these goals from a language understood by the consultation group into a language understood by the family, thus putting the problem into a new cognitive frame and activating a new set of interactions.

The importance of changing the cognitive perception of a problem has been elegantly described by Watzlawick and his colleagues (18).

> To reframe, then, means to change the conceptual and/or emotional setting or view point in relation to which a situation is experienced and to place it in another frame which fits the "facts" of the same concrete situation equally well or even better, and thereby changes its entire meaning. . . . (Reframing) *teaches a different game*, thereby making the old one obsolete. The other "now sees something different and can no longer naïvely go on playing."

Such a notion can perhaps be traced to the pre-Socratic philosopher Epictetus who, in the first century, wrote: "Men are disturbed not by things, but by the views which they take of things." In this century, the idea has been the cornerstone of the cognitive therapies, most notably in the rational-emotive psychotherapy of Albert Ellis (3, 4).

In evaluating how best to reframe a problem or design a task, we will assess the family from three perspectives:

1. What attitudes and values does each family member hold dear?
2. Which family member is most likely to follow a directive?
3. What language and/or incentives will motivate family members to follow directives?

The members of the Salter family were all clearly committed to the value of family togetherness. The parents, particularly the mother, were intensely child-oriented. The father, who had worked his way through the ranks of the armed services, valued achievement and appropriate social behaviour. All family members seemed to seek and value approval from authority figures. The object of strategic therapy is not necessarily to change these basic values but rather to alter the manner in which family members work with them.

In the mid-group discussion, we decided that I would take a "go slow" approach with the Salters—simply to reframe the problem, support the parents, and gather more specific data. When I returned to the family with the group's message, they sat up in their chairs, looking extremely alert and a little nervous. The following exchange occurred:

> Therapist: The group and I are extremely impressed by what a caring and sensitive family you are. There is no question in our minds that you (to parents) are deeply concerned about your daughter and will do every-

thing you can to help her. (The parents looked quite pleased at this point.) We feel that Serena's problems are in some way connected with her intense caring and loyalty and that she has chosen to sacrifice her well-being in order to help the family in some mysterious way. (The father now looks less pleased.) For us to get a better idea about how we can help with this problem, we would like you to fill out the following chart for the next three weeks. We want you to list every time Serena gets sick and what each person in the family does when she gets sick. In the last column, we would like to know what mother and father do after they sit down together and discuss the problem. (The parents look very surprised after hearing this last statement.)

Father: I don't know what you mean. We already discussed this, and we don't know what to do.

Therapist: (realizing that the father had somehow assumed we were implying negligence) Oh, I know you discuss the problem. We would simply like you to write down what you decide, just so we have the information.

Father: I don't know about all this. I think Serena is sick, and the doctor hasn't found the problem yet. I think she needs more tests.

Mother: (meekly to the father) He is a good doctor. I don't know . . . he gave her a lot of tests. I don't know where else to take her.

Therapist: (to the father) Do you think he is a lousy doctor? Do you want to take her to another doctor?

Father: Well, I don't know. I just don't know about all this business.

Therapist: Well, look. I'm not sure either. Obviously Serena is quite sick, and it's a real mystery. The doctor hasn't found anything, so he sent you here to see if there is any way that you, as a whole family, can work together to help her. We are interested in working with you on this. Personally, I think it's worth a try.

Mother: It's probably worth a try.

Father: I suppose so.

Therapist: By the way, there was one other thing I wanted to mention to you about what the group said. They really think that you (looking at husband) have an attractive wife, and they are confused why a good-looking woman like you (looking at wife) isn't out enjoying the finer things in life—like dancing and socializing. They find it quite surprising.

Mother: (becoming quite defensive) Well I don't really like that stuff. I like being at home. I like my children, my house. . . .

Therapist: (cutting her off quickly) Well, I don't know either. I don't know how important it is. I just thought I'd let you know that the group did mention that. We look forward to seeing you all again in three weeks.

My wording in this exchange is representative of our approach. In reframing the symptom, I used the verb "to choose" to lift the symptom from the frame of "helplessness" to one suggesting conscious control and decision-making. When confronted with resistance, therapists constantly return to a positive description of the current and future behaviour of the family, to avoid a head-on battle, not because we are afraid of confrontation but because such an argument might lead to a symmetrical escalation or to feelings of defeat. Because of the anonymous consultation group, the therapist can "take sides" with the family—the enemy to be resisted is "out there" behind the mirror. The therapist can pretend to be as unsure about the meaning of the directives as the family, hence the frequent use of "Well, I don't know. . . ." In addition, the group's message about Serena's symptoms was worded rather vaguely: "To help the family in some mysterious way." It is extremely difficult for families to refute such vagueness. Lastly, the ground was laid for a later exploration of the mother's reclusive behaviour. It is significant that, even when this ancillary problem was broached in a relatively flirtatious and non-condemning way, the mother reacted as though she were being attacked. Her attitude alerted us to the necessity of wording our intentions in the most positive and noble of terms, to provoke co-operation rather than resistance.

In the post-session meeting, the group discussed how Serena's face had seemed to brighten as I delivered the group's message, a reaction I had not noticed because all my efforts had been towards engaging the parents and disarming them. Nevertheless, we were not predicting much change by the next session and thought that perhaps the family might somehow "lose" or "forget about" the chart. We are generally as cautious as possible about a family's response to our prescriptions, so that we will not be caught unprepared. We inevitably find that, despite our most rigorous efforts at predicting outcomes, families still surprise us.

Session II: Prescribing a Ritual

In the pre-session meeting three weeks later, I discussed my tentative approach. Hoping that the family had at least partially done their homework, I was going to try to restructure the parents' solution to the problem, encourage Serena to develop autonomy with her problem (by assigning her a personal worry list), and perhaps investigate the mother's anxieties further.

At the beginning of the session, the mother quickly handed me the chart. Both parents assured me that Serena was "greatly improved." In fact, there were only four reported incidents of illness, and the parents had written that "we decided to try and get her interested in other things. Maybe getting out more and back to doing gym in school. Keeping her busy." When I asked what specifically they were getting her to do, they replied that Serena was being asked to do the dishes and some light housework, requests she had apparently agreed to without a fuss. I was told (mostly by the mother) that Serena was not spending nearly as much time lying on her bed and that she was "back to normal." Closer questioning revealed this to be an exaggeration: although Serena was less symptomatic, she still complained about school and chest pains, and she did not go out with friends. I then returned to the consultation group for the mid-session meeting.

We were in a quandary. The girl's symptoms having abated far more rapidly than expected, we were left without the leverage of her problems to motivate the family to make the structural changes we felt were crucial. Without the pressure of worry—about a child, for example—families are rarely motivated to go through the bothersome business of changing habits. In fact, little other than Serena's symptoms had seemed to change: Serena and her brother still appeared timid and withdrawn; the mother was still intensely anxious. The parental coalition did, however, seem strengthened. We decided that I would reinforce the parents for their united stand, yet predict a backslide in an attempt to re-intensify the concern for the daughter. We also decided to prescribe a ritual, often found extremely helpful in stemming the tide of family interactions. As Selvini-Palazolli (16) has written, rituals, which are a series of specific actions and words involving all family members, both engage the group in striving towards a common goal and provide a new interactional game to replace the old dysfunctional one. In addition, rituals allow the therapist to introduce meaningful change without commenting on the dysfunctional norms, thereby avoiding the risk of alienating the family. The following exchange occurred when I returned to the therapy room:

Therapist: Well, I want to tell you that the group and I are struck by the manner in which you, Mr. and Mrs. Salter, have taken some definite united action in regard to Serena.

Father: I don't think we did anything we weren't doing before.

Therapist: Well, I don't know. It seems as though she has improved and I can only attribute this change to the decision you two have made. Anyway, there is something important that I want to tell you. While the group members are impressed, they are also worried. I know this might sound a little strange—it took me a while to see their point— anyway, they are concerned that Serena is getting better too fast and that this is dangerous for the whole family. They think that Serena's illnesses are her way of worrying for the whole family. (Parents begin to protest.) I know this sounds strange, but the group is very firm: they think that Serena is the family's vent and that she will get sick again to help the family. However, we have come up with a way probably to prevent such a relapse, by having you all share the worrying with her. You must do this in a very organized way. Every night I want you to sit down as a family for exactly forty minutes. You will each have ten minutes in which to present your individual worries to the rest of the family, and then the others are to offer suggestions for helping. I want you each to come up with as many worries as you can in the time period. I want you, Serena, to save up your worries for this nightly worry session and not discuss them with anyone during the day. However, I would like you to record them privately and give the list to me next time.

Sam: I don't have that many worries. I don't know what I would say.

Therapist: For the sake of your family, Sam, you must make up pretend worries if you can't think of real worries because it is crucial that you all get the practice of expressing worries and helping each other.

I then had Sam talk about a worry and had the family do a trial run. I also had the parents specify the exact time and place for the nightly ritual.

There were several reasons for establishing the ritual:

1. It provided a specific structure, thus limiting the amount of worry that the family members experienced.
2. Engaging all family members in helpful give-and-take would break the exclusive mother-daughter alliance.
3. The ritual carried with it the implication that experiencing and expressing concerns and worries is normal and necessary in *everyone's* life, thus taking the focus and burden off Serena as the "problem" in the family.
4. The ritual would give Serena the opportunity to help her family overtly, through spoken advice rather than covertly through psychosomatic problems.

We also hoped these nightly sessions would provide additional material for our next session. In assigning Serena the task of keeping a private worry list, I was attempting to establish a break between her and her mother, with whom she was still sharing various vague woes, and thus to encourage more age-appropriate autonomy.

Session III: Refocussing the Problem

Before the third session, the group and I agreed that, if the family had performed their ritual, I would deal more directly with the mother's anxieties and the difficulties in the marriage.

Sam was absent from the session because of exams in school. The rest of the family reported having done the ritual quite often, although not every night. They said that they had enjoyed the experience and had found each other quite helpful. When I asked what concerns had been raised, the parents described the children's problems, but rarely mentioned their own. They admitted, however, that the children had made helpful comments and suggestions to them. Serena gave me her private worry list containing just six items, all of which related to school. It appeared that her symptoms had virtually disappeared, and the mother seemed quite eager to end therapy right then and there. When I carefully questioned the father about other worries to do with his children, he commented that they did not seem as involved in extra-curricular activities as other children. He quickly qualified the statement by denying the implication that he wanted them to "run wild" like many other teenagers and expressed great pleasure with them. The father had offered me a new "lead" which I followed enthusiastically. I pressed Mr. Salter to talk about what he thought might happen if his children did not socialize more. I praised him as an authority on the subtleties of dealing with the outside world since he had, so successfully, advanced himself in his profession. I suggested that he would not want his children to have social handicaps (which I described nonchalantly in excruciating detail). I then questioned the parents extensively about their social lives and discovered the mother to be almost agoraphobic in her avoidance of going outside. She would spend hours getting dressed and made-up before going anywhere, much to the father's frustration. I encouraged the father to express his annoyance in an effort to elicit some conflict.

At mid-session, the group discussed how to manipulate social handicaps in getting the family to make necessary structural changes. We realized we could use the family's value of togetherness to induce more appropriate behaviour in the mother and between the parents. We decided that I would explain to the parents that they needed to teach their children how to socialize. I would give the parents specific directions, and the task would be introduced as having come from a member of the group who was an expert in adolescent development. We also decided that the message and directions would be sent by letter to each family member. When I returned, I read the family the following message:

> The group and I are very pleased that Serena has been feeling much better lately. However, we understand that Mr. and Mrs. Salter are still concerned that Serena and Sam are not very involved with other young people. The group and I believe that the solution to this problem rests with mother and father. We believe that in this family the children have great respect for their parents and look to them as examples of how to behave. We also see the children as being at a crucial age for learning the skill of how to get involved with friends without getting out of control. We believe that Serena and Sam can best learn this skill from their parents.
>
> Thus we recommend that the parents teach the children how to get involved with the outside world in a proper way. Since we know that children learn best by following what their parents *do*, we recommend the following:

1) Once a week Mr. and Mrs. Salter go out on a date in the evening. Mr. Salter will decide on the time and place of the date and Mrs. Salter will spend exactly one half-hour getting ready for the date. The next day the children are encouraged to carefully question their parents about their date and the parents are to stress the positive and fun aspects of going out on a date.
2) Once a week, Mrs. Salter is to go out and visit someplace or someone. That evening she will describe to the family her day in detail and emphasize the positive and fun aspects of her experiences with the outside world.

The group and I are aware that we are asking the parents to inconvenience themselves by doing things that are out of the usual pattern. However, we really feel that it is far better that children learn from their parents than from anyone else.

Although Mrs. Salter became quite agitated, I emphasized that I thought the recommendation necessary, maintaining that, if the children did not learn these skills from their parents, they might learn them from "other sources," which could lead them astray. As support, I echoed the mother's own words, "Like mother, like daughter." In addition, I stated that, although the group doubted whether the parents could carry out this difficult task, I had no question that they would dedicate themselves to becoming leaders and teachers of their children. This is an example of making a therapeutic triangle of the consultation group (14), allowing the therapist the flexibility of encouraging and discouraging change.

We had several reasons for mailing each family member a copy of the prescription:

1. The prescriptions and directions were fairly long and complicated, easy to forget if simply heard.
2. When families receive a written message at home, they cannot argue with the therapist about the contents, thus disqualifying the directive. Furthermore, the written message often commands respect and compliance.
3. Although Sam was absent from the session, he would remain involved in the intervention if he received a copy of the instructions.
4. Sending copies to each member of the family reinforces individuality. Moreover, it maximizes the potential impact of the message and the possibility that at least one person will react to it.
5. The message indirectly required the children to observe their parents' behaviour. Sending the message to each family member increased the pressure on the parents to abide by the directive for the sake of the children.

Session IV: Reinforcing the Change

In the pre-session meeting, we discussed our prediction that the parents would not carry out the tasks. We had been struck by the intensity of the

mother's anxiety upon hearing the message. We considered using a paradoxical prescription of the system, normally adopted only after families
show themselves resistant to carrying out compliance-based directives. If
the task had not been carried out, we planned that the group would
interrupt by phone to state that I had pressured the family to change "too
much too fast" and that the mother would be treated as an invalid by all
family members (thus prescribing and exaggerating the system). I would
then side with the group and discourage the change I had previously
encouraged.

The family was to surprise us:

> Upon entering, all family members, the mother in particular, looked
> markedly changed. There was an air of gaiety and happiness. The mother
> appeared very bubbly and proud as she reported having exceeded the
> requirements of the directive by spending more time with friends than we
> had suggested and less in primping. The parents had had a number of
> enjoyable outings. I expressed delight and surprise, emphasizing that the
> tasks had certainly been difficult and that the parents had surpassed our
> expectations. When I asked if the parents had noticed such changes
> having any immediate effect on the children, the mother reported that
> Serena was much happier at school. Serena pleasantly concurred, evi-
> dence that she had learned from her mother how better to cope with the
> outside world.

In the mid-session meeting, we decided that the family had made
significant progress towards our original goals and that the presenting
symptoms had disappeared. It was time to reinforce the changes and say
goodbye to the family. In reinforcing change, we not only praised the
family, but also carefully attributed all improvement to family members'
changes in behaviour and attitude. Our goal is for families to leave therapy
with a heightened sense of their own competence.

> Therapist: The group would like to tell you how happy they are for you
> and to congratulate you on your success.

> Father: Yes, I think we are all doing better and Serena's really back to her
> old self—she screeches and is always talking on the phone.

> Therapist: Well, what do you think has caused this change?

> Father: For one thing, maybe she's not worrying so much about other
> people (glancing over at the mother).

> Therapist: (feigning surprise) Oh, so you think that Serena was too
> worried about her mother?

> Father: Could be.

> Therapist: Well, that's a very interesting theory, very interesting indeed,
> almost as though she worried herself sick.

Father: Kinda.

Therapist: Well, what do you think, Mrs. Salter?

Mother: Oh well, I think she has learned not to take things so seriously. She was too much of a worrier before.

Therapist: I agree with you and I also think that she learned how to control her worrying from you, because of the changes you have made with yourself and with your husband.

Mother: Well, maybe.

Therapist: You know, the group told me that there is no question in their minds that Serena has gotten better because the family has co-operated, pulled together, and shown her that she really doesn't have to carry everyone's troubles on her back, that you can each carry your own pack of worries and be okay.

Therapy was ended after the fourth session.

Interpersonal Dynamics of the Consultation Group

One of our main objectives for a consultation group was to create a pool of expertise in this area of therapy. Because most members of the group had been trained in other modes, we all had to work at adopting ideas of problem causality and change quite alien to our training and experience. Given our dissimilar backgrounds, we found our early meetings characterized by confusion and grossly diverging conceptualizations of the problem. To bring order out of chaos, we devised a credo of rules, expectations, and theoretical premises, which we made verbal commitments to accept and follow. Our prescribed task was akin to an initiation ritual, and it improved group functioning. In addition, we set aside time to discuss the books and articles that we were all reading on the subject.

It would be inaccurate to imply that all the group's difficulties disappeared following these innovations. As a group, we are always vulnerable to the same problems in interaction and errors in thinking as the families we work with. For example, when it has, at times, been unclear who is ultimately to decide the form and content of the intervention, the results are uncertainty and delay. Thus, although we call ourselves a peer consultation group, we realize the need to designate the therapist as having final word and responsibility for his or her family. The structural hierarchy of the consultation group became flexible, not horizontal; each group member now takes a turn occupying the "executive" position. Another realization is that we can still be trapped by linear thinking, blaming the problem on one family member. To counteract this tendency, we repeatedly attempt to discuss the answer to the question: "How is each family member contributing to the problem?" A final challenge is to function productively although we do not have the same values or world views. Although the dissimilarity of our backgrounds generates a variety of suggestions and ideas about a case, it can also lead to value clashes and dissonance. In these situations, we have found it helpful to delineate the opposing views and agree to disagree.

Why, despite such difficulties, have we continued working as a group? First, the existence of the group has greatly supported our move from the linear and individual conceptual model of therapy to a model that is circular and systems-oriented. Second, the presence of the group forces us to be more specific and precise in our hypotheses. Third, by being accountable to our peers, we become more rigorous in our approach. Fourth, group members help us present interventions. In strategic therapy, the therapist needs to be quite forthright and firm, a behaviour at odds with the non-directive empathic posture we have been trained to adopt; therefore, we frequently rehearse the delivery and wording of a message in the mid-session meeting and accept criticism. A fifth advantage of a consultation group is that phone calls to the therapist interrupt dysfunctional repetitive cycles of interaction. By calling a therapist out for a meeting, the group can save him or her from being overwhelmed by a family's protest against, and resistance to a message or directive. Furthermore, the anonymous peer group can lend great support to the therapist's directive and can form a triangle with the therapist, thereby forcing the family to choose an ally. Papp (14, 15), Selvini-Palazzoli and her colleagues (17), and Coppersmith (2) report even greater benefits.

Strategic Family Therapy in Context

The assumptions of strategic family therapy are in clear conflict with the more established ideology of the intrapsychically oriented therapies. In strategic family therapy, the past is not crucial, the traditional theory of suppressed emotions as the cause of problems is irrelevant, and the therapeutic focus is on the family rather than on the individual child. Family therapy tends to challenge the professional hierarchy in which psychiatrists maintain superiority. With family therapy, all professionals, regardless of training and discipline, must be able to work with more than one person. Professional discipline and specific skills (like psychological testing or extensive case histories) become less valued. With this shift in clinical functions, staff of various disciplines may no longer accept differential salaries and, therefore, may pressure the administration. Such changes may threaten the status quo of a clinical setting and consequently encourage resistance from other staff and administration.

The strategic family therapy group at our clinic has been spared many of these struggles because of its inception when most staff had already become open to, and interested in, family therapy. In addition, the administration had already begun to equalize professional job descriptions and salary. Nevertheless, for the first two years, the group came under repeated attack for being "manipulative and unethical." Some staff viewed us as a group of conniving therapists who spent our time devising diabolical ways of tricking clients into changing and who were insensitive to the family's "true" needs. The implication was that good family therapy required complete honesty, openness, and spontaneity, and that the therapist should be a model of a "healthy" person for the "less healthy" family members. Only after considerable discussion with staff about basic notions of therapy and the roles of therapists did some of these concerns and reservations disappear.

The reactions might have been less negative had we, from the beginning, been more open about our rationale. When we first started the group, we were so excited that we rather arrogantly assumed all other staff would automatically understand the innovativeness and importance of the approach. Confrontations forced us to become much clearer and more specific about the values underlying strategic techniques and the role and responsibility of the therapist to direct the family toward productive solutions. (This role-definition contrasts sharply with the traditional definition of therapist as consultant and/or gentle facilitator.) Consistent with the definition is the mandate to plan interventions carefully and to be keenly aware of how therapists influence their clients. We believe that clients with long-standing problems do not usually change or respond reasonably when the therapist gives them supposedly objective observations of their behaviour. In addition, we believe it normal for most clients to resist changing familiar patterns and that dramatic measures are often necessary. By paradoxically encouraging a symptom or a system's dysfunctional behaviour, we are trying to free clients from their problems. In being selective and reframing the information that we feed back to clients, we are trying to relate to their idiosyncracies and beliefs. In planning strategies, we are trying to help families change as quickly as possible.

After discussing our rationale, and after observing our sessions, and listening to edited tapes of complete cases, the staff modified its description of us from "manipulative and unethical" to "directive and tactical." Slowly, many of the techniques that we had been using were adopted. At present, several staff members are experimenting with a variation of strategic family therapy by working in pairs, with one therapist behind the one-way mirror, and by using phone calls and mid-session meetings to devise tasks and strategies.

In summary, the experience of working in a strategic family therapy, peer consultation group has liberated and lifted the restrictions of traditional therapy both within the group and within the agency. Just as families learn alternate ways of functioning and problem-solving, so we have learned alternate ways of intervening and of taking advantage of our various backgrounds to achieve our goal of helping families change.

References

1. Andolfi, M. *Family Therapy: An Interactional Approach*. New York: Plenum Press, 1979.
2. Coppersmith, E. "Expanding Uses of the Telephone in Family Therapy." *Family Process*. 19(4): 411-417.
3. Ellis, A. *Reason and Emotion in Psychotherapy*. New York: Lyle Stuart, 1962.
4. Ellis, A., and Harper, R. *A new guide to rational living*. Englewood Cliffs, N.J.: Prentice-Hall, 1975.
5. Haley, J. "Why a Mental Health Clinic Should Avoid Family Therapy." *Journal of Marriage and Family Counselling*. 1 (1975): 3-12.
6. Haley, J. *Problem-Solving Therapy*. San Francisco: Jossey-Bass, 1976.
7. Haley, J. *Leaving Home*. New York: McGraw-Hill, 1980.
8. Liddle, A.H. "The Emotional and Political Hazards of Teaching and Learning Family Therapy." *Family Therapy*. 1978, 5(1).
9. Liebman, R., Minuchin, S., Balcer, L., and Rosman, B. "The Role of the Family in the Treatment of Chronic Asthma." In P. Guerin, ed. *Family Therapy, Theory and Practice*. New York: Gardner, 1976.
10. Madanes, C. *Strategic Family Therapy*. San Francisco: Jossey-Bass, 1981.
11. Minuchin, S. *Families & Family Therapy*. Cambridge, Mass.: Harvard University Press, 1974.
12. Minuchin, S., Rosman, B., and Baker, L. *Psychosomatic Families*. Cambridge, Mass.: Harvard University Press, 1978.
13. Minuchin, S., and Fishman, H.C. *Family Therapy Techniques*. Cambridge, Mass.: Harvard University Press, 1981.
14. Papp, P. "The family who had all the answers." In P. Papp, ed. *Family Therapy Full Length Case Studies*. New York: Gardner, 1977.
15. Papp, P. "The Greek Chorus and Other Techniques of Paradoxical Therapy." *Family Process*. 19 (1, 1980): 45-57.
16. Selvini-Palazzoli, M. *Self-Starvation*. London: Chaucer, 1974.
17. Selvini-Palazzoli, M., Boscola, L., Cecchin, G., and Prata, G. *Paradox and Counterparadox*. New York: Jason Aronson, 1978.
18. Watzlawick, P., Weakland, S., and Fisch, R. *Change*. New York: Norton, 1974.
19. Watzlawick, P. *The Language of Change*. New York: Basic, 1978.
20. White, M. "Structural and Strategic Approaches to Psychosomatic Families." *Family Process*. 18 (3, 1979): 303-314.

10
Strategic Family Therapy ...
Feedback and Response*

Allon Bross

This article focusses on two aspects of a therapeutic encounter. The first is the therapist's perception of the family as he engages, assesses, and manoeuvres the family into a position which requires its members to change. The second aspect is the family's perception of what took place during the therapy, as recorded by the mother.**

Introduction

Rarely is the therapist furnished with an account of his work as viewed by the client. The following case, which is representative of my approach to family therapy, presented such an opportunity.

Five months after Mrs. Laura X., age 32, terminated therapeutic sessions that had resolved the family problem to be described, she revisited the clinic complaining of stress-induced back and chest pain. Once this situational stress was alleviated, using strategic methods, Laura, a social service student, asked whether she could interview me for one of her college courses. Discussion concerning my method and approach to problem-solving led to a reference to our previous contact. I asked specifically what she could recall that seemed to have produced changes in herself or members of her family. I suggested that she write about our contact from Sessions one through four as she remembered them. Her full account appears in its original form.

My role in therapy is to intervene in the relationships between family members that maintain dysfunctional behaviour, to induce change, and thereby to eliminate the problem. In order to do so I must clearly understand (a) the specific family system, (b) the problem, precisely defined, with which the family has come, and how it is useful in the solution of other difficulties, and (c) the sequence of events, that is, the predictable pattern of behaviour that helps maintain the problem. Once I have examined these data I select those interventions that I hope will lead to the desired changes.

---

*Reprinted with the permission of *The Journal of Strategic and Systemic Therapies.*

**The names of those involved in the case have been changed to ensure the confidentiality of our contact. I am exceptionally grateful to the family for the helpful comments.

First Contact

The X family was referred to the clinic by a school public health nurse. Armed with a résumé of the family background and the nurse's perception of the problem, I telephoned Mrs. Laura X. She explained that Paul, age 11, was having problems at school which "affect his character and school-work." Laura, who had been separated from her husband four and one-half years prior to our contact date, believed that Paul had not accepted the loss of his father. As the story later bears out, the meaning of "loss of father" had far different implications for me than for my client.

Generally, I take very little information about the problem over the telephone, preferring to investigate it when the family arrives. I asked Laura to bring in the entire family, Paul, Marty, age 9, and Nora, age 6.

The Initial Interview—March 10, 1977

As I greeted the family in the waiting room I noticed that the three children were well-behaved and at ease. The mother, however, was visibly anxious. During the interview Laura's comments and concerns focussed on Paul's behaviour. She reported that, since she and her husband had separated, Paul had become disrespectful and "bossy" within the family. He frustrated his mother by telling everyone what to do, usurping her parental authority. Laura said Paul's demands placed severe constraints on her time and energy.

As I began to ask the children questions directly, Laura volunteered their answers. This micro-transaction which repeatedly occurred, indicated that Laura was an over-protective mother. Laura's anxiety, as a device to protect her children, would be the key to the solution of this family's difficulty.

Laura, as a common example of the head of a single-parent family in transition, had failed to make a necessary adjustment in her role. Laura, systemically—in relation to her husband, a strict and harsh disciplin-arian—was afforded the role of being soft and protective of her children. From my perception, Laura maintained her protective role, felt bad about her children losing their father, and placed herself in an ineffectual position vis-à-vis her eldest son. Paul, in this same transitional shift, assumed more of a parental function in order to help his mother; however, his role of inappropriate parenting caused heightened conflict between mother and son.

The more the mother felt that she was being a strict parent, the more the son misbehaved. In fact, the more that Laura became upset, the more helpless she felt. Laura interpreted her frustration as the result of the failure of her attempts to be strict.

My therapeutic goal was to mobilize Laura's helplessness into a position of strength in order for her to set clear parental limits for Paul. In doing so I would shift the control and power from the child to the mother, breaking the dysfunctional repetitive sequence of events that perpetuated the problem.

Session 2—April 6, 1977

The family met with the consultant psychiatrist who confirmed a family-pattern disturbance and recommended continued work with the family.*

Session 3—May 3, 1977

In order to become as selective as possible about my interventions, I collect as much data as possible to confirm a working hypothesis.

This was the family's second session with me. I drew a family genogram based on my original therapeutic "hunches." In using this technique of drawing a map of the interrelationships of the family, I (a) obtained additional data to confirm my working hypothesis, (b) began to create some therapeutic distance between myself and the family via the use of a blackboard, and (c) granted some power to myself as the therapist in order that my intervention would be effective. The family genogram clearly illustrates that the child's problem is a family affair. By the end of the session I had enough data to plan an interventive pretext for change.

Session 4—June 7, 1977

Laura's protectiveness would be difficult to deal with directly. I had to mobilize a change by either avoiding her resistance or using the energy of the resistance to produce the change. Laura's ability to take control of her children's behaviour, especially Paul's, without feeling guilty about being non-protective, needed to develop. She had to accept responsibility for being the "parent" in this family. If she succeeded, Paul's behaviour would improve and some normal expectations of his role of eldest son in a father-less family could be established.

I staged an enactment that would result in a failure. An enactment refers to the construction of an interpersonal scenario in the session in which a dysfunctional transaction is played out. With the X family I encouraged Laura to speak to Paul about a couple of problems that she felt must be resolved. When she spoke to Paul, he refused to pay attention until she began shouting. At the point where Laura's voice was raised I instructed her to pursue another problem because Paul was not paying attention. Upon her failure to obtain his compliance, I defined Paul's behaviour as being "mother deaf," and unable to hear anything she said. Laura agreed in discouragement.

It was important to use her discouragement in order to reverse this

---

*All families attending the Child Guidance Clinic are assessed by the staff consultant psychiatrist.

painful and problem-maintaining behaviour. The moment at which Laura displayed discouragement (giving up, helplessness) was the time that an intervention was needed for the therapy to move forward.

I told Laura that, somehow, Paul being "mother deaf" served a useful function in this family and that it ought to continue. I suggested that his behaviour served to prevent her from becoming lonely, or that he was simply trying to assist the family by taking control. I also advised Laura to remain helpless in order to please Paul. After all, she did not want to add to her guilt, and this was understandable. I then instructed her to chart the behaviour of all the children, noting how often she had to speak before they listened and obeyed. Perhaps we could determine why Paul had to be "bossy" and disobedient.

Laura verbally complied. However, the look on her face was one of dismay.

In fact, I encouraged Paul's misbehaviour with the hope that it would disappear. By encouraging him, I expected to convert Laura's discouragement into action. My prediction was that Laura would have to leave my office with the difficult task of resolving my "seemingly" anti-therapeutic message. My hunch was that, if Paul's behaviour continued, mother's would not, or if mother's behaviour continued, Paul's would not.

The pretext given for Paul's behaviour was a paradoxical intervention designed to unbalance the sequence of events that maintained the dysfunctional behaviour.

Session 5—June 14, 1977

Laura reported a noticeable change in the family and specifically in Paul's behaviour. Laura told me about repeated incidents where Paul and the other children refused to listen, but she had "put her foot down" and soon found compliance. She did not understand what had occurred; however, she wanted to continue for another session. I expressed surprise at what had happened and I applauded the turn of events. I continued to encourage Laura to do what was working for her.

It was my impression that I had successfully broken the dysfunctional transactional patterns and that this would allow the transitional shift in this family to occur. I felt that the work could be completed in one or two sessions.

Session 6—Not Attended

Laura telephoned to say that Paul had been kidnapped by her ex-husband and that we could not meet. She reported that Paul was continuing to do well, as was she. She felt that further sessions might not be needed. I instructed her to call and let me know how things developed concerning the kidnapping.

In early September Laura called. She told me the kidnapping incident was solved quickly, and there was temporary upset in the household. In addition she stated that Paul's behaviour had improved significantly both at home and at school. She felt that further sessions were not needed and that if assistance was required in the future, she would call me.

Mrs. Laura X.'s Written Account

Following an interview with the school vice-principal and public health nurse, at which time I expressed concern for my eldest son, arrangements were made for counselling. I received a call from Mr. Bross. An appointment was set up for March tenth, at ten a.m.

Mr. Bross asked that the entire family be present. I began to have a few doubts, since the words mental health implied to me that this clinic was for kids with real problems mentally and Paul didn't fit in this category, though my concern was partly due to his not doing well in school since his father and I separated. I also resented the idea that the entire family be involved but decided that following our initial visit, counselling would be concentrated on Paul.

March 10

After a frantic search and wading through numerous hospital halls, proper instructions finally led us to our destination some twenty minutes late. Shortly after giving our name to the receptionist, a gentleman arrived and introduced himself as Mr. Bross and we were led to a sitting room on the second floor. I was somewhat annoyed that Mr. B. was young, as I had doubted at the time of our telephone conversation and thought to myself, "They've likely given us someone who's just starting out. That's all I need."

Mr. B. joined us a few minutes later and started to speak to each one of us, by asking various getting-acquainted questions.

Marty sat very quietly only talking when spoken to, while Nora was a little more talkative and decided to try out different chairs in the process. Paul appeared somewhat uncomfortable with the entire situation and possibly feared this experience as all the blame centred on him. I was slightly nervous since this was my first such experience and I kept on wondering: "What next?"

I expressed my fear in Paul not accepting reality. That his father and I had been separated for four years with no chance of reconciliation. We discussed the behaviour problems—doesn't listen when spoken to; in fact, he totally ignores what I say. He is terribly bossy with his younger sister and brother. All this annoying me terribly.

Mr. Bross asked Paul how he felt about what was being said and at one point, had me look at Paul and speak to him directly, telling him how I felt. Mr. B. pointed out that whenever I spoke the message given was, "I don't like what you do Paul, but I love you." He suggested, "Stop telling him you love him—he already knows that." This was not being done knowingly and made me think of parents who discipline their kids (spanking) then love them to release guilt feelings. This brought a new awareness.

He discussed our next appointment to be made with a Dr. Brown, a psychiatrist, and warned that she usually runs half an hour behind time. This visit was to include the entire family as well.

I left with mixed feelings—wondering what was ahead and if indeed any good would come out of it, but at least I went away with something to think about—awareness of my behaviour.

April 6

We arrived twenty minutes prior to the appointment and nearly three hours later we were still waiting. The children were now getting restless, giddy, and active, while I could feel my anger mounting. Finally we were directed to Dr. Brown's office. No apology was given except that it was one of those days when everything had gone wrong, and how she had a terrible cold. At this point I couldn't sympathize with her and thought, "Big deal, lady, that is your problem, I have better things to do than waste three hours while trying to keep three kids quiet." I was too angry to say anything so I did very little talking, but the boys more than made up for this. They started to talk about an unrelated incident and started to laugh uncontrollably. I felt like an outsider looking in and thought, "My God, she'll really think he's kooky (Paul), even though I know that they were tired and nervous. To this day I don't know how Dr. Brown assessed the interview, but I'm not sure I want to know. I left wondering if she considered me unable to control my own children.

May 3

I wasn't too enthused with the idea of returning; however, I was curious with the outcome of our interview (the assessment made), and Dr. Brown did indicate that counselling was needed.

We arrived late once again (due to bus connections) and this, along with our own previous experience or incident, had me feeling pretty uptight so that when Mr. B. appeared, I thought to myself, "Don't you dare say a word about our being late."

Once settled and having discussed how things were since our last visit, Mr. B. proceeded to draw and explain a genogram and how all this related to our family dynamics. We discussed how each member of the family felt at the time of the separation and what happened as a result. Time up, we were once again asked to return—the entire family.

I felt this was a better visit and now resented less the idea that we all be present instead of just Paul, but I was still ambivalent about the whole thing.

June 7

We quickly re-discussed the genogram and proceeded with role play which emphasized the results or behaviour I was getting from Paul when speaking to him, e.g., asking that he please do . . . or be told to go to bed. The results were negative—he was "mother deaf," totally ignoring anything I'd say regardless of my being calm and polite, until I'd get angry and start yelling due to having repeated the same things over and over again.

Mr. B. said that he felt "Paul's behaviour had a function in this family" and told him to continue his pattern of behaviour—it's O.K. . . . I was asked to chart the behaviour of all three children—noting how often I had to speak before each listened.

I was stunned by what had been said to Paul and could say or do nothing, but nod my head—"Yes, I understand."

Then I began to wonder "What is going on?" I came here to get help, NOT to have someone reinforce Paul's undesirable behaviour by siding with him. This is my child, I know him, and you don't tell a child like Paul something like that. After only a few visits, you can't claim to really know him.

I could see the expression on Paul's face. First, one of surprise, then "Oh, great! This will be fun." Within ten minutes we boarded the bus and due to the cool wind, I told Paul not to open the window. He promptly replied (loud enough to be heard by all and arousing curiosity), "you know what he told me," and proceeded to open the window. I was furious and said, "I don't care what he said, you'll do as I say."

I was fuming all the way home and kept wondering "Why?—did he have an ulterior motive or had he simply meant just that?" I decided to take him aside next time and find out. If there was a reason—what was it? If not—I was prepared to tell him that I could kill him, if I was still sane by then.

I consulted a couple of close friends—told them what had been said and asked how they felt, then told them that I had reacted the same way. Again I began to wonder if Mr. B. was perhaps young and inexperienced— perhaps I should ask to see someone else.

I wasn't too consistent in recording the children's behaviour since it seemed as if I was constantly running for a pen and the piece of paper. I found this annoying.

June 14

I realized that I forgot to bring in the requested information but decided to try and follow it through next time. On our way to Mr. B.'s office, Paul and Marty walked closely behind him and, as they approached the doorway, Paul pushed past Marty to get a particular seat (which they had discussed in the waiting room—then I had warned them to behave). This went unnoticed by Mr. B., though they just missed pushing him.

I followed, grabbed Paul by the arm and sitting him in a chair opposite the one intended, I thought "There, I don't care Mister what you have to say about this."

Now taking note, Mr. B. asked what happened and telling him, I was shocked when he replied, "That's good." I had expected a negative comment. I sat down more bewildered than ever. How can he side with Paul and now approve what I just did—it doesn't balance.

June
Sessions ended abruptly (due to kidnap attempt by father). I noticed an improvement in Paul's behaviour but was unable to identify the reasons for it.

September
By this time I began to get a greater insight into the entire situation and realized the extent that I had contributed to Paul's undesired behaviour.

Factors contributing to this were:

1. Paul played on my guilt feelings (denying him a father).
2. I was unconsciously projecting images of his father on Paul rather than seeing him as unique.
3. My inner feelings of insecurity contributed, as I didn't have the ability to take a stand, mean what I'd say, and carry it through.
4. I was more anxious about the future and what could happen in five to ten years time in preference to dealing with the here and now.

Now as I reflect on the past year, I realize that I was denying to myself that in reality I was responsible.

11

Intergenerational Continuity and Strategic Family Intervention: A Case Study

Patricia H. Lindsey

Non-clinical families tend to retain significant and enduring contact with their effective kindred. With respect to clinical families, the involvement of kindred is thought either to be associated with the blurring of intergenerational boundaries (the "boundary" perspective) or to be the source of distorted intra-psychic introjections which, in turn, are the bases of family problems (the "intergenerational" perspective). Examination of the case of the S family suggests that in certain respects, these apparently divergent positions may be reconciled. The clinical and theoretical implications of such a reconciliation are discussed. In particular, the intergenerational continuity of dysfunctional family themes is explored.

Introduction

Throughout this century in North America, on average, not less than 90% of all single adult men and women have eventually married (18). Such an event links not only two individuals, but also two previously unrelated families into a patterned network of relations, that is, a kinship network or system (58, 59). With the recent increase in the rates of divorce and remarriage (18), such networks can become extremely complex, forming, in some cases, what Bohannan (12) has called "divorce chains" of linked households.

From the existence of such networks, however, it does not necessarily follow that the nuclear family maintains an ongoing relationship with its extended family members. Indeed, until approximately 1950, it was widely accepted that the family was relatively isolated from kin (26, 73, 74). This view was based on the assumption that the social differentiation and diversity associated with industrialization and urbanization tended to dissolve primary group bonds, including those of the extended family (62, 78, 28, 53). Accordingly, it was argued that the geographic and social mobility characteristic of North America was fundamentally incompatible with the maintenance of extended family ties (63, 64).

In the intervening 30 years, however, data have rapidly accumulated indicating that this view of the relationship (or lack of it) between the family and its extended kin was and is largely or wholly invalid. As of this writing, there is almost complete consensus in the literature concerning at least the following three points:

1. Implicit in the foregoing formulation is the notion that modern industrialization and urbanization destroyed the three-generation co-residential extended family. This necessarily assumes that such a family form not only existed in the past, but was quite prevalent. Available historical data, however, strongly suggest that this idealized family form in fact never did exist in large numbers, either in North America or Europe (20, 21, 30, 45, 46, 28, 35). That such a view of the past continues to persist says more about our jaundiced view of the present than it does about the facts of our agrarian past.

2. Far from being isolated, current evidence suggests that the nuclear family tends to maintain close, significant ongoing ties with the extended family (47, 39, 74, 50, 51, 52, 68, 2, 3, 69, 70, 71). Such involvement tends to (a) particularly involve the activity of the mother, especially with respect to her own married daughters (3, 71, 39); (b) include residential propinquity (19); (c) be especially important among working-class and certain ethnic-group families (4, 80, 56); and (d) extend throughout the life cycle (70, 71).

3. The relationship between the family and the extended family tends to promote the welfare of both systems through a variety of forms of mutual support (59). With respect to crises, for example, Caplan (17) notes that the extended family acts to mediate stress in the following ways: by acting to collect and disseminate information; by operating as a feedback guidance system; by providing a source of ideology; by acting to guide and mediate problem-solving; by serving as a source of practical services and aid; by providing a haven for rest and recuperation; by operating as a reference and control group; by serving to validate members' family identity; and, by helping members to achieve a sense of emotional mastery (see also 67, 27, 54).

Collectively, these data clearly indicate that the relationship between the non-clinical family and its extended family is, in general, significant, enduring, and reciprocal. They have little to say, however, concerning the role of the extended family in either the development and/or the maintenance of family dysfunction. This is presumably the province of the clinical (i.e., family therapy) literature and, in light of the foregoing review, would be expected to have much to say. In fact, the contrary is the case. Available data are scanty, scattered, and divergent.

More specifically, two disparate themes characterize the relevant literature.* The first concerns the issue of the maintenance of optimal

---

*A novel, third formulation has recently been advanced by Reiss (67). In oversimplified terms, this holds that the family's relationship to its extended family is a function of the family's paradigm, that is, its assumptions and premises about the nature of the world. Conversely, the kin network may significantly affect the shape of that paradigm, particularly during periods of crisis when it is most susceptible to reorganization.

boundary permeability. Marriage requires reorganization of the family system. This produces a temporary disequilibrium around the need to establish the separateness of three connected families (66). Family dysfunction tends to be associated with family systems whose boundaries deviate sharply from some moderate level of permeability, either being inappropriately open to the influence of the extended family (8) or completely impervious to that influence (23).

A related formulation is advanced by Haley (34) and Minuchin (57). This holds that effective family functioning requires hierarchical organization involving clear, distinct boundaries between levels, both within the family system (between parents and children) and between the family and its extended family (between parents and their parents). In this context, family dysfunction tends to be associated with the blurring of intergenerational boundaries characterized by covert cross-generational coalitions. Such coalitions, moreover, tend to be symmetrical; a coalition between parent and child will tend to be balanced by an isomorphic coalition between the other parent and a grandparent (see 38). Such coalitions, insofar as they interfere with the various tasks which family systems must perform, if they are to remain viable, result in distress to all participants in the kin network.

In both cases, these formulations imply that the involvement of the extended family (a) is directly associated with the maintenance of dysfunctional patterns of family interaction; (b) prevents the resolution of conflict, either within and/or between the systems in question; (c) impedes the process of individuation crucial to child socialization; and (d) is transacted in the present, as part of the ongoing processes which characterize the kin network, such that therapy is focussed on the client-family.

The second theme concerns the issue of the intergenerational transmission of irrational ways of thinking and feeling. Exemplified by the work of Framo (24, 25), Bowen (15, 42), and Whitaker (60, 77), this view holds that current family difficulties largely stem from efforts to overcome intrapsychic conflicts and transference distortions which initially arose in the family of origin.* The difficulties in question may reside solely in the previous generation (Framo, Whitaker) or may represent increasingly reduced individual differentiation culminating over several generations (Bowen). Whatever the time scale involved, perpetuation of the problem requires selection of a spouse whose attributes either bear some resemblance to the individual's family of origin (Whitaker) and/or which exhibit split-off and denied aspects of the self (Framo). Consequently, the seeds of family dysfunction exist in the past and, in most cases, positively require the

---

*Related formulations may be found in Lidz (48, 49), Ackerman (1), Meissner (55), Boszormenyi-Nagy and Spark (14), Boszormenyi-Nagy and Ulrich (13), Haas (31), Paul and Paul (65), and Headley (36).

involvement of members of the family of origin (at least for part of the treatment process) in order to achieve problem resolution.

The differences between these formulations are apparent. With respect to the "boundary" perspective: (a) dysfunctional family processes are located in the present in the ongoing interaction among family members; (b) while there may be historical linkages between past experience and present behaviour, these may be disregarded for both explanatory and therapeutic purposes; (c) the involvement of extended family members in therapy, if it occurs at all, is primarily designed to strengthen, clarify, and reaffirm family boundaries and hierarchical organization; and (d) the bases of mate selection are outside the purview of this formulation.

In contrast, with respect to the "intergenerational" perspective: (a) dysfunctional family processes are located in the members' psychic representations of past events as these are acted out in the present; (b) there is a direct causal relationship between introjected past events and current interactional processes, such that these introjects are critical for both explanatory and therapeutic purposes; (c) the involvement of extended family in therapy is the only way to effectively resolve the conflicts and distortions which underlie the family's current difficulties; and (d) the bases of mate selection are central to the explanation of, and successful intervention in current family problems.

Given such divergence, can these perspectives be reconciled or is one forced to select one formulation and reject the other? In the remainder of this paper, I explore this question, using as a vehicle for this purpose the case history of the S family.

Assessment

The S family was seen in treatment for a total of six two-hour sessions. The therapy team consisted of myself and a consultant who remained behind a one-way mirror throughout, communicating with me by telephone with comments, observations, and suggestions.

At the time that it entered treatment, the nuclear family consisted of Don, age 15, the identified patient; his mother, Rose, age 35; and mother's live-in boyfriend, Les, age 36. Their "effective kindred" (67, p. 276) consisted of Rose's mother, Joan, age 62; her father, Bill, age 75; and her brother, Jim, age 26, who resided with his aged parents who also provided him with some financial support.

Present in the first four sessions were Rose, Don, Les, and Jim. Joan attended the last two sessions, while her husband Bill attended not at all, although it was never entirely clear whether this was because he had refused to attend or because my request that he attend was never passed on to him. As events unfolded, reliance on the family to recruit Bill was seen in retrospect as a serious intervention error (10). While he did not attend in the flesh, his presence in "ghostly" form (cf. 44) significantly shaped our therapeutic encounter.

In what follows below, I present the history and presenting problems of the S family as these emerged during the first four sessions. The tidiness and coherence of this portrait, however, is misleading, for these data emerged haltingly, piecemeal, and with much overlap and inconsistency among members' accounts. In this sense, what follows is my reconstruction and thus may diverge on particulars from the members' accounts. Moreover, in light of my preference for a strategic approach (see 16), the critical importance of historical data in this case marks a significant departure, one that I will return to in the discussion.

The single most salient feature of the family's history concerns the unsatisfactory nature of the marital relationship between Joan and Bill. Experiencing Bill as sullen, withdrawn, distant, and uncommunicative, Joan was deeply distressed but apparently resigned to her fate. Her opportunity for relief from her isolation came with the birth of her first child, Rose, from whom she sought support, "triangulating" her in the process (57, 15). Simultaneously, this acted to increase the distance between Bill and herself, a position he apparently retains to this day. The intensity of this relationship between Joan and Rose also affected her later child, Jim, who, like his father, felt and continues to feel somewhat distant from Joan.

Initially satisfying for both Joan and Rose, this state of affairs became increasingly unsatisfactory with time, as adolescence brought implicit demands for individuation, autonomy, and separateness (37, 43). Rose felt that she was being "suffocated." The result was a relationship that oscillated wildly between approach and avoidance, intimacy and anger, much in the fashion of Watzlawick et al.'s (76) classic "nag-withdraw" cycle. Eventually, these swings became intolerable for Rose who, despite her parents vehement objections, "escaped," at age 17, into marriage with George R., a 25-year-old truck driver.

This escape, however, was short-lived. An alcoholic, George was no less withdrawn than her father Bill, only one of several parallels between Rose's marital and family experience and that of her family of origin. While this relationship was to limp on for nine years, and to yield a son, Don, it was obviously doomed from the start (see 60) and ended in separation nine years ago.

Rose, deeply disturbed by the experience and badly in need of support, turned to her mother for help, moving in with her parents shortly thereafter. While the relationship between Rose and Joan continued to be tense and conflictual at times, it remained relatively satisfying for both of them until approximately two years ago. At this time, Rose again made a bid for independence and moved out to live with Les, whom she had met through her mother. For Rose, this involved two important transitional shifts: first, into a common-law marital relationship; and, second, into the position of taking on the full responsibility for parenting Don. Further, her relationship with Les, while more satisfactory than that of her first husband, remained relatively distant and quite circumscribed, with Rose refusing to allow Les any real responsibility for parenting Don, a situation not unlike the relationship between her parents.

Joan responded to Rose's relationship with Les with rage. Ostensibly, this was related to the fact that they were living together while unmarried. Less obviously, her response related to the fact that once again she was left alone with her husband and son, neither of whom provided her with any sense of support and intimacy. Over time, disappointment and frustration with Rose took the form of a covert coalition between herself and her grandson Don against Rose.

As this relationship developed, Don began showing signs of distress, culminating, on April 7, 1981, in Don being admitted on an emergency basis to a community general hospital because of an overdose of 30 tablets of Imiprimine. Subsequently transferred to our in-patient psychiatric unit, it became clear that Don was deeply unhappy, was in almost constant conflict with his mother, was experiencing difficulties at school (including truancy), got on poorly with his peers, and specifically complained of his mother's inability to provide adequate parental controls.

Presentation of Members

Rose presented as a competent, concerned woman who appeared angry and frustrated about her lack of control over her son's behaviour. She related this to the fact that every time she had a row with him, he "took off" to his grandmother's, who allowed Don to stay with her rather than sending him back to mother to accept the consequences of his behaviour. She explained Joan's behaviour by relating it to the tense, conflictual relationship she has had with her since she was an adolescent. Rose maintained that this conflict has continued to this day and is now centred around Don. Interestingly, while she was only too willing to talk about her relationship with Joan, when asked about the relationship between her parents, her responses became short, clipped, and relatively uninformative. With respect to this issue, the same was true of her brother Jim.

Les, Rose's boyfriend, presented as a passive, non-confronting individual who admitted being involved with Don's problems only when mother requested help from him. He reported that he was often confused about his role in the family and was quite uncertain about the source(s) of Don's difficulties or about his part in them.

Next, Jim, mother's brother, was a likeable but immature and rather confused young man, who indicated that he was involved in Don's problems. For example, whenever Don came to his mother's house, grandmother would often recruit Jim to help deal with Don.

Finally, Don was a handsome but rather sullen, angry adolescent, who denied any responsibility for his problems. However, both he and mother reported that they had always been very close during the past year or so.

Interaction between Members

Interaction between Don and his mother was predominantly characterized by conflict. Mother made attempts to understand Don's position but when he defied her, she became angry and made ineffective attempts to control Don, who continued to behave in a provocative manner.

Les interacted with Don to a limited extent, but spent most of his time comforting mother when she appeared upset. Mother and Don appeared to pay little attention to his input, thus emphasizing his peripheral position in the S family.

In contrast, the relationship between mother and brother appeared tense. Mother verified this interpretation when she said that Jim was "interfering" in her efforts to parent Don. For example, Jim had gone to Don's school to check up on his behaviour without consulting his sister and had repeatedly supported grandmother's relationship with Don against mother.

However, despite the conflict between mother and brother, they were in complete agreement about at least one issue: their relationship with their mother was extremely tense. For example, they stated that they had to "walk on eggshells" whenever they were around her. Further, they concurred that grandmother played a very important role in mother's conflictual relationship with Don, intruding where she was not wanted. Despite their objections, they felt helpless to stop grandmother's intrusion. Indeed, by the end of the second session, Jim had shifted his perception of his sister from that of an incompetent mother to that of a "victim of their mother's interference." At no time did either relate their current difficulties to the relationship between their parents, nor did they overtly recognize any role that their father Bill might play. Ironically, Bill's peripheral position in the family was strikingly similar to that of Rose's boyfriend Les.

Formulation

In light of the theoretical issue raised in the introduction, what is especially salient about this case is that neither "boundary" nor "intergenerational" perspectives can fully account for all the assessment data given in the preceding three sections. Put differently, a complete and coherent formulation with respect to this case is not possible without some combination of elements from both perspectives.

On the one hand, the data show clearly that Don is caught in the knot of two interpersonal "triangles" involving, first, an over-involved mother and a peripheral "father" figure; and, second, an ineffectual mother and an over-intrusive grandmother, with his uncle Jim shifting loyalties between the two, first to grandmother, then to mother, and so on. The resulting blurring of intergenerational boundaries simultaneously (a) rendered Rose helpless and incompetent to effectively set limits and controls, while (b) directing attention away from the still smouldering conflict between mother and grandmother, mother and brother, and grandmother and grandfather. In effect, Don had become the "medium" through which family members talked while failing to really communicate.

On the other hand, this formulation does not account for (a) the striking parallels between Rose's marital experience and her family of origin—the peripheral nature of the husbands in both families, the closeness and conflict of mother-child ties, and the tendency to "escape" problems rather than confront them; and (b) the specific configuration of the coalitions that characterize this family system.

Both issues, however, are consistent with an intergenerational formulation. Specifically, two themes (cf. 37) show manifest intergenerational continuity in the S family: *differentiation* and *intimacy*. With respect to the first, all members of the family are characterized by incomplete differentiation—Joan's almost "symbiotic" involvement with her daughter, Rose's repeated efforts to achieve complete autonomy, Jim's continued dependence on his parents, and Don's flight into care, all suggest a shared family "rule" (cf. 40): no member may initiate activities that are completely separate from all other members. Thus, in the S family, efforts at demonstrating concern and commitment take the form of Ashby's (5) too richly cross-joined system, with reduced differentiation as one consequence.

With respect to the second theme, all relationships in the S family avoid, at least to some extent, true intimacy and mutuality. The distant relationship between grandmother and grandfather represents the prototype for all others, suggesting a pervasive fear of intimacy codified in such implicit rules as the following: intimacy is dangerous; intense feelings of either joy or anger are to be avoided; confrontation threatens the sanctity and integration of the family system; and, contentious issues are best left alone.

Significant in this context is the realization that in both cases the themes in question extend across three generations of the S family. In other words, the dysfunctional system in question is neither that of Rose and her immediate family nor that of Joan and hers, but rather that of the extended S family itself (cf. 6). While this formulation tends to emphasize the *shared* aspects of these family themes (67) rather than their intrapsychic representations, the former is not incompatible with the latter.

This intergenerational perspective also helps illuminate the specific configuration of the family's coalitions. In this context, the relationship between Joan and Bill may be seen as a "leading part" (32) in the S family system. On the assumption that interactional processes in family systems represent adaptive efforts in the face of perceived problems (75, 76), Joan's distant relationship with her husband and her intense relationship with her daughter appear as complementary facets of the same process. In turn, they help explain Joan's involvement with her grandson as a metaphor for her relationship with her daughter, while Rose's distant relationships with Les and Jim echo the distance characteristic of her family of origin.

The results of these family themes and triangles for the participants were as follows:

1. Don was being prevented from fully individuating and becoming autonomous. At the same time, it was difficult for him to work out an appropriate degree of closeness and distance from his grandparents, his uncle, and his "stepfather." As well, he could not develop a realistic picture of his mother.

2. Rose was prevented from performing her parental functions and was made to feel incompetent as a result. Further, she was not dealing as an adult with the hostile feelings she had with grandmother, brother, and boyfriend. Finally, she was prevented from establishing a clear, firm boundary around her own nuclear family.

3. Les, mother's live-in boyfriend was prevented from unambiguously becoming involved in parenting. He was also prevented from supporting his girlfriend against grandmother and brother; furthermore, he was in a position where it was difficult to make a decision about staying in the family as a full member or withdrawing entirely.

4. Jim, to a lesser extent than Don, was prevented from fully individuating as a result of his continual conflictual relationship with his sister and his mother. This, in turn, made it difficult for him to have an adult, supportive relationship with his sister which he would have preferred.

5. Finally, grandmother was prevented from working out her conflict with her daughter directly, thus preventing her from having a mutually supportive relationship with her daughter, which would be more satisfying for both of them. It was speculated that grandmother's over-involvement with her daughter was necessary as a result of a negative relationship between herself and her husband, who was reported as difficult but peripheral.

Given this formulation, the following treatment goals were derived:

1. To clarify and strengthen the boundaries around the nuclear family, thus excluding grandmother and brother from parenting functions, while affirming mother and boyfriend's executive powers.
2. To exclude Don from the marital dyad, thus reducing his power in the family and transferring it to mother and boyfriend. This would facilitate an agreement between them about parenting, thus helping them to take a united stand towards Don so that they could effectively set limits and controls on him.
3. To help to reduce the distance between Joan and Bill, thus allowing them to more effectively meet each other's perceived needs while simultaneously weakening the intensity of the relationship between Joan and her daughter.

Of these goals, I was most confident of achieving the first while considerably less confident with respect to goals #2 and #3. This uncertainty arose on two bases: first, that the relationship between Rose and Les appeared so tenuous that it might not be able to sustain the pressures and conflicts of executive power; and, second, that the guarded responses from Rose and Jim to questions about their parents' relationship were such as to raise doubts about the practicability of persuading either or both of them to join the therapeutic process. As will shortly become evident, these uncertainties were well grounded.

Intervention

Whitaker (in 41) has suggested that 80% of the therapy battle is having the right people present. With respect to the S family, this pointed to the critical importance of bringing the grandparents into the therapeutic process, because so many of the conflicts at hand were directly or indirectly related to them.

Pursuant to this end, the first three sessions were directed at preparing the way by (a) defusing the immediate crisis precipitated by Don's attempted suicide; (b) giving the family hope that change was not only possible but probable; and (c) reframing Don's behaviour as a family, rather than a personal problem. These efforts were successful. By the fourth session, Don's panic and despair and mother's distress had subsided substantially, and everyone was in a hopeful, if guarded, frame of mind.

At this point, I decided to push for the inclusion of the grandparents in what was to be the turning point of the case. Expecting resistance to this idea, I was not disappointed when I got it. With respect to grandmother, Rose and Jim's response to my suggestion shifted from outright denial, to argumentative negation, and finally to fear. Specifically, they felt that grandmother would be so angry that she would withdraw from them completely, a prospect which left them literally shaking with fear. Such behaviour was eloquent testimony to the power of extended family bonds in a family marked by lack of differentiation—this despite the anger and resentment which Rose and, later, Jim had so forcefully directed at Joan just the session before. It was with great reluctance, then, that they approached Joan. They were shocked when she readily agreed to attend.

With respect to grandfather, however, they were adamant and unmovable. Patiently but with determination they explained at length and in detail how crotchety and irascible he was, and that he didn't speak to anyone anymore. Indeed, as their recital unfolded, they so heightened and exaggerated grandfather's muteness that it almost seemed as if he had no mouth. In a sense, of course, they were perfectly correct; to suggest that grandfather "had no voice" in family affairs was an apt metaphor for the extreme distance that had evolved in their relationship with him. Indeed, so powerful was this notion that it assumed the proportions of a "family myth" (22), protecting them from the need to revivify old wounds, thus placing stress on a relational structure which they perceived to be brittle, fragile, and dangerous.

In practice, then, they refused to approach grandfather because it was clear to them at least that he "couldn't come" to therapy. In fact, it was a double entendre encompassing his alleged infirmity and the disastrous consequences that would surely, they felt, attend his participation. From fear of disrupting the significant progress already made, I reluctantly agreed.

Accordingly, Session Four focussed on my first objective outlined in the treatment plan. Towards this end, it was initially important to focus grandmother and mother's attention on their conflictual relationship in the hope of achieving some resolution. This was crucial in order to block grandmother's attempts to sabotage mother's parenting efforts. In an effort to confront them with this issue, I initiated an enactment, directing grandmother to give verbal support to her daughter, telling her that she was a good mother who could handle her own son. At the same time, she was directed to embrace her daughter in order to assure her that she really was supportive of her. I reasoned that, their conflict notwithstanding, the relationship between Rose and Joan was fundamentally based upon feelings of intense concern and attachment. This enactment sought to use these feelings as the lever to persuade Joan to relinquish all parenting responsibilities to Rose.

The results were explosive, producing an intensely emotional scene—with mother and daughter holding each other, crying and swaying back and forth—in which they appeared to make real emotional contact for the first time in a long while. Even Jim was deeply affected, as he observed the scene with tears in his eyes.

Having established a different and more positive emotional climate between mother and grandmother, it was now important to continue toward the treatment goal and increase the distance between mother and grandmother around the issue of parenting. In effect, it was important to get grandmother to "lend" her executive power to mother, thus supporting mother in her position as parent to Don. This was achieved by directing mother to tell Don that when they had a disagreement, he was not to go to grandmother's. I then directed mother to ask grandmother whether she would support and agree to this. Grandmother agreed to this. Throughout this exchange, Don sat quietly and appeared to accept what was being proposed.

At this point, I decided to proceed towards objectives two and three. However, in terms of the presenting problem, their importance was now considerably weakened. The removal of grandmother had produced more change than I had originally anticipated. Don's behaviour had dramatically changed: he had completely stopped acting out, had begun to co-operate with mother's instructions, and, when conflict did occur, he did not seek out grandmother's support.

Furthermore, Jim indicated that he had come to understand his part in maintaining Don's disruptive behaviour and so willingly agreed to withdraw. Like grandmother, this had the effect of transferring whatever executive power he had to mother.

These data suggested that the triangle of mother, grandmother, and Don was so powerful in this family system that when it was altered, it produced corresponding changes in the other triangles, namely, that of mother, "stepfather," and son.

To test this out, I then shifted emphasis in order to focus on the relationship between mother and boyfriend. I now suspected that in fact the relationship between mother and boyfriend was quite tenuous and that efforts to intervene would precipitate its dissolution. In other words, I suspected that Les was so peripheral that he really was not an authentic member of this family system at all, certainly neither at the level of meaning nor affect. While he remained physically present, his relationship with the S family was literally confined to that of "mother's boyfriend." Accordingly, I suggested that mother and boyfriend attend the next session alone.

However, at the sixth and last session mother arrived alone, explaining that Don's problems were resolved and that she did not want to work on her relationship with Les because she planned to end it in the near future. Abruptly, she then terminated, over-riding my comment that a number of additional outstanding issues had yet to be resolved. In essence, I interpreted her action as isomorphic with the family's refusal to deal with the relationship between Joan and Bill. To do otherwise would have contravened the two central themes which gave structure to this family, and, as such, the prospect of doing so was probably experienced as generating overwhelming anxiety.

At this point, Don's behaviour had been reversed completely. He had ceased to act out and no longer exhibited any signs of depression or suicidal ideation. His mother was firmly in charge and no longer had difficulty establishing rules and limits. Grandmother and brother were no longer involved in parenting, although they maintained a warm and supportive relationship with mother. Finally, boyfriend's position remained peripheral and somewhat ambiguous, although not disruptive of the relationship between mother and Don.

In these terms, the treatment of the case was seen as a success. In light of the means by which Rose effected termination, no follow-up was planned. From a larger perspective, however, only a partial success can be claimed, for one of the most problematic relationships in the family, that between Joan and Bill, had yet to be addressed. That it had not been addressed suggested, on the one hand, that a central dysfunctional process in the S family remained intact; and, on the other hand, that some other manifest family problem might be expected to arise at some point in the future.

Discussion

The S family presented with an adolescent, Don, who had attempted suicide. Strategic family intervention revealed that Don's acting out behaviour was directly related to twin interpersonal triangles, especially one involving a longstanding conflictual relationship between mother and grandmother. Resolution of these triangles freed Don to return to his status of "child" and relinquish his role of family mediator; allowed mother to fully accept and effectively implement her executive responsibilities; and, allowed brother, grandmother, and boyfriend to support mother in these efforts. In this sense, the presenting problem that brought the S family into treatment, namely, Don's acting out, was resolved.

Such resolution, however, tended to conceal the underlying structure of this family as being based on the twin themes of undifferentiation and the avoidance of intimacy extending over three generations. That structure, as metaphorically but covertly centred on the relationship between the grandparents, was emotionally charged and intensely defended. It remained largely impervious to therapeutic destabilization. Consequently, case termination paradoxically involved symptom resolution in a family that, at best, only functioned "adequately" (7) and, at worst, is likely to exhibit serious dysfunction at some point in the future.

This case permits the derivation of a number of implications, some of them straightforward, others more contentious.

With respect to the former, this case provides empirical support for Bateson's (6) prohibition against "chopping up the ecology." Put simply, the client-family requiring treatment in this case was the S family extended-kin network. To have done otherwise would have involved significant distortion of the problematic issues at hand, would have concealed several critical processes maintaining the problem, and, without the involvement of the brother and grandmother, would have made it impossible to intervene effectively. More generally, this suggests that the definition of the system requiring treatment may not be decided a priori, but rather must be determined in situ. This includes not only the extended family but, indeed, any other systems (e.g., school, work, church, neighbourhood, etc.) whose involvement appears to maintain the problem and whose inclusion in treatment is therefore necessary for problem resolution (see 38).

Further, the evidence of this case is consistent with Bell's (8) formulation that the relationship between extended and nuclear families may be crucial in the maintenance of a problem in either or both of them. Interactional processes that may be highly dysfunctional for the nuclear family, for example, may be highly functional for the larger extended family system. In this case, Don's behaviour was dysfunctional in that it kept him from individuating and assuming responsibility for his own behaviour, that is, achieving a measure of autonomy. Conversely, Don's behaviour kept all members of the family involved and served to maintain and stabilize the conflictual relationship among the adult members.

With respect to the more contentious issues, one implication of the case is that one need not choose between "boundary" and "intergenerational" perspectives; rather, some reconciliation between formulations is both desirable and practical. While the interpersonal coalition structure of the S family may have been proximally associated with the family's presenting problem, the intergenerational continuity of the family's thematic structure, together with the interactional processes that operated to maintain it, are just as clearly distally related.

Having made this statement, the reformulation of the intergenerational perspective implicit in it is worthy of note. Specifically, I am suggesting that intergenerational thematic continuity is a shared family construct and, as such, is not easily amenable to interpretation in terms of intrapsychic states or processes. The transactions that maintain the themes in question are simultaneously interpersonal and covert, that is, largely unnoticed (11). As such, individual cognitive and memory capacities, with their vulnerability to error and decay (79), are singularly inappropriate repositories for these critical family processes (67). Rather, they are "stored" in the ongoing interaction among members in the present and thus are continuously being reinforced, corrected, and embellished. In turn, this necessarily requires some degree of interpenetration among family members and their effective kindred, a process that clearly has the potential to render such themes rigid (61) and ritualized (22), or flexible and adaptive (67).

In this sense, the implicit dichotomy between the longitudinal data of the intergenerational approach and the cross-sectional data of the boundary approach is false. Rather, longitudinal data are critical to the interpretation and selection of those cross-sectional data that will serve as the basis for intervention. Clearly, this tends to support the present focus of proponents of the strategic approach (16), but calls in question their exclusive reliance on current data. While such an approach would, in all probability, have achieved an outcome similar to that accomplished with the S family, it would have made it extremely difficult to recognize the intergenerational processes which predict problem recurrence or the critical importance of intervention in the grandparent relationship as a means of preventing recurrence.

An additional facet of this reformulation concerns the importance of mate selection for intergenerational thematic continuity. Proponents of the intergenerational perspective (see *Introduction*), based on clinical data, essentially postulate that continuity is a function of familial homogamy with respect to intrapsychic attributes. If replicable in more normative samples, this represents an important finding. Even so, it begs the question of the mechanisms underlying the development and maintenance of family structural configuration. Given the immense complexity and diversity of family systems, union of two such systems that are identical or at least similar in most respects is a statistical improbability (leaving aside the question of how such similarities are recognized and negotiated during courtship); some important differences, at the individual and/or the family level, will prevail.

Data from the case of the S family suggest that intergenerational thematic continuity will be directly related to the strength of the bond between the spouses and their respective sets of parents, and the degree of interpenetration between nuclear and extended families.

As noted above (see *Introduction*), of all parent-child ties, the mother-daughter tie tends, in general, to be the strongest and the most enduring. Furthermore, the wife tends to be the primary representative of the family in its relations with its effective kindred. This would tend to mean more frequent and more regular contact between the family and the wife's extended kindred than that of her husband's counterpart. In turn, this implies greater reinforcement of those interaction patterns which characterize the wife's response repertoire than that of the husband's.

If, at the same time, the interpenetration between the family and its effective kindred is high, then divergent patterns embodied by the husband's experience of his family of origin is likely to be submerged and integrated into the larger extended family system of the wife's. In effect, a complementary, one-up relationship is established (76) by virtue of the wife's relationship with her family of origin.

Add to this the selection processes postulated by proponents of the intergenerational perspective and intergenerational thematic continuity of a particular set of interactional processes is, barring chance variety (see 9), all but assured. In short, this means that intergenerational thematic continuity can be better explained by reference to ongoing transactional processes in the present than by intrapsychic introjection of such themes in the past.

Finally, the case of the S family suggests that, at least in some cases, limited structural reorganization may be sufficient to produce symptomatic relief. It is widely accepted among family therapists that dysfunctional interactional processes necessarily encompass all family members. It follows that symptomatic relief requires structural reorganization of the entire family system (57). The present case suggests that this proposition, while valid, has only limited potential for generalization. While the relationship between Don and his mother was the focus of Don's acting-out behaviour, this relationship was not the centre of direct intervention; rather, reorganization of the relationship between mother and grandmother was sufficient to produce symptomatic relief.

At the same time, however, this suggests a cautionary note. A strategic approach coupled with a focus on the presenting problem (e.g., 33) may blind the clinician to the need to develop formulations which take account of *all* relevant data. In the case of the S family, the intergenerational processes underlying the presenting problem required a focus encompassing both interventive and preventive components. To the extent that the latter was not possible in the present case labels it only a partial success. To think otherwise would be to do a disservice to the client-family.

References

1. Ackerman, N.W. *The Psychodynamics of Family Life.* N.Y.: Basic, 1958.
2. Adams, B.N. *Kinship in an Urban Setting.* Chicago: Markham, 1968.
3. Adams, B.N. "Isolation, function and beyond: American kinship in the 1960's." *Journal of Marriage and the Family.* 32 (1970): 575-597.
4. Aldous, J. "Intergenerational visiting patterns: Variation in boundary maintenance as an explanation." *Family Process.* 6 (1967): 235-251.
5. Ashby, W.R. *Design for a Brain.* London: Chapman & Hall, 1969.
6. Bateson, G. *Mind and Nature: A Necessary Unity.* N.Y.: Dutton, 1979.
7. Beavers, W.R. "Healthy, midrange, and severely dysfunctional families." In F. Walsh, ed. *Normal Family Processes.* N.Y.: Guilford Press, 1982.
8. Bell, N.W. "Extended family relations of disturbed and well families." *Family Process.* 1 (1962): 175-193.
9. Benjamin, M. "General Systems Theory, Family Systems Theories, and Family Therapy: Towards an Integrated Recursive Model of Family Process." Chapter 2 in this volume.
10. Benjamin, M., and Bross, A. "Family Therapy: A Typology of Therapist Error." Chapter 3 in this volume.
11. Berger, P., and Kelner, H. "Marriage and the construction of reality." In H.D. Dreitzel, ed. *Recent Sociology.* No. 2. N.Y.: Macmillan, 1969.
12. Bohannan, P. "Divorce chains, households of remarriage, and multiple divorces." In P. Bohannan, ed. *Divorce and After.* N.Y.: Doubleday, 1970.
13. Boszormenyi-Nagy, I., and Ulrich, D.N. "Contextual family therapy." In A. Gurman and D.P. Kniskern, eds. *Handbook of Family Therapy.* N.Y.: Brunner/Mazel, 1981.
14. Boszormenyi-Nagy, I., and Spark, G.M. *Invisible Loyalties.* N.Y.: Harper & Row, 1973.
15. Bowen, M. *Family Therapy in Clinical Practice.* N.Y.: Jason Aronson, 1978.
16. Bross, A., and Benjamin, M. "Family therapy: A Recursive Model of Strategic Practice." Chapter 1 in this volume.
17. Caplan, G. "The family as a support system." In G. Caplan and M. Killilea, eds. *Support Systems and Mutual Help.* N.Y.: Grune & Stratton, 1976.
18. Cherlin, A.J. *Marriage Divorce Remarriage.* Cambridge, Mass.: Harvard University Press, 1981.
19. Cohler, B.J., and Geyer, S. "Psychological autonomy and interdependence within the family." In F. Walsh, ed. *Normal Family Processes.* N.Y.: Guilford Press, 1982.
20. Demos, J. *A Little Commonwealth: Family Life in Plymouth Colony.* N.Y.: Oxford University Press, 1970.
21. Demos, J. "Images of the American family: Then and now." In V. Tufte and B.

Meyerhoff, eds. *Changing Images of the Family*. New Haven, Conn.: Yale University Press, 1979.

22. Ferreira, A.J. "Family myth and homeostasis." *Archives of General Psychiatry*. 9 (1963): 457-463.

23. Flomenhaft, K., and Kaplan, D.M. "Clinical significance of current kinship relationships." *Social Work*. 13 (1968): 68-75.

24. Framo, J.L. "Family of origin as a therapeutic resource for adults in marital and family therapy: You can and should go home again." *Family Process*. 15 (1976): 193-210.

25. Framo, J.L. "The integration of marital therapy with sessions with family of origin." In A.S. Gurman and D.P. Kniskern, eds. *Handbook of Family Therapy*. N.Y.: Brunner/Mazel, 1981.

26. Freeman, D.S. "The family as a system: Fact or fantasy." In J.G. Howells, ed. *Advances in Family Psychiatry*. Vol. 1. N.Y.: International Universities Press, 1979.

27. Goldsmith, J. "The postdivorce family system." In F. Walsh, ed. *Normal Family Processes*. N.Y.: Guilford Press, 1982.

28. Greer, S. "Urbanism reconsidered: A comparative study of local areas in a Metropolis." *American Sociology Review*. 21 (1956): 20-25.

29. Graven, P. *Four Generations: Population, Land and Family in Colonial Andover, Massachusetts*. Ithaca, N.Y.: Cornell University Press, 1970.

30. Goode, W.J. *World Revolution and Family Patterns*. N.Y.: Macmillan, Free Press, 1969.

31. Haas, W. "The intergenerational encounter: A method in treatment." *Social Work*. 13 (1968): 91-101.

32. Hall, A.D., and Fagen, R.E. "The definition of system." *General Systems Yearbook*. 1 (1956): 18-28.

33. Haley, J. *Problem-Solving Therapy*. San Francisco: Jossey-Bass, 1976.

34. Haley, J. "Toward a theory of pathological systems." In P. Watzlawick and J. Weakland, eds. *The Interactional View*. N.Y.: Norton, 1977.

35. Hareven, T.K. "American families in transition: Historical perspectives on change." In F. Walsh, ed. *Normal Family Processes*. N.Y.: Guilford Press, 1982.

36. Headley, L. *Adults and Their Parents in Family Therapy*. N.Y.: Plenum Press, 1977.

37. Hess, R.D., and Handel, G. *Family Worlds: A Psychosocial Approach to Family Life*. Chicago: University of Chicago Press, 1959.

38. Hoffman, L. *Foundations of Family Therapy*. N.Y.: Basic, 1981.

39. Irving, H.H. *The Family Myth*. Toronto: Copp Clark, 1972.

40. Jackson, D.D. "The study of the family." *Family Process*. 4 (1965): 1-20.

41. Kaslow, F.W. "Involving the peripheral father in family therapy." In A.S. Gurman, ed. *Questions and Answers in the Practice of Family Therapy*. N.Y.: Brunner/Mazel, 1981.

42. Kerr, M.E. "Family system theory and therapy." In A.S. Gurman and D.P. Kniskern, eds. *Handbook of Family Therapy*. N.Y.: Brunner/Mazel, 1981.

43. Kuten, J. *Coming Together—Coming Apart: Anger and Separation in Sexual Loving*. N.Y.: Macmillan, 1974.

44. Laing, R.D. *The Politics of the Family*. Toronto: C.B.C. Publications, 1969.

45. Laslett, P. *The World We Have Lost*. London: Methuen, 1965.

46. Laslett, P., and Wall, R., eds. *Household and Family in Past Time.* Cambridge, Eng.: Cambridge University Press, 1972.
47. Leichter, H.J., and Mitchell, W.E. *Kinship and Casework.* N.Y.: Russell Sage Foundation, 1967.
48. Lidz, T. *The Family and Human Adaptation.* N.Y.: International Universities Press, 1963.
49. Lidz, T. *The Person.* Rev. ed. N.Y.: Basic, 1976.
50. Litwak, E. "Occupational mobility and extended family cohesion." *American Sociology Review.* 25 (1960): 9-21.
51. Litwak, E. "Geographical mobility and extended family cohesion." *American Sociology Review.* 26 (1960): 258-271.
52. Litwak, E. "Extended kin relations in an industrial democratic society." In E. Shanas and G. Streib, eds. *Social Structure and the Family: Generational Relations.* Englewood Cliffs, N.J.: Prentice-Hall, 1965.
53. Locke, H.J. "Mobility and family disorganization." *American Sociology Review.* 15 (1940): 489-494.
54. Lovelene, E., and Lohmann, N. "Absent fathers and black male children." *Social Work.* 23 (1978): 413-415.
55. Meissner, W.W. "The conceptualization of marital and family dynamics from a psychoanalytic perspective." In T. Paolino and B. McCrady, eds. *Marriage and Marital Therapy.* N.Y.: Brunner/Mazel, 1978.
56. McGoldrick, M. "Normal families: An ethnic perspective." In F. Walsh, ed. *Normal Family Processes.* N.Y.: Guilford Press, 1982.
57. Minuchin, S. *Families and Family Therapy.* Cambridge, Mass.: Harvard University Press, 1974.
58. Murdock, G.P. *Social Structure.* N.Y.: Macmillan, 1949.
59. Nye, F.I., and Berardo, F.M. *The Family: Its Structure and Interaction.* N.Y.: Macmillan, 1973.
60. Napier, A.Y., and Whitaker, C.A. *The Family Crucible.* N.Y.: Harper & Row, 1978.
61. Palazzoli, M.S., Cecchin, G., Prata, G., and Boscolo, L. *Paradox and Counterparadox.* N.Y.: Jason Aronson, 1978.
62. Park, R., Burgess, E., and McKensie, R. *The City.* Chicago: University of Chicago Press, 1967 (original publication 1925).
63. Parsons, T. "The kinship system in contemporary United States." *American Anthropologist* 45 (1943): 22-28.
64. Parsons, T. "The social structure of the family." In R. Anshen, ed. *The Family: Its Function and Destiny.* N.Y.: Harper & Row, 1949.
65. Paul, N.L., and Paul, B.B. *A Marital Puzzle.* N.Y.: Norton, 1975.
66. Radcliffe-Brown, A.R. "Introduction." In A.R. Radcliffe-Brown and D. Dorde, eds. *African Systems of Kinship and Marriage.* London: Oxford University Press, 1950.
67. Reiss, D. *The Family's Construction of Reality.* Cambridge, Mass.: Harvard University Press, 1981.
68. Reiss, P. "The extended family system: Correlates of an attitude on frequency of interaction." *Journal of Marriage and the Family.* 24 (1962): 333-339.
69. Shanas, E. "Living arrangements of older people in the United States." *The Gerontologist.* 1 (1961): 27-29.

70. Shanas, E. "Family-kin networks and aging in cross-cultural perspective." *Journal of Marriage and the Family.* 35 (1973): 505-511.
71. Shanas, E. "Social myth as hypothesis: The case of the family relations of old people." *The Gerontologist.* 19 (1979): 3-9.
72. Sussman, M.B. "Relationships of adult children with their parents in the United States." In E. Shanas, and G.F. Streib, eds. *Social Structure and the Family: Generational Relations.* Englewood Cliffs, N.J.: Prentice-Hall, 1965.
73. Sussman, M.B., and Burchinal, L. "Kin family networks: Unheralded structure in current conceptualization of family function." *Marriage and Family Life.* 24 (1962): 231-240.
74. Szinovacz, M.E. "Role allocation, family structure and female employment." In J.G. Howells, ed. *Advances in Family Psychiatry.* Vol. 2. N.Y.: International Universities Press, 1980.
75. Watzlawick, P. *The Language of Change.* N.Y.: Basic, 1978.
76. Watzlawick, P., Weakland, J., and Fisch, R. *Change.* N.Y.: Norton, 1974.
77. Whitaker, C., and Keith, D. "Symbolic-experiential family therapy." In A. Gurman and D.P. Kniskern, eds. *Handbook of Family Therapy.* N.Y.: Brunner/Mazel, 1981.
78. Wirth, L. "Urbanism as a way of life." *American Journal of Sociology.* 44 (1938): 1-24.
79. Yarrow, M.R., Campbell, J.D., and Burton, R.V. *Recollections of Childhood: A Study of the Retrospective Method.* Monograph Soc. Res. Child Development 1970, 35, Serial No. 138.
80. Young, M., and Willmott, P. *Family and Kinship in East London.* London: Penguin, 1957.

The Family Therapist's
Reference Manual

Allon Bross

This manual is a summary of essential ideas in the practice of Strategic Family Therapy. The content of the manual includes many but not all of the ideas of the previous chapters. Additionally there are ideas expressed, with particular reference to the section on the treatment of sexual dysfunctions, which have not been included in any of the articles of this text. The intention of the manual is for the reader to use it as an ongoing reference guide.

I. Assumptions

General Systems Theory—
A Model for Family Therapy Practice

1. A theory is needed that views causality, based on the interrelationships between man and his ecological systems, over time.

2. A theory is needed that can abandon notions of the individual, in a vacuum, independent of, or superior to his or her context.

3. A theory is needed that has implications for change.

Systems Theory

1. A system is defined as any set of two or more elements that interact in a pattern and stable manner over time, despite environmental fluctuations.

2. Systems theory is a theory of explanation and not a theory of intervention. It has implications for theories of intervention. It is a way of thinking and organizing data about people and their interrelationships with the environment.

3. Systems theory looks at the circular process of interaction between people and their environment. It views the reciprocal relationships between all the parts of any given field:

    a) A system has a set of units with relationships among them.
    b) Relationships within systems remain stable over time.
    c) The interrelationships of the component parts of a system are greater than the sum of its individual parts.
    d) A change in one part of the system affects the system as a whole and all of its parts.

4. Systems theory involves circular thinking as compared to the linear thinking on which most models of psychotherapy are based.

5. Feedback is defined as a communications network that produces action in response to an input of information and includes the result of its own action in which new information modifies subsequent behaviour.

6. Boundaries are defined as interactional patterns that differentiate members of one system from those of another.

Systems Theory and Its Relationship to Family Therapy*
1. Family therapy is not just another procedure, like group or play therapy, but a different way of beginning to understand and conceptualize problems between people.

2. Working with families means looking at the family as a self-governing unit that maintains homeostatic balance. This unit is responsible for problem-formulation and problem-resolution. The individual is not seen as superior to the rest of the family.

3. A client's history, which is used a great deal in individual-oriented therapies, is more or less irrelevant. The client's problem is seen in the here and now, and it is the current process between people that must be adjusted and changed. The past is mediated and serves its purpose in the present.

4. The need for "traditional" psychiatric taxonomies in family work is no longer required. Diagnosis with families is based on the interpretation and formulation of feedback following intervention. Diagnosis is continual and focusses upon the interactional processes that maintain dysfunction.

5. The therapist is part of the system and, therefore, is part of the ongoing diagnosis of the therapy.

6. Family therapy is the method that explores and attempts to shift the balance of dysfunctional family relationships so that new forms of relating become possible, with the goal of problem-resolution.

Assumptions about Families and Family Therapy
1. Dysfunctional behaviour in a human being is a product of the relationship between that human being and the members of his or her family system. It is the interrelationships that are producing and maintaining the problem.

---

*Although systemic principles apply to other interactional units (e.g., workplace, school), this manual will only focus on the family unit.

2. Families are part of problem-formulation, therefore they are part of the solution of the problem.

3. Family structure is an invisible set of rules that governs transactions among family members. The change of one of these transactions may or may not affect the underlying structure, while structural transformation will have ripple-effects on family patterns (Minuchin, 32).

4. Family structure becomes visible in the behavioural transactions among family members. Each transaction is related to specific circumstances but observation of isomorphic (parallel structures at different levels of abstraction) transactions highlight structural patterns. Out of these behavioural observations the therapist constructs a map of family organization (Minuchin, 32).

5. All families create interactional realities. Interactional reality is the reality of a second order (Watzlawick, 53), whereby people attribute meanings and values to other objects and people. Thus, we attribute or create realities that produce and maintain problems. Once reality is created, the logic as a result of the reality is iron-clad and all subsequent behaviour must therefore follow.

6. Problem families engage in predictable sequences of behaviour around the problem. Sequences are repeated transactions that occur in a predictable manner. Family therapy is designed to change the sequences of relationships among people and additionally change the interactional reality among those relationships.

7. The solution to the problem generally is the problem.

8. The goal of family therapy is the resolution of specific problems that clients bring to the therapist. Clients generally suffer for long periods of time before seeking help.

9. The course of family therapy is planned.

10. Therapeutic change occurs when there is a change in the interactional reality, plus a change in the existing sequence of events that maintains a problem.

11. The process of family treatment is a test re-test, hypothesis-creating process. A hypothesis is a predictive statement among two or more variables. A hypothesis is a conjecture, guess, or assumption with a great deal of probability.

12. The duration of treatment is related to the time required to resolve the problem. There is no a priori justification for a treatment to be a long, slow process.

The Role of the Family Therapist—Assumptions
1. The therapist takes charge of the therapy by (a) collecting data, (b) maintaining the relationships between self and the family members, and (c) introducing change strategies.

2. The therapist attempts to create the change first. Insight will follow.

3. Change occurs quickly and it does not require long time periods.

4. The therapist focusses on clearly defined problems, ones that are solvable.

5. The therapist is responsible for the success or failure of the therapy. The therapist takes credit for all failures, and the family takes credit for all success. The therapist plans strategies to bring about the change that the client desires.

6. The family is an "open system" that maintains its state by utilizing internal and external inputs. The therapist could become the external input that changes the family, but his or her input could maintain the family organization unchanged.

See Figure 1.1, Chapter 1

II. Family Assessment

Clinical Families
1. A family consists of a minimum of two people with a shared network of *relationships* including a past history, a present reality, and a future expectation of interconnected relationships. NOTE: Criteria are not biological. NOTE: Criteria are not necessarily legal criteria.

2. In order to be in a *relationship* four conditions must exist.
   a) There must be a fulfilling of survival needs, which includes food, clothing, shelter, water, and touch.
   b) There must be a reciprocal psychological and emotional investment. "I am invested in you as much as you are invested in me."
   c) Individuals in a family relationship must feel as if there is a sense of belonging to that relationship and the ability to feel a sense of being separate from the relationship in some ways at some times.
   d) There must be an ontic quality to the relationships.

3. Observations about relationship include:
   a) Relationships never end, they only change form.
   b) Relationships that take up all of one's psychological energy will produce symptoms (Zentner, 56).
   c) To be totally separate in a relationship reflects dysfunction.

    d) In relationships there are "relationship" issues and content issues. These decide who has the power in relationships. Power in the relationship is with the person who has the ability to define the experiential state of the other.

    e) When a relationship is in conflict, content cannot be addressed properly.

Family Transactions

1. All family systems involve transactional patterns:

> Transactions occur as to how, when, and to whom to relate. A transaction in any relationship will define one person in relation to another in context of time and place. These transactions regulate behaviour.

2. In families there are rules governing organization:

    a) All creatures organize and form a status, or power ladder, in which each member has a place in the hierarchy.

    b) Hierarchies are not necessarily good or bad. Hierarchies are maintained by all the participants.

    c) There must be a power hierarchy in which parents and children have different levels of authority.

    d) When family hierarchy is confused it may be caused by lack of boundaries, where superior and peer cannot be distinguished; or too rigid boundaries, where a superior forms a coalition with a member of another level and violates the rules of the hierarchy and organization.

    e) When family members enter coalitions across hierarchical lines problems will emerge! Coalitions refer to a process of joint action *against* a third person. Alliances refer to shared interest between family members but not shared by a third!

    f) Family expectations between members reflect ideas about family loyalty, obligations, and limits.

    g) Families establish rules (both explicit and implicit) and meta-rules that determine and govern behaviour.

    h) Family rules are inferences made by an observer about redundant interactional sequences.

3. A functional family has the ability to engage in alternative transactional patterns in the existing relationships in response to situational stress.

4. "Family dysfunction" would be reserved for families that develop, in the face of stress, an increase in the rigidity and predictability of a sequence of events that violates the hierarchy and boundaries of

systems—resulting in symptoms; with symptoms, the hierarchical arrangement is confused, and interactional realities are established that maintain the problem.

Family Boundaries

1. Family boundaries refer to interactional patterns which differentiate members of one system from those of another:

   a) The boundaries of a family subsystem define who participates.
   b) Family boundaries must be clear in order to allow varied functions and behaviours without interference.

Family Subsystems

1. Subsystems within a family system include the individual, the marital relationship, the parental relationship, and the sibling relationship.

2. The *spouse subsystem* is the foundation of the family and it has vital tasks. These include:

   a) developing support, co-operation, and negotiation in a number of areas;
   b) yielding part of one's separateness in order to belong to the relationship;
   c) having the ability to be intimate and close and the ability to be apart;
   d) preventing children from entering the parents' subsystem.

3. The *parental subsystem* requires:

   a) both parents to be accessible to their children;
   b) parents to nurture their children;
   c) the use of authority in order to guide and control their children;
   d) parents changing and adapting to the developmental stage of the family.

4. The *sibling subsystem* is where children learn to compete, co-operate, and negotiate; therefore, siblings should be protected from adult interference.

The Initial Interview

1. The *goal* of the initial interview is to clearly define a resolvable problem.

2. The therapist decides a) who is to attend the initial interview; b) where to have it; c) the length of the interview; and d) the timing and technology of change.

3. The therapist observes a) how the family organizes to attend the first interview; b) the mood of the family; c) the tempo of the family; and d) the language and non-verbal behaviour of the family.

4. The therapist remembers that a) clients come to therapy in pain; b) the client is never really sure of what the problem is; c) the client has tried many remedies and the problem now is the existing solution; and d) clients expect therapy to take a relatively short time.

5. Areas that are highly charged and considered taboo must not be avoided by the therapist. These areas include: a) sex, b) violence, c) retardation, and d) death.

6. The therapist must learn cultural differences in order to assess accurately families with ethnic differences.

7. The therapist is always in charge and is the leader of the therapy. Therefore he or she must be a) a source of hope by communicating that there are alternatives; b) able to join, confirm, and respect all members of the client system; and c) an alert responder to system feedback, by accepting dependency on the system, for in order to lead, one must follow.

8. The therapist must *not* a) interpret or get the client to see things differently; b) offer premature advice; and c) argue with clients.

9. The therapist attempts to collect as much assessment data as possible, attending primarily to the "process" and ignoring the content of communication.

10. In making an assessment, the therapist must obtain and understand a) the sequence of behaviour around the stress point or symptom; b) how that relates to the hierarchy of the family; c) the function of the symptom; and d) the family's meaning systems (interactional realities).

11. Initial observations are important but tentative. Be flexible. Each observation can and should be tested. Develop a working hypothesis that allows you to intervene.

12. Debrief other therapy experiences.

13. Ending the initial interview includes a) setting up the next interview; b) making sure who is to be there and arranging for it; and c) devising a preliminary directive that encourages the family to return.

14. There is at least one person in the family with the power to bring the family back. That person must be convinced by the therapist that it is important to return.

III. Family Problem Formulation
Common Dysfunctional Family Constellations
For further elaboration read the works of J. Haley (21) and S. Minuchin (32).

Intact Family
1. One parent sides with a child against the other parent. The result is an intense symptom-bearing relationship, which excludes the other parent.

2. The child becomes the focus of the marriage, for example:
   a) Mother has an intense relationship with son.
   b) Son misbehaves.
   c) Father is called to solve the problem.
   d) Mother attacks father's solution or may threaten to leave.
   e) Father withdraws.
   f) Mother and son continue relationship until a problem arises.

Variations
Mother and grandmother are in a struggle for the child, and the father is excluded.

Therapeutic Strategies
1. Facilitate one parent abandoning a previous position by joining the other parent against the child.

2. Begin working with the marital relationship so that the differences can be negotiated.

3. Be aware of: a) rapid change and reversal; and b) potential on-going conflict which may imply separation as a consequence.

Chronic Boundary Problems
This is seen when stress in one subsystem is negotiated through another. This can be seen when parents consistently use one child to deflect spouse conflicts.

The goal is to restructure the subsystem organization according to parent-child functioning.

Therapeutic Strategies to Achieve Goal
1. The therapist blocks the child, taking total responsibility for the child's symptom. This will promote the child's autonomy and spousal interaction.

2. Define spousal relationship in positive terms in order to increase the partners' affiliation with one another. The therapist must then affiliate with the excluded child.

3. Restructure the parents in a coalition against the child.

The Extended Family — Single Parent

1. When such a family comes into therapy, it is clear that mother is incompetent in the presence of her own mother. The purpose of the children's misbehaviour is to involve mother.

2. The overall goal of therapy is to join mother and grandmother together in the parental subsystem in a position of complementarity and mutual support. Boundaries between mother and grandmother must be clarified.

Therapeutic Strategies to Achieve Goal

1. Grandmother observes her daughter parenting without her participation.

2. Sessions include only grandmother and mother, whereby the therapist includes himself or herself in an alliance of executives.

3. The therapist positions himself between the adults and children, clarifying the boundary around mother and grandmother.

Family with Parental Child (PC)

In the dysfunctional family with the parental child, the overall goal in therapy is to return the parental child into the sibling subgroup, but allowing him or her to maintain a position of leadership. The boundary between mother and child must be clarified; for example, the parental child has a role of leadership only in the absence of mother. The other children will then be permitted direct access to their mother.

Therapeutic Strategies

1. Join the mother in a coalition that moves the parental child into the sibling subsystem.

2. Clarify the boundaries regarding access to mother, and who is in charge of the family. The parental child is in charge during mother's absence.

Temporary Loss

This is a transitional situation to which the family must adapt. If a father, for example, has spent time away and returns, both spouse and parental transactions must be re-negotiated. For example, a mother and children are observed in a coalition against the father. The children interrupt spouse transactions, and the father is excluded from parenting transactions. The therapeutic goal is to increase the strength of the boundary around husband and wife, excluding the children from spouse transactions and permitting father to take on parental functions.

Therapeutic Strategies to Achieve Goal

1. The therapist affiliates with father, increasing his involvement.

2. The therapist blocks the mother-child transactions, setting a boundary between father and children and moves the mother toward father.

3. The therapist joins with parents in coalition against children to make parents form a parental unit.

Divorced Families

The overall goal is to allow both mother and father to maintain separate relationships with the children. Seeing mother and father separately with the children will reinforce this. The state of the marital situation must be made clear so that the children will not interfere. Any spousal disagreements are to be dealt with directly rather than through the children.

Blended Family

A family situation in which one or both parents have previously been married, and bring with them children from the first marriage.*

One parent refuses to give power to the other thus forcing disengagement.

Therapeutic Strategies to Achieve Goal

1. Shift of power from overinvolved parent to step-parent in order to let the latter establish rules autonomously.

2. The problem is one of borrowed power when two families become one. The mother only allows the stepfather to have control.

3. Have uninvolved father establish rules and give him total power.

4. Have involved mother stay out. Remember:

   a) that children in blended families can have dual memberships in families;
   b) to ensure clear boundaries and open links of communication which will result in a functional system for all;
   c) that the therapist can check the sibling subsystem for the one who "mirrors" the apparent marital difficulties.

Death in the Family

1. Assess whether the grieving process is related to the current family dysfunction.

   a) In a family where prior to death there was dysfunction, and the family is grieving appropriately, treat the dysfunction.

---

*For a more extensive discussion of these topics see Wolpert-Zur and Bross, "The Formation of the Reconstituted Family System: Processes, Problems, and Treatment Goals" in this volume.

b) In a family where death has occurred and the family has not grieved, trigger the grieving, by direct enquiry about death, the family member, memories, etc., then allow the family to mourn.
   In an unresolved grief situation, often children will be parentified. Grief is unresolved.

c) In a family where grieving has continued beyond a "normal" level, the goal is to end this process.

2. There are cultural differences as to the appropriate length of grieving. Guidelines can suggest anywhere from three months to two years.

The Assessment and Treatment of Sexual Dysfunctions

1. Sexual dysfunction is a major problem area in family functioning.

2. The therapist must record a sexual history to differentiate the sexual dysfunction and dysfunction from sexual boredom.

3. All sexual dysfunctions include a physiological component and an interactional component.

Male Sexual Dysfunctions

Erectile Dysfunction—Impotence

1. There are three types of erectile dysfunctions. They are:

a) organic—there is some anatomical defect in the reproductive or central nervous system;

b) functional—this includes physiological difficulties due to alcohol abuse, the effects of medications, circulatory problems, and physical exhaustion;

c) psycho-interactional—the individual's sexual beliefs and feelings are combined with a dysfunctional interactional behaviour:

   i) Primary impotence refers to a male who has never been able to achieve or maintain an erection of sufficient firmness to engage in coitus.

   ii) Secondary impotence refers to a male who fails to achieve an erection of sufficient firmness during coitus in approximately 25% of his sexual attempts.

2. Treating erectile dysfunctions includes:

a) removing the male fear of failure;

b) changing the spectator role to one of involved participation;

c) removing the woman's fear of her partner's impotency (Masters and Johnson, 30, 31);

d) not forcing treatment stages.

3. The major treatment strategies for erectile dysfunctions include:

    a) focussing on pleasure and relaxation without focussing on erection;

    b) encouraging a firmness-flaccid-firmness sequence of behaviour between the couple;

    c) moving to extra-vaginal orgasm, either by manual or oral stimulation;

    d) encouraging coitus in the female superior position; female guidance, moving to male extra-vaginal ejaculation;

    e) encouraging coitus and orgasm (Masters and Johnson, 30, 31).

Premature Ejaculation

1. This dysfunction is dependent on the interactional behaviour of the couple.

2. Ejaculation is premature if the man cannot delay it long enough after penetration to satisfy his sexual partner in at least half of their acts of intercourse.

3. The major treatment strategies for premature ejaculation include:

    a) getting the couple to recognize the signs of imminent orgasm; and

    b) implementing the "squeeze technique." Upon female stimulation, the male signals partner to stop. The female "squeezes" the penile glands by placing the thumb below the frenulum and two fingers above. The male is permitted to ejaculate on the last trial of each training session. After four or five of these sessions, couple is ready for coitus. At sign of ejaculation, apply "squeeze" technique.

Retarded Ejaculation

1. Retarded ejaculation is defined as the male's difficulty in ejaculating during penile penetration in the female's vagina.

2. The major treatment strategies for retarded ejaculation include:

    a) implementing manual, oral, and manipulative techniques to stimulate extra-vaginal ejaculation; and

    b) encouraging repetition and then penile insertion.

3. A variation in treating this disorder includes having the male masturbate to achieve erection, then perform coitus in order to facilitate female satisfaction, and then having the male masturbate to orgasm, ejaculating intra-vaginally.

Female Sexual Dysfunctions

Orgasmic Dysfunction

1. Primary orgasmic dysfunction is the inability of the woman to achieve orgasm through any method of sexual stimulation.

2. Situational orgasmic dysfunction refers to women who have experienced orgasm, but no longer do.

3. Whatever the cause, the physiological result is an involuntary inhibition of the orgasmic reflex.

4. The major treatment strategies in orgasmic dysfunction include:

    a) encouraging the female to focus on sensations associated with mounting sexual excitement, utilizing any means appealing to the woman (e.g., fantasies) in order for her to experience orgasm;
    b) involving her partner by having him stimulate her (manually or with vibrator), until she experiences pleasurable vaginal sensations;
    c) positioning the male and female so that both can stimulate the clitoris, moving to pelvic thrusts and orgasm.

Vaginismus

1. Vaginismus results when penile penetration leads to vaginal pain. There is contraction of the muscle tract of the vagina.

2. The major treatment of vaginismus includes:

    a) encouraging the woman to relax;
    b) directing the woman's self-exploration of the vaginal opening using her fingertip, progressing to using a finger (to begin to control muscles), and then two and three fingers;
    c) having the male partner lubricate his penis and move slowly to penetration until a comfort level is achieved by the female.

Dyspareunia

1. Dyspareunia refers to painful coitus, experienced in either the vagina, cervix, uterus, or bladder. This may be caused by lack of vaginal lubrication.

2. Sometimes the pain can be alleviated by using a commercial lubricant.

3. This dysfunction *may require a medical* or surgical procedure. *Refer* appropriately.

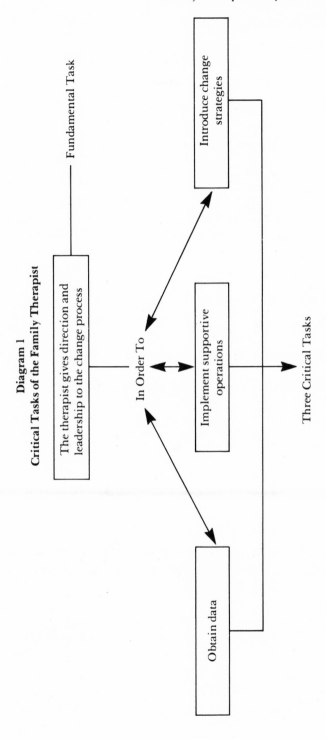

Diagram 1
Critical Tasks of the Family Therapist

Fundamental Task

The therapist gives direction and leadership to the change process

In Order To

Introduce change strategies

Implement supportive operations

Obtain data

Three Critical Tasks

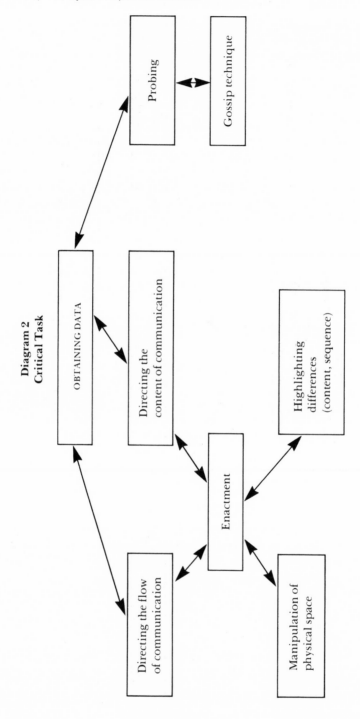

Diagram 2
Critical Task

IV. Tasks, Tactics, and Strategies

Three Critical Tasks of the Family Therapist

1. The fundamental task of a therapist is to be in charge of, and to give direction to the change process. He or she becomes the leader and director of what occurs in the relationship between self and the client; and by so doing is able to manoeuvre the relationship to achieve treatment goals.

2. The critical tasks of the therapist, in relation to the client system, are threefold: *First*, the therapist must be able to obtain the necessary data in order to pinpoint those variables that maintain the problem. *Second*, the therapist must be able to implement supportive techniques in order to sustain a continuing relationship throughout the entire process. *Last of all*, the therapist's ability to implement change strategies will dictate how, and in what manner a successful outcome can be achieved (see Diagrams 1, 2, 3, 4).

Data Collection

Probing

1. The therapist must elicit necessary assessment information about the variables involved in maintaining the client's problems and the variables that are important in problem resolution.

2. To obtain a full and accurate description of the problem, the therapist must be able to raise questions about the problem in context. In specific transactions, questions are formulated and designed in order to:

    a) recover missing data or missing information;
    b) elicit relational information, i.e., who is involved and under what circumstances;
    c) specify any unclear information.

These guidelines, when implemented, force clarity and precision.

NOTE: To actually prevent obtaining relevant information the therapist can assume that he or she understands what the client is reporting and that the client's report is accurate. Client yes/no responses will prohibit acquisition of an adequate data base.

Directing the Content of Information

1. The need to obtain data in content areas other than those offered by the client system requires action by the therapist.

2. Content, in the initial interview, is often dictated by the client system. Areas of content avoidance between the therapist and the client are most often in stressful and taboo areas, such as:

a) sexual functioning;
b) physical violence;
c) retardation;
d) death and dying, etc.

Directing the Flow of Communication

1. The technique of enactment (32), is based on the assumption that only limited data can be obtained from the verbal descriptions of the client system. This method of data collection is useful when a therapist is interviewing more than one member of a family, and when the worker assumes that the relationship between two or more family or system members is maintaining an individual's problems.

2. To facilitate an enactment, the therapist directs certain family members to interact with each other, under specific conditions, and prescribes the flow of content. For example, an instruction might be, "Talk to your wife about establishing some rules for your son." The role of the therapist is to observe the transactions and to follow the flow of content.

3. Opening various channels of communication closes others. The therapist must be aware of how and what ways he or she directs the communication flow in order to obtain data.

Manipulation of Physical Space

Extending the enactment technique to include the manipulation of physical space requires that the therapist give an accurate pretext for the physical movement of one member of the client system in relation to another. This technique is primarily implemented where there is more than one family member involved in the treatment, and in relation to directing the flow and content of communication. Implementation occurs depending on the assessment need.

Highlighting Differences (Content, Sequence)

1. Perceiving discrepancies in the client's communication to you, and your ability to feed this communication discrepancy back to the client in a manner in which it is understood is one way of highlighting differences. Carkhuff (10, 11) has referred to this technique as confrontation. Spooner and Stone (48) define confrontation as: "Any statement that calls the client's attention to something of which the client may not be aware. The statement challenges the client, points out discrepancies, or offers a point of view different from the client's."

2. When the client system includes more than one person, the therapist feeds back and highlights differences between members of the client

system. Between-people discrepancies, in both content and sequence of behaviour, can be highlighted.

Gossip Technique (Selvini-Palazzoli)

This technique is implemented by requesting one member of the family to report on the relationships of another family dyad, e.g., "Mother, what happens when there is a disagreement between father and your son?"

Summary

The techniques of data collection require detailed probing or searching by the use of both verbal and direct techniques and non-verbal and indirect techniques. Diversity in technique selection in the initial phase of treatment can vary according to who is in treatment and the nature of the data desired. However, the implementation of data collection techniques needs to be synthesized, in the service of the treatment goals.

Supportive Operations—Critical Task

1. Supportive operations are those interventions designed directly to reduce the psychological distance between therapist and client. It is this writer's opinion that implementing supportive operations is fundamental to the total change process; if neglected, *all attempts at obtaining data and implementing change strategies will fail.*

2. Supportive techniques are designed to validate the client, provide encouragement and approval for client actions, and to convey respect and understanding.

Attentive Listening

1. Attentive listening is the therapist's communication of verbal and non-verbal cues that the client perceives as conveyed interest. Although the technique of attentive listening tends not to challenge the client, it does not require the communication of agreement.

2. In the initial treatment phase the ability to be an attentive listener is perceived as a confirmation of the information that the client gives, and also of respect for the client. By accepting the client's communications the therapist will ratify his or her position as the leader of the therapy process.

3. Techniques that encourage attentive listening are empathy, reinforcing strengths, respecting individual differences, and imitation.

Empathy

1. Empathy is considered one technique designed to make the client feel as if he or she has been understood, as a result of behaviour communicated by the worker.

2. This technique is a two-step process, which includes an accurate understanding of the client's communication and "The verbal facility to communicate this understanding in a language attuned to the client's feelings." (Truax, 49)

3. This technique, although communicated verbally, requires non-verbal cues, which match those of the client. This may include a change in voice tempo, a shift in body position, or perhaps a shift in mood. Empathy expands the Rogerian technique of "reflecting back." Communications theory, alone, necessitates the expansion.

Reinforcing Strengths

1. The therapist's understanding of the client's strengths and communication of those strengths to the client will reduce the distance in the worker-client relationship. The initial phase of treatment requires searching for and reinforcing client strengths.

2. The family therapist who supports a client, recognizing the dysfunction, maintains a functional sequence of events between himself and the client.

Imitation

1. Imitative operations are those in which the therapist's communication of verbal and non-verbal behaviours approximates the client's communication. In the initial phase of treatment, utilization of this technique can be in adopting the client's language, cliches, and voice tempo, joining the client's mood, matching the breathing rate of the client, and mirroring the client's sitting position.

2. The nature of imitative operations are subtle, but have a strong effect on enhancing the worker-client relationship. This technique is one way that the therapist can lead the relationship, by following the client's lead.

Respecting Client Differences

1. The therapist must honour and respect client differences. Respect-variables to think about include age, culture, sex, roles, and levels of expertise.

2. The simplest formula for conveying respect is to acknowledge the differences and inquire about them.

3. Being sensitive in respecting the client system will enhance the likelihood of a successful relationship.

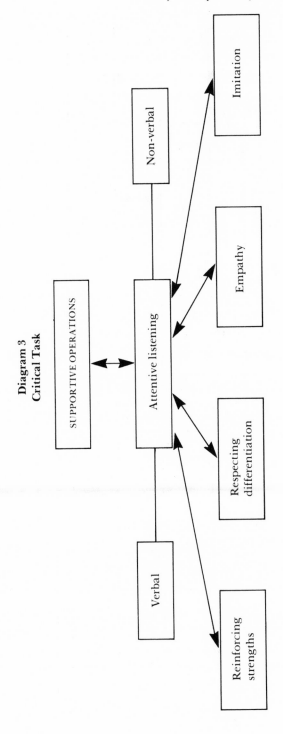

Diagram 3
Critical Task

Diagram 4
Critical Task

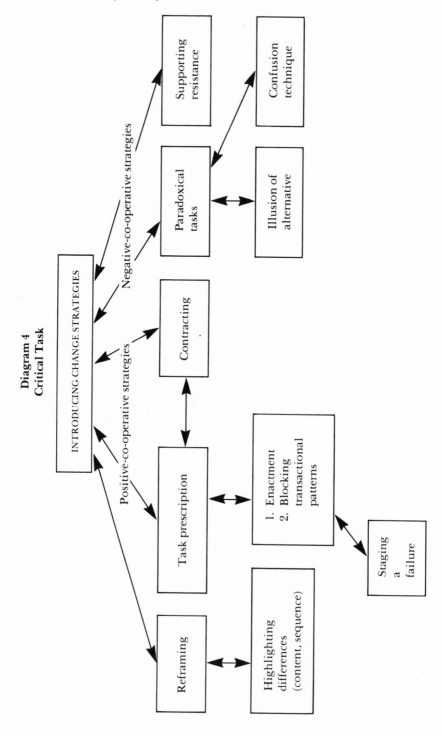

Summary

Supportive operations allow the therapist to blend as closely with the client as is possible. Incorporation of these techniques during the course of the treatment are critical to continuation of the change relationship.

Introducing Change Strategies—Critical Task

1. Introducing change strategies is based on the purpose of the therapeutic relationship-problem resolution.

2. These strategies are selected to the extent that they help change a problem-maintaining situation and service the goals that the therapist and client set.

3. It is assumed that change strategies are introduced based on having accurate data about the problem-maintenance featured and on the fact that sufficient supportive operations have been introduced.

4. In process, change strategies occur as a result of planned preparation by the therapist and are the result of a series of manoeuvres which, contextually, are designed for the client.

5. Two categories of change strategies will be offered:

   a) First, are positive-co-operative strategies. These techniques include contracting, in session, homework tasks, and reframing problems.
   b) Second, is a series of negative-co-operative strategies, which include paradoxical tasks, creating an illusion of alternatives, confusion techniques, and supporting resistance.

Contracting

1. From a communications perspective, the transactions between the worker and client are a contract (Rothery, 42).

2. The technique of contracting has many variations, but fundamentally it is designed to establish agreement between the therapist and the client about the nature of the problems and the goals for change.

3. Initially, contracts may be more vague, but as the process evolves so does the nature of the contract or changing contract.

4. Structural contracting refers to the explicit agreement between the worker and client about the logistics of the relationship. Variables include the location of treatment, who is to attend, the help requested, the frequency of sessions, their duration, payment procedures, time, etc. The degree of contract agreement evolves and changes with the process of treatment.

Systemic Tasks

1. The communication of a directive from the therapist to the client for a definite piece of work to be done constitutes a task. Tasks, therefore, can be assigned both for use in the session and for "homework."

2. The assumption involved in task assignment is that the client agrees to the task, is willing to commit an effort towards it, and is prepared to implement it.

3. Tasks, which are assigned for homework, extend the therapeutic process beyond the immediate session. Tasks service the treatment goal and are alternatives to existing behaviours. Additionally, homework tasks can intensify the relationship between the worker and client.

4. Reid and Epstein (40) list two guidelines for task creation. They insist that tasks must be feasible, that is to say the task can be accomplished, and that tasks must be desirable. Desirability is determined by assessing the negative consequences of accomplishing the task.

5. Haley (21) emphasizes the delivery of the tasks. He suggests that tasks be given clearly, rather than suggested, to be sure that the task is not left undone, caused by lack of clear understanding.

Reframing Problems

The technique of reframing occurs when the therapist communicates a message "which attempts to change the conceptual or emotional setting or viewpoint in relation to which the client experiences the situation. The therapist must try to place it in a different frame which fits the facts equally well or even better, and thereby changes its entire meaning." (Watzlawick, 53)

Paradoxical Tasks

1. The technique of prescribing a paradoxical task occurs when the therapist wants the client to change by proving him or her wrong.

2. Operationally, the therapist communicates encouragement of more of the same undesirable behaviour in the context of the necessity for change. Haley (21) writes that the paradoxical approach always has two levels in which the message is communicated: "change" and, within a framework, "don't change." To be successful the client achieves the treatment goal by proving to the worker that he or she is wrong.

3. The manner in which paradoxical tasks are delivered, combined with an accurate use of pretext, is often more difficult than knowing what problem needs to be encouraged.

Supporting Resistance

1. There are occasions when the client will openly resist or disagree with the directives of the therapist. At these times the therapist can transactionally create a situation where the alternative consideration can be implanted as well as having the client perceive worker flexibility, sometimes, to his or her dismay.

2. To do so, the therapist must stop the content of his or her own communication to the client and adopt and agree with the client's communication and reasoning. In doing so there comes a reversal of the existing transaction and the possibility for alternative thinking by the client. While supporting resistance, consistency in direction reversal is required in order for this technique to be successful.

Confusion Technique

This technique is indicated for clients who tend to intellectualize everything. It is designed to produce intellectual confusion by means of "complex pseudo-logical explanations, through ponderous, complicated, and therefore confusing references to trivial facts" (Watzlawick, 53). Out of it must come a piece of meaning which is therefore grasped and held on to with tenacity. Paradoxically, clarity of purpose is required in order to implement this technique.

Illusion of Alternatives

1. The "illusion of alternatives" (Watzlawick, 53) is a technique used when the therapist wants to give the client the impression that there are apparent choices from which to select.

2. These choices are only two choices within a limited set of alternatives, and, in fact, there is a super-ordinate pair of opposites that are true choices.

Staging a Failure

The therapist designs a task that the family cannot accomplish, in order to obtain another treatment goal.

Blocking Transactional Patterns (see Enactment)

These techniques are used to produce stress by blocking the flow of conversation along its normal channels.

Alliances or Coalitions

A strategy that produces stress when the therapist allies with a family member for a period of time against someone else.

Strategies for Dealing with Members Who Don't Attend Sessions

1. Have the family bring in the missing member.

2. The therapist can phone the missing member, indicating the importance of attendance.

3. The therapist can send home a note, accepting the apparent reason for non-attendance and reinterpreting the non-involvement as involvement.

4. The therapist can use guilt to influence the missing member.

V. Error, Resistance, and Termination

Sources of Therapist Error

1. Three outcomes of therapeutic intervention include:

   a) success—these are changes at *both* the level of meaning and of the behavioural sequences;
   b) partial success—these are partial changes in either meaning or interactions *but* not both;
   c) failure—this refers to *no* change at any level. This is a result of therapist error or client-resistance.

2. There are three types of therapist error:

   a) beneficial errors—these are interventions that result in data collection, case formulation verification, or in a change, in spite of their original intention;
   b) neutral errors—these are errors that neither help nor hinder the client or therapist;
   c) destructive errors—these errors create distress or deterioration in the client-family in addition to the apparent problems.

3. There are five sources of therapist error:

   a) assessment error—these are primarily errors of information;
   b) formulation error—working on an inaccurate hypothesis results in formulation error;
   c) tactical error—these errors occur through the use of interventions;
   d) support error—failing to reduce the distance between the therapist and the family and each of its members results in supportive errors;
   e) evaluation error—the inability to read family feedback accurately is an evaluation error.

Resistance

Dealing with Resistance

Four ways of dealing with client resistance are: a) work through it, b) direct confrontation, c) the use of the "illusion of alternatives" technique, or d) supporting the resistance.

Purpose of Resistance

The purpose of resistance is to preserve the sense of adequacy and independence of both the individual and the system, and to protect the existing set of relationships.

Types of Resistant Operations

1. Actively controlling manoeuvres:

   verbosity—talking about everything but the problem;
   introducing red herrings;
   talking around the problem but missing the point;
   literal interpretations of content;
   intellectualization;
   rationalization;
   blaming the other person;
   hostile behaviour;
   withholding information;
   breaking appointments;
   confusing the issues.

2. Passive controlling manoeuvres:

   seeming compliance;
   meagre responses;
   blaming self.

3. Evasion and avoidance manoeuvres:

   minimizing issues;
   half-truths;
   introducing other topics;
   forgetting;
   withholding facts;
   seeming reasonable;
   isolation;
   symptom development;
   breaking appointments;
   ending contact abruptly.

4. Relationship responses as resistance:

   flattery;
   seduction;
   bribery;
   subtle insults;
   questioning personal adequacy;
   questioning adequacy of training.

Termination
Termination of the relationship between a therapist and a client can be a result of:

    a) recognizing health or absence of a problem;

    b) a problem where family therapy is contraindicated;

    c) the client terminating, without success;

    d) the therapist terminating, without success;

    e) the client terminating, with partial success;

    f) a mutual agreement between the therapist and client-family about the achievement of the treatment goals.

Do's and Don'ts of Family Therapy

1. Do learn about hypnosis, witchcraft, and magic in order to learn how to deliver a message and create scenarios that will lend power to you as a therapist.

2. Do take at least one acting course.

3. Don't prescribe child abuse, violence, or suicide.

4. Don't ever react to change with excitement, as the family will resist it if they do it for you.

5. Never argue with a client.

6. If you're lucky enough to see change and it works, never take credit for it.

Recommendations

1. Avoid places where focus is on the personality of the therapist rather than the skills to bring about change. Supervisors and teachers should not get involved in the personal lives of their students and trainees.

2. Avoid a limited population.

3. Avoid rigid places—where there is no experimentation.

4. If the focus is on diagnosis, you will hear little about change.

5. Generally avoid in-patient settings.

6. Have control over home visits.

Places

1. Look for centres with live supervision, one-way mirrors, and video-tapes.

2. Select a setting where the focus of intervention is on problem-resolution.

Family Therapy Bibliography

1. Aponte, H., and Hoffman, L. "The Open Door: A Structural Approach to a Family with an Anoretic Child." *Family Process.* Vol. XII, No. 1, March, 1973.
2. Bandler, R., and Grinder, J. *The Structure of Magic,* Vol. 1. Palo Alto, Cal.: *Science and Behaviour,* 1975.
3. Bateson, G. "The Biosocial Integration of Behaviour in the Schizophrenic Family." *Exploring the Base. loc. cit.,* pp. 116-122.
4. Bateson, G., et al. "Towards a Theory of Schizophrenia." *Behavioral Science.* No. 1 (1956): 215-264.
5. Bateson, G., and Jackson, D.D. "Some Varieties of Pathogenic Organizations." *Disorders of Communication, No. 42.* Research Publications, Association for Research in Nervous and Mental Diseases, 1964.
6. Bateson, G., and Ruesch, J. *Communication, the Social Matrix of Psychiatry.* New York: Norton and Norton, 1951.
7. Bertalanffy, L. Von. *General Systems Theory.* New York: Braziller, 1968.
8. Biestok, F. *The Casework Relationship.* Montreal: Loyola University Press, 1957.
9. Bross, A. *Treatment of Families — A Manual.* Unpublished work, Toronto, 1980.
10. Carkhuff, R. "Training in the Counselling and Therapeutic Process: Requiem or Reveille?" *Journal of Counselling Psychology,* 13 (1966).
11. Carkhuff, R., and Truax, C. "Training in Counselling and Psychotherapy: An Evaluation of an Integrated Didactic and Experiential Approach." *Journal of Consulting Psychology.* 29 (1965).
12. Carter, E., and McGoldrick, M. *The Family Life Cycle.* N.Y.: Gardner, 1980.
13. Compton, B.R., and Galaway, B. *Social Work Processes.* Homewood, Ill.: The Dorsey Press, 1975.
14. Framo, J.L. "Family Treatment of Schizophrenia," *Family Process.* 1 (1962): 119-131.
15. Germain, C.B. "Social Study, Past and Future." *Social Work Processes.* Ed. B.R. Compton and B. Galaway, 1975.
16. Goldstein, H. *Social Work Practice: A Unitary Approach.* Columbia, S.C.: University of South Carolina Press, 1973.
17. Haley, J. "An Interactional Description of Schizophrenia." *Psychiatry.* 22 (1959): 321-332.
18. Haley, J. *Changing Families: A Family Therapy Reader.* New York: Grune & Stratton, 1971.
19. Haley, J. "Family Therapy." *International Journal of Psychiatry.* 9 (1970-1): 233-242.
20. Haley, J. *Leaving Home.* New York: McGraw-Hill, 1980.
21. Haley, J. *Problem Solving Therapy.* San Francisco: Jossey-Bass, 1976.
22. Haley, J. *Strategies of Psychotherapy.* New York: Grune & Stratton, 1963.
23. Haley, J. "The Art of Being a Failure as a Therapist," *Changing Families.*
24. Haley, J. "The Art of Being Schizophrenic." *Voices,* 1965.
25. Haley, J. "The Power Tactics of Jesus Christ." *The Power Tactics of Jesus Christ and other Essays.* New York: Grossman, 1969.
26. Haley, J. *Uncommon Therapy.* The Psychiatric Techniques of Milton Erickson. New York: Ballantine Books, 1973.

27. Haley, J., and Hoffman, L. *Techniques of Family Therapy*. New York: Basic, 1967.
28. Jackson, D.D., Riskin, J., and Satir, V. "A Method of Analysis of a Family Interview." In D.D. Jackson, ed., *Communications, Family and Marriage*. Palo Alto, Cal.: Science and Behaviour Books, 1968, pp. 230-250.
29. Laing, R.D. *Politics of the Family*. Massey Lectures. Toronto: C.B.C. Publications, 1968.
30. Masters, W., and Johnson, V. *Human Sexual Inadequacy*. Boston: Little, Brown, 1970.
31. Masters, W., and Johnson, V. *Human Sexual Response*. Boston: Little, Brown, 1970.
32. Minuchin, S. *Families and Family Therapy*. Cambridge, Mass.: Harvard University Press, 1974.
33. Minuchin, S. "Family Structure, Family Language and the Puzzled Therapist." *Family Theory and Family Therapy of Female Sexual Delinquency*. O. Pollack, ed. Palo Alto, Cal.: Science and Behaviour Books, 1967.
34. Minuchin, S. *Psychosomatic Families*. Cambridge, Mass.: Harvard University Press, 1978.
35. Minuchin, S. "The Child in Context: A Systems Approach to Growth and Treatment." An unpublished article.
36. Minuchin, S., et al. *Families of the Slums*. New York: Basic, 1967.
37. Papp, P. *Family Therapy*. New York: Gardner Press, 1977.
38. Parsons, B.V. *Family Therapy Training Manual*, University of Utah, unpublished paper.
39. Perlman, H.H. *Social Casework: A Problem Solving Process*. Chicago: University of Chicago Press, 1957.
40. Reid, W.J., and Epstein, L. *Task-Centred Casework*. New York: Columbia University Press, 1972.
41. Rogers, C. "The Necessary and Sufficient Conditions of Therapeutic Personality Change." *Journal of Consulting Psychology*, 21 (1957): 95-103.
42. Rothery, M. "Contracts and Contracting." *Clinical Social Work*. 8(3), Fall, 1980, Chapter 5 in this book.
43. Satir, V.M. "Conjoint Family Therapy, A Guide to Theory and Technique." Palo Alto, Calif.: *Science and Behavior*, 1964.
44. Selvini-Palazzoli, M. *Self-Starvation*. London: Chaucer, 1974. (N.Y.: Brunner/Mazel).
45. Selvini-Palazzoli, M. *Paradox and Counter Paradox*. N.Y.: Jason Aronson, 1978.
46. Selvini-Palazzoli, M. "The Treatment of Children through the Brief Therapy of their Parents." *Family Process*. 13 (1974): 13-14.
47. Shah, S. *The Way of the Surf*. N.Y.: E.P. Dutton and Co., 1970.
48. Spooner, S., and Stone, S. "Maintenance of Specific Counselling Skills Over Time." *Journal of Counselling Psychology*, 24 (1), 1977.
49. Truax, C.B. "A Scale for Rating of Accurate Empathy: The Therapeutic Relationship and its Report." In C. Rogers, et al., eds. *The Therapeutic Relationship and its Report*. Madison, Wisc.: University of Wisconsin Press, 1967.
50. Watzlawick, P. "A Review of the Double Bind Theory." In D. Jackson, ed.

Communication, Family and Marriage. Palo Alto, Calif.: Science and Behavior Books, 1968.

51. Watzlawick, P. *The Language of Change*. New York: Basic, 1978.
52. Watzlawick, P., Beavin, J.H., and Jackson, D.D. *Pragmatics of Human Communication*. New York, 1967.
53. Watzlawick, P., Weakland, J., and Frisch, R. *Change: Principles of Problem Formation and Problem Resolution*. New York: Norton, 1974.
54. Whitaker, C., and Miller, M. "A Re-evaluation of 'Psychiatric Help' When Divorce Impends." *American Journal of Psychiatry*, 126, No. 5 (November, 1969): 611-616.
55. Wynne, L., et al. "Pseudo-mutuality in the Family Relations of Schizophrenics." *Psychiatry*. 21 (1958).
56. Zentner, E. *Manual for Planned Short-Term Treatment Techniques*. Waterloo: Wilfrid Laurier University, 1973.
57. Zuk, G. "The Go Between Function in Family Therapy." *Family Process*, 5: 162-178.

Journals

American Journal of Orthopsychiatry
1775 Broadway
New York, N.Y. 10019

The Family
Center for Family Learning
10 Hanford Avenue
New Rochelle, N.Y. 10805

The Family Coordinator
National Council on Family Relations
1219 University Avenue, S.E.
Minneapolis, Mn. 55414

Family Process
Box P
Stockbridge, Ma. 02162

Journal of Family Counseling
Box 2124 Hillside Manor
New Hyde Park, N.Y. 11040

Journal of Family Process
Nathan W. Ackerman Family Institute
149 E. 78th St.
New York, N.Y. 10021

Journal of Family History
National Council on Family Relations
1219 University Avenue, S.E.
Minneapolis, Mn. 55414

Journal of Marriage and Family Counseling
American Association of Marriage and Family Counselors
225 Yale Avenue
Claremont, Ca. 91711

Journal of Marriage and the Family
National Council on Family Relations
1219 University Avenue, S.E.
Minneapolis, Mn. 55414

Journal of Sex and Marital Therapy
Behavioral Publications
72 Fifth Avenue
New York, N.Y. 10010

Journal of the Family Therapy Institute of Marin
1353 Lincoln Avenue
San Rafael, Ca. 94901

The Relationship
Academy of Psychologists in Marital and Family Therapy
107 W. Welcome Avenue
Mankato, Mn. 56001

Clinical Social Work Journal
Mary L. Gottsfeld
Behavioral Publications
1852 Broadway
Morningside Heights, N.Y. 10025

Social Work
2 Park Avenue
New York, N.Y. 10016

Index